THE
NORTHERN
SEA ROUTE

AND THE ECONOMY OF THE SOVIET NORTH

THE

NORTHERN

SEA ROUTE

AND THE ECONOMY

OF THE SOVIET NORTH

by Constantine Krypton

PUBLISHED FOR THE

RESEARCH PROGRAM ON THE U.S.S.R.

HE
848
.K78
1976

GREENWOOD PRESS, PUBLISHERS
WESTPORT, CONNECTICUT

Library of Congress Cataloging in Publication Data

Krypton, Constantine, pseud.
   The northern sea route and the economy of the
Soviet north.

   Reprint of the ed. published for the Research
Program on the U. S. S. R. by Praeger, New York,
which was issued as no. 14 of Studies of the
Research Program on the U. S. S. R.; and as no. 42
of Praeger publications in Russian history and
world communism.
      Bibliography: p.
      Includes index.
      1. Northeast Passage--Economic aspects.
2. Siberia--Economic conditions. 3. Russia,
Northern--Economic conditions. I. Title.
II. Series: East European Fund. Research Program
on the U. S. S. R. Studies ; no. 14.
[HE848.K78 1976]   330.9'47'2   76-9087
ISBN 0-8371-8886-5

The preparation and publication of this study were
made possible by a grant from the Research Program
on the U.S.S.R. (East European Fund, Inc.)

The views of the author are his own and do not necessarily represent those of the Research Program on the
U.S.S.R. or of the East European Fund, Inc.

First published in 1956 by Frederick A. Praeger Publishers,
New York

Reprinted with the permission of Praeger Publishers, Inc.

Reprinted in 1976 by Greenwood Press,
a division of Williamhouse-Regency Inc.

Library of Congress Catalog Card Number 76-9087

ISBN 0-8371-8886-5

Printed in the United States of America

CONTENTS

AUTHOR'S PREFACE

The continuing scientific and technological advances of the twentieth century are opening up new possibilities in the Soviet Arctic regions. What was previously considered a frozen and impassable region is rapidly developing into a maritime transportation route, an air route between continents, an accessible source of raw materials and semifinished products, and a vantage ground for scientific research on natural phenomena which affect areas far beyond the Arctic borders. Thus the Soviet Arctic compels the interest of the economic geographer, the strategist, the economist, the scientist, and the specialist in Soviet affairs.

The present study was undertaken primarily to examine the actual and potential economic role of the Northern Sea Route, the seaway along the Arctic coast between Novaya Zemlya and the Bering Strait, which has long been looked upon as the key to Soviet penetration into the Arctic. The study is a continuation into the Soviet period of the author's earlier work on the prerevolutionary development of the Northern Sea Route.* In addition to analyzing its economic significance, the study attempts to assess the strategic value of the Route and of Soviet polar aviation in order to throw light on the noneconomic motives for Soviet work in the Arctic.

The economic issues raised in this study undoubtedly would long ago have been the subject of public debate by re-

---

* Krypton, Constantine, *The Northern Sea Route: Its Place in Russian Economic History Before 1917*, New York, Research Program on the U.S.S.R., 1953.

sponsible persons in the Soviet Union were it not for the pressures engendered by the Soviet regime. An objective examination of economic policy on the present and future development of the polar region and the Northern Sea Route's place in it, however, has been impossible in that country; published works on the subject have been subjected to severe criticism or simply banned and withdrawn from circulation, while their authors have incurred disfavor.

Before leaving the U.S.S.R. the author was head of the economics section of a research institute concerned with the study of the North. One of his responsibilities for many years was to lecture on the economics of the Northern Sea Route and Arctic aviation. In the course of this work he collected and kept up to date a body of relevant data from the Planning Department of the Main Administration for the Northern Sea Route (Glavsevmorput'), the Department of the North of the R.S.F.S.R. State Planning Commission and other economic and administrative organizations, as well as from the archives of the Committee for the Northern Sea Route (Komseverput'). The information was obtained either from responsible officials of the organizations or from the files to which the author had access. Unfortunately in most cases it was permissible only to take down the data without the name or source of the document. Therefore, although the author is still in possession of his original notes, he can usually cite as authority only the organization which supplied the data. As a representative of the research institute with which he was associated, the author traveled in the North and spoke with innumerable local officials and residents. The present study is, of course, based also on published materials, which are listed in the appended bibliography.

The author wishes to express his sincere thanks to the Research Program on the U.S.S.R. and its director, Professor Philip E. Mosely, for making possible the writing and pub-

Author's Preface

lication of his two studies on the Northern Sea Route. He is greatly indebted to Mr. Robert Slusser, Associate Director of the Research Program, for his constant help and encouragement. His thanks are also extended to Mrs. Esther Corey, who made the original translation of the Russian manuscript, Mr. Nicholas N. Krijanovsky of the American Geographical Society for preparing the map, and Mr. Irving Haber of New York City for his work with the author in the preliminary stages of editing. Miss Louise E. Luke, Assistant Director of the Research Program, working together with Mr. Richard Sorich of the Research Program editorial staff, carried through the final editing of the manuscript, for which the author is deeply grateful. Finally, his thanks go to Dr. Terence Armstrong of the Scott Polar Research Institute and Professor Oleg Hoeffding of Columbia University for their valuable criticisms of the original manuscript. The author takes full responsibility for statements of fact or interpretation.

Constantine Krypton

May 1955
Fort Lee, New Jersey

THE
NORTHERN
SEA ROUTE

AND THE ECONOMY OF THE SOVIET NORTH

I. RATIONALE OF SOVIET WORK IN THE ARCTIC

The active interest in the Arctic region which the Soviet government has displayed since the first months of its existence[1] has been attributed by Soviet writers to three fundamental policies: the even distribution of productive forces, the regeneration of the northern national minorities and the development of the Arctic as a "weather kitchen" for the entire country. Soviet publications still advance substantially the same views. I. Spirin in his account of the operation of the polar station North Pole 1 states:

> Without these planned, diversified explorations all this would have been impossible—the conquest and exploitation of the Northern Sea Route and its conversion into a normal, active seaway, the broad cultural and economic development of the Arctic, the regeneration of the peoples of the extreme North and their absorption into the life of the whole Soviet people constituting Communist society.[2]

The objectives proclaimed are genuine, although they do not constitute the full explanation of Soviet interest in the Arctic regions.

The economic drive to master the Arctic was of course prompted by the wealth and variety of the natural resources in the northern regions. The decision to exploit these resources without delay was dictated in part by the fact that certain idle facilities were already available for the purpose. Such utilization afforded the opportunity to rescue and draw some economic benefit from investments made before the Revolution. For example, it was desirable to find some commercial use for the Murmansk Railroad (since January 1935 called the Kirov Railroad), which had been constructed during

1

World War I for military purposes. One of the ways to make use of the railroad was to develop the Barents Sea fisheries, which the tsarist government had left in poor condition despite efforts at improvement.[3]

The condition of the northern minorities, the second object of Soviet concern in the Arctic, was officially described in 1924 as a "catastrophic situation, one of complete disorganization and isolation from the Soviet structure."[4] In that year the Committee for Assistance to the Nationalities of the Northern Borderlands, better known as the Committee of the North, was organized under the Presidium of the All-Russian Central Executive Committee. Its purpose was to promote the economic development, cultural growth and political re-education of the northern nationalities and to supply the area with consumer and producer goods via the Northern Sea Route.[5]

Mistakes made by subordinate Party organizations in religious matters and in breaking up traditional institutions had aroused hostility toward the Soviet system among the national minorities in the Arctic.[6] Resentment was aggravated by the government's demand that the northern peoples surrender the furs they had collected to state agencies at prices set by Moscow, instead of selling them commercially. Violators of this law were severely punished.[7] The northerners were further antagonized when the government failed to provide them with the supplies, especially guns and ammunition, which they needed for hunting. Some of the mistakes of ignorant functionaries in the lower Party organizations might have been corrected, but no change was possible in the policies affecting the fur trade and supplies. The government refused to retreat in the matter of furs, which were an important source of foreign exchange. As to supplies, it was incapable of providing them in sufficient quantities. Experiments with a new type of economic system in a country crippled by war had created a shortage of the goods essential for the northern trading population. Moreover, the transportation problem remained very difficult.[8]

The strong discontent that arose as a result of the serious situation in districts such as the Chukotsk Peninsula turned the population toward the outside world. Occasionally boats crossed the Bering Strait between Alaska and the peninsula, and shipments of goods were received from the American continent.[9]

Beginning with the early twenties the Soviet government intensified its efforts with regard to the national minorities in a series of measures directed toward the cultural and material regeneration of the backward minorities which had "previously been oppressed by Russian tsarism."[10] The primary concern, however, in the formation of the Committee for Assistance to the Nationalities of the Northern Borderlands was not the well-being of the nationalities, but the economic and political significance of the regions.[11]

Soviet scientific interest in the Arctic was defined by the All-Union Arctic Institute in its report to the Seventeenth Party Congress in 1934 which stressed the need for additional polar observation stations:

> At present the significance of meteorologic and aerologic factors in the Arctic for the southerly latitudes is generally known and recognized. . . . It is obvious what tremendous importance long-term weather forecasts have for our country, where agriculture plays such a large role.[12]

The rationale behind Soviet work in the Arctic is much more complex than the conventional explanation suggests.

The end of the nineteenth century and the beginning of the twentieth introduced a new phase in the history of the Arctic Ocean. Navigation by Russian and foreign vessels began in the Kara Sea, until then known only as the "ice cellar."[13] For Russia this change created critical economic, strategic and political problems. As a result of the increasing possibility of navigation in northern waters, international relations in the Arctic grew more complicated, and it became necessary to define the sovereign rights of interested states in the water and land spaces of the Arctic Ocean. The question was a delicate one, since foreign vessels also sailed off the Siberian shores. In fact, the first passage of the northeast sector of the sea route on a through voyage was made by a Swede, Professor Nordenskiöld (1878-1879). When a foreign expedition, shortly before World War I, asked permission to enter the Kara Sea, the Russian government answered cautiously and evasively.[14] Fears regarding Russian sovereign rights in the Arctic Ocean were also evident in the note sent by the Ministry of Foreign Affairs on September 4, 1916, to "the governments of allied and friendly states."[15] The pretext for the note was the successful voyages of Captain Vil'kitski. The real purpose, however, was to point out Russian rights in relation to newly discovered as well as previously known islands in the Arctic Ocean. These rights were claimed on two legal grounds: (a) discovery and geographic explorations and (b) the proximity of the islands to the Russian mainland. The Ministry of Foreign Affairs could not very well refer to the basic principle of international law, "effective occupation," inasmuch as it was clear that Russia did not have the means to occupy effectively the territory it claimed.

The Soviet government addressed itself energetically to the problems of international rights which it had inherited in the Arctic.

An event after the Civil War pointed up the urgency of this task. In 1921 a Canadian expedition, organized on the initiative of the well-known polar explorer Vilhjalmur Stefansson, landed on Wrangel Island, which had been claimed in the note of 1916 as an "indivisible part of the Russian empire." The head of the expedition raised the British flag on the island and left the following proclamation:

Rationale of Soviet Work in the Arctic

KNOW BY ALL THESE PRESENTS, That I, Allan Rudyard Crawford, a native of Canada and a British subject and those men whose names appear below, members of the Wrangel Island Detachment of the Stefansson Arctic Expedition of 1921, on the advice and council of Vilhjalmur Stefansson, a British subject, have this day, in consideration of lapses of foreign claims and the occupancy from March 12th 1914 to September 7th 1914 of this island by the survivors of the brigantine Karluk, . . . the property of the Government of CANADA chartered to operate in the Canadian Arctic Expedition of 1913-1918 . . . , raised the Canadian flag, raised the British flag and declared this land known as WRANGEL Island to be the possession of His Majesty GEORGE, King of GREAT BRITAIN and IRELAND and the Dominions beyond the Seas, Emperor of INDIA, etc., and a part of the BRITISH EMPIRE.

Signed and deposited in this monument this sixteenth day of September in the year of our Lord one thousand nine hundred and twenty one.

Allan Crawford, Commander; E. Lorne Knight, Second in Command; F. W. Maurer; Milton Galle.

WRANGEL ISLAND, Sept. 16th, 1921. GOD SAVE THE KING.[16]

Stefansson himself later commented:

If nearness were the controlling element, [the Falkland Islands] should belong to Argentina, but they do belong to the British Empire. . . . They are in times of peace a part of the commercial sea power of the Empire. We wanted Wrangel Island to remain British as a part of her developing air power for dirigibles and planes to use as schooners and cruisers have used the Falklands.[17]

According to Soviet sources Stefansson also expressed the hope that Wrangel Island would become a source of valuable furs and walrus bone.[18]

Settling Wrangel Island proved difficult, however; almost all the members of the first party perished from hunger. In 1923 a new group of Canadians, provided with food and supplies for two years, arrived and continued the exploitation of the island's natural resources. Thereupon in connection with the second expedition and the campaign conducted in the British press, the People's Commissariat of Foreign Affairs categorically protested the actions of the Canadian government, in notes of May 24 and 28, 1923.[19] The position of the Soviet government, incapable of remedying the situation on the island, was not a pleasant one. It was only three years later that the crew of the gunboat "Krasnyi Oktyabr' " (Red October), formerly an icebreaker of the port of Vladivostok, succeeded in reaching Wrangel Island through the ice, took the Canadians into custody and raised the Soviet flag there.[20]

Many of the other possessions claimed by the U.S.S.R. were even less accessible than Wrangel Island, which is separated from the continent only by a strait. Despite its 1924 and 1926 declarations of extensive rights in the Arctic Ocean, it was not until 1929 that the Soviet government was able to accomplish its next annexation, of the archipelago of Franz Josef Land.[21]

In view of the uncertainty about international rights in the Arctic, the Soviet government moved to define its own position in that region. In 1924 it sent a note to all foreign states reaffirming the 1916 declaration of rights in the Arctic by the tsarist government. The note read in part:

> Reiterating once more. . . that these islands belong to the R.S.F.S.R., the Government of the Union [of Soviet Socialist Republics] emphasizes that the United States of America was obligated to make no claims to the above-mentioned islands and lands in the waters contiguous to the northern shore of Siberia and situated west of the line defined as the boundary by Article One of the Washington Convention of March 18-30, 1867, between Russia and the United States of America. The Government of the U.S.S.R. directs the serious attention of all powers whose official or private explorers and vessels are visiting or will visit the indicated waters and territories of the [U.S.S.R.] to the above-mentioned facts. The Government of the U.S.S.R. trusts that all governments concerned will take the necessary measures to warn their citizens against violation of the sovereignty of the U.S.S.R. over these territories.[22]

The note of 1924, referring only to the Asiatic part of the U.S.S.R., left the full scope of Soviet sovereign rights still to be defined. A categorical definition was given a year and a half later by a decree of the Central Executive Committee of the U.S.S.R., issued April 15, 1926, which stated:

> The Union of Soviet Socialist Republics proclaims as territories all lands and islands already discovered or discovered in the future which at the time of publication of this decree are not recognized by the Government of the Union of Soviet Socialist Republics as territories of any foreign state and which lie in the Arctic Ocean north of the shores of the Union of Soviet Socialist Republics up to the North Pole between the meridian 32°04'35" E. long. from Greenwich, running along the eastern side of Vaida Bay through the triangular marker on Cape Kekurski, and the meridian 168°49'30" W. long. from Greenwich, bisecting the strait separating the Ratmanov and Krusenstern Islands of the Diomede group in the Bering Strait.[23]

The decree of 1926 disturbed a number of officials in the Commissariat of Foreign Affairs. The cartographic offices of the Arctic Institute, Glavsevmorput'[24] and the geographical publishing houses began to receive communications on the advisability of publishing maps of the Arctic Ocean showing the boundaries of the Soviet sector. Some of the letters expressed anxiety about the prestige of the Soviet Union in case of a landing by foreign planes on any of the islands in the sector shown as Soviet. There was a fully justified fear that no proof of "effective occupation" by the U.S.S.R. could be offered to prevent such an occurrence.

In 1925 the American jurist David Hunter Miller proposed that the Arctic be divided into conical sectors projected to the Pole from the eastern and western extremities of the countries bordering on the Arctic Ocean.[25] This proposal appeared to offer a good basis for a general division of the Arctic. Miller's ideas were reflected in some Soviet legal and scientific works on the Arctic published between 1926 and the beginning of the 1930's.[26] The official position of the Soviet government, however, was more accurately represented by the views expressed in an article written in 1932 by a high official of the

7

Commissariat of Foreign Affairs under the pseudonym of *Aktivist* O. A. Kh.:[27]

> An argument about the existence of sectors according to which the Arctic may be divided has begun to appear in the pages of Soviet literature. . . .[28]
>
> From our point of view the sector theory must be opposed with very serious political objections. In evaluating this theory, as well as other political matters, there are fundamental differences between the Soviet approach and the theories of bourgeois jurists and politicians. . . .[29]
>
> Any notion of dividing the Arctic into spheres or any such categories, adroitly transplanted from the dictionary of colonial terminology to the snow and ice of the Arctic, is categorically alien to the Soviet power and its ideology. When the Soviet Union in a special decree of its highest organ of authority defined its northern borders, it did so in order to fix those Arctic territories where it has the right to extend its sovereignty for the establishment of a socialist economy. These acts, of course, do not imply any deal with the imperialist states subjacent to the Arctic. . . .[30]

Furthermore, the Soviet government did not explicitly declare its support for the sector principle as applicable either to the U.S.S.R. or to other countries subjacent to the Arctic.[31]

The motivation behind this equivocal position can be seen in Soviet press comments at the same time on the inactivity of the capitalist countries in the Arctic and on their alleged inability to explore and develop the region, in contrast to the vigorous efforts of the U.S.S.R. Soviet laws and decrees concerning the Second International Polar Year, August 1, 1932 —August 31, 1933, stressed the vital importance to the U.S.S.R. of carrying out its program of exploration and study of the Arctic without regard for the efforts or lack of efforts by the capitalist countries.[32] Thus the Soviet Union simultaneously ignored the rights of other countries and asserted that they were unable, because of their "capitalist nature," to develop the Arctic economically. Relying on the world economic crisis at that time and the inherent "weakness" of the capitalist states to keep them from any further activity in the

Arctic and consequently anticipating no competition there, the Kremlin hesitated to tie its hands for the future.

During World War II the Soviet point of view on international rights in the Arctic changed. The *Short Soviet Encyclopedia* (1943) defines the Arctic briefly as "polar lands of the northern hemisphere. Divided into five sectors. The largest is the Soviet sector."[33]

The sectors of other nations were given more detailed recognition in 1950 by the *Large Soviet Encyclopedia:*

> After World War I the Arctic region, encompassing the islands and the Arctic Ocean up to the Pole, was divided into five sectors, Soviet, American, Canadian, Danish, and Norwegian. The largest is the Soviet sector, with an area of about 9 million square kilometers, of which 6.8 million are covered by seas. . . .[34]
>
> Without any special juridical acts it became usual in the cartographic practices of bourgeois countries to show American, Canadian, Danish, and Norwegian sectors on their maps of the Arctic.[35]

There is no explanation why the "cartographic practices of bourgeois countries" which had begun after World War I received the recognition of the U.S.S.R. only after World War II. Nor is there any such explanation in a textbook on international law issued in 1951 by the Law Institute of the Soviet Academy of Sciences, which treats problems of the "so-called polar sectors" in a paragraph on "composition of state territory."[36]

An analysis of Soviet theory on international law need not detain us here, although its history is very instructive. We need only note that after World War II the Kremlin was confronted with a changed world; the economic crisis had passed, and the "bourgeois" powers had come out of the war with highly developed technological resources. Statements about the helplessness in the Arctic of western countries, which have no planned economy or other attributes of the Soviet system, stopped completely. Invidious comparisons between Soviet and "capitalist" explorations of the Arctic before the war now merely ascribed the latter to an interest in breaking records.[37]

While thus recognizing, or partly recognizing, the sectors of other countries, the Soviet government at the same time hastened to extend its own claims. The 1950 article goes far beyond the 1926 decrees, which mentioned only islands, and announces:

> In Soviet scientific thought it has become the established view that Siberian seas of the gulf type, such as the Kara, Laptev, East Siberian, and Chukotsk, are historically Russian seas; the stupendous work of the Russian and Soviet navigators who envisioned and carried out the navigation of these seas, as well as historical precedents (Ukase of 1619 on the Kara Sea), supports this view.[38]

Irrespective of the views of Soviet science, however, the Soviet government has always regarded the Northern Sea Route as a passage through its territorial waters. A rule for polar navigation issued in 1933 reads: "Foreign vessels are to be escorted under the command of Soviet masters on their outbound and return runs [east of the Kara Strait]."[39] After World War II it was noted in Western Europe that the U.S.S.R. was preparing to declare part of the Arctic Ocean, and consequently the air spaces over it, a possession of the Soviet Union.[40] In 1951 B. V. Kostritsyn treated the legal status of the Soviet Arctic as being completely settled. To him the Soviet Arctic Ocean is the ocean of "our ancestors," "the frigid sea." He supports his view with historical, economic and strategic arguments.[41] A 1952 article then clinched its argument that the Northern Sea Route is a national seaway and that the Arctic seas through which the route runs— the Kara, Laptev, East Siberian, and Chukotsk—are also closed national waters by invoking the sector principle:

> The sector system has recently come under fierce attack in the reactionary American press. . . .[42]
>
> To the attack of the imperialists on the sector principle in the Arctic, we must counterpose our defense of this principle and of

Rationale of Soviet Work in the Arctic

Soviet sovereignty over our own polar regions . . . including our Arctic seas.[43]

The development of aviation by the Western powers during World War I made the Soviet position in the Arctic especially critical. Aviation provided new resources for the study and development of transportation lines in the Arctic and also raised the question of air rights.[44]

In 1924, on the initiative of the German captain Walter Bruns and the famous polar authority and Russian *émigré* L. L. Breitfuss, the international society Aeroarctic was formed to study the Arctic Ocean by means of dirigibles. The first meeting of the society took place in Berlin in November 1926.[45] The Soviet Union participated actively in Aeroarctic, and the second meeting was held in Leningrad in 1928.[46] Soviet specialists even flew in a German dirigible and explored the Arctic jointly with the Germans.[47]

The active collaboration and cooperation of the U.S.S.R. with capitalist countries in exploring the Arctic arose entirely from necessity. The Western countries after World War I had a more highly developed technology and much unused equipment, including aircraft. The Soviet Union, however, had to import even agricultural equipment for over ten years after the Revolution.[48] During this time construction of planes, dirigibles and other technical equipment remained only a goal. Compelled to rely on the experience and technology of the West and to participate in Aeroarctic, the Soviet government allowed Bruns to make special explorations of the Kola Peninsula on the instructions of the international society.[49]

The general purpose of Aeroarctic could not, of course, arouse any real sympathy in the Soviet government. At the Leningrad meeting the chairman of Aeroarctic, Professor F. Hansen, declared:

> We hope that other nations as well will support the cultural aims of the society, which are of basic importance from the standpoint of world economy.[50]

11

The concept of a world economy contradicted official Soviet doctrine, which at that time denied the possibility of a unified world economy and proclaimed the inevitability of conflict between the socialist and capitalist systems. Appeals for co-operation in the name of a world economy represented, in the opinion of the Kremlin, nothing but an attempt to undermine the Soviet state.

The behavior of Soviet participants in Aeroarctic and other joint Arctic expeditions was regulated accordingly. Their task was to get all information possible from the capitalist countries and at the same time to conceal Soviet data, even of a purely theoretical or scientific character. Written instructions to follow this practice were issued to Soviet personnel at the Arctic Institute. The unwillingness of the U.S.S.R. to cooperate in good faith was again demonstrated in 1931, when R. L. Samoilovich, the director of the Arctic Institute, was required, in a public lecture on the joint expedition in the German dirigible, to stress the superior ability of the Soviet personnel and the resulting disagreements with the Germans over details of the work.[51]

The potentialities for developing air routes depend on the state of the air theater, that is, the whole complex of airports, communications, fuel supplies, housing and other facilities. The difficult flying conditions of the Arctic necessitate many special installations, such as land-based radio stations for directing planes. In order to provide for such facilities and thus to assure itself control of the Arctic air spaces, the Soviet government continued to press its claims to all islands in the Arctic Ocean, both discovered and undiscovered, as set forth in its 1926 declaration.

The Soviet press took a hostile attitude toward the activities of other countries in the Arctic. Development of air transportation and other technical achievements of the West were regarded by the Soviet government solely in relation to the concepts imperialism and aggression. In addition to the familiar terms "militarism" and "navalism," the term "aeronautism" appeared briefly, to connote not only air armament but also air aggression. The greatest danger from this new type of "imperialist aggression," it was felt, was its threat to Soviet polar possessions.[52] Great Britain was accused of attempting to create and control a chain of polar air stations on territory belonging *de jure* to Norway.[53] The alleged danger from the United States was mentioned quite openly.[54]

Research conducted by "imperialist" countries in the Arctic by means of expeditions and other methods especially irritated the government of the U.S.S.R. From the Soviet point of view such investigation was a dangerous "fever," calling for vigorous protection of Soviet rights, some of which had already been violated.[55]

The accusatory tone sharpened after World War II. On December 31, 1947, in one of Moscow's large lecture halls, a noteworthy lecture was given on the topic "Polar Strategy and Polar Expansion." In view of its special significance, the text was printed and distributed as a separate pamphlet by *Pravda*. The speaker, Yermashov, after a preliminary reference to the "great investments," economic progress and scientific achievements of the Soviet Union in the Arctic, where its sovereignty "extends over almost half the entire Arctic basin, including a great number of islands along the northern extremity of the Eastern Hemisphere,"[56] launched into an attack on America's Arctic operations, interpreted as directed against the U.S.S.R. and as evidence of "American imperialism." For contrast to the postwar situation, Yermashov revived the old assertion that other countries with Arctic possessions had paid little attention to them before the war, although he now omitted the earlier jibes at "capitalist" ineffectuality in the area—since the purpose of the lecture was to point out the excessive activity of the United States in the

Arctic. In substantiation, the lecturer adduced "facts" on American air and naval routes in the Arctic, on the introduction of military training in the U.S. and on the subjugation of Arctic countries with the aim of transforming the Arctic Ocean into an "American sea." The lecturer summed up by stating that what might be called the first circle of American world expansion had been established in the Arctic.

Somewhat earlier, in November 1947, the Leningrad journal, *Zvezda* [Star] had published an article of similar import, entitled "Polar Fever in America," by V. Golant.[57] In 1950 an article in *Izvestiya* discussed a recently published geographic symposium on the American North,[58] under the heading "Alaska in the Plans of American Aggressors."[59] The purpose of these and similar articles was to make known Soviet postwar policy and to explain the increased efforts demanded of leading civil and military figures in the conquest of the Arctic, especially by means of air routes.

The Northern Sea Route promised to be the means of unlocking the storehouse of natural resources in the Arctic regions and of integrating the northern aborigines with the rest of the population. The stable sea communications required for economic development would also provide a basis for establishing and maintaining scientific observation stations and the facilities of an Arctic air theater and enable the government to give effect to the declarations of Soviet diplomacy on international rights in the Arctic.

The use of a northern sea lane revolutionizes communications between the western and eastern regions of the U.S.S.R. From Murmansk to Vladivostok the distance by sea via the Bering Strait is about 11,000 kilometers; via the Suez Canal it is doubled. In comparison with overland and river shipping between the central European areas of the U.S.S.R. and northern and eastern Siberia, the Northern Sea Route offers great

Rationale of Soviet Work in the Arctic

advantages. The route from Moscow to Tiksi, for instance, is over 4,000 kilometers longer via the Siberian railroads and the other facilities involved in overland communication than it is via the Northern Sea Route:

Table I. Distances from Moscow to Tiksi (kilometers)

Northern Sea Route		Overland and river route	
Moscow-Archangel		Moscow-Irkutsk	
railroad	1,133	Trans-Siberian	
		Railroad	5,031
		Irkutsk-Yakutsk	
Archangel-Tiksi		highway	254
sea route	4,158	river	2,465
		Yakutsk-Tiksi	
		river	1,671
Total	5,291	Total	9,421

East of Tiksi this differential increases still more in favor of the sea route. In addition, the sea route, requiring less transshipment and freed from dependence on local routes, both land and river, permits speedier delivery.

In addition to these advantages, the shorter communications between east and west—through Soviet-controlled waters— had an obvious significance for U.S.S.R. naval operations.

As a channel for trade between southwestern Siberia and western Europe, the Northern Sea Route affords the possibility of cheaper transport by the combined use of the sea route and the great Siberian rivers.

These were all potential advantages offered by the Northern Sea Route. Their realization depended upon the willingness and ability of the Soviet government to pursue the policies and invest the resources which would lead to this end.

NOTES

[1] On July 2, 1918, V. I. Lenin, Chairman of the Council of People's Commissars, signed a decree authorizing an expedition of several ships assisted by aviation to conduct explorations in the Arctic Ocean. The

The Northern Sea Route

Civil War, however, prevented carrying out the expedition. Archives of Komseverput'. *Spravka ob uzakoneniyakh i rasporyazheniyakh sovetskovo pravitel'stva po voprosu morskikh plavanii vdol' sibirskikh beregov 1917-1927* [Memoranda on Laws and Ordinances of the Soviet Government Concerning Navigation Along the Siberian Coasts, 1917-1927]. V. Yu. Vize describes the plan for the expedition as a "tremendous research project." *Na "Sibiryakove" i "Litke" cherez Ledovitye morya* [Through Arctic Seas in the "Sibiryakov" and the "Litke"], Moscow-Leningrad, Glavsevmorput', 1946, p. 45.

[2] Spirin, I., *Pokoreniye Severnovo polyusa* [The Conquest of the North Pole], Moscow, Gosudarstvennoye izdatel'stvo geograficheskoi literatury, 1950, pp. 313-14. In Soviet usage the term "extreme North" describes the territory above a line running approximately through the following points: Kandalaksha, Kozhva, Tobol'sk, Yeniseisk, Sovetskaya Gavan'. For the law of 1931 defining the territory included under the term "extreme North," see Taracouzio, T. A., *Soviets in the Arctic: An Historical, Economic and Political Study of the Soviet Advance into the Arctic*, New York, Macmillan, 1938, p. 455. The population of the extreme North, excluding prisoners, has increased steadily, as the following figures show: 1913, 480,000; 1926, 645,000; 1937, 1,400,000. *Kursy politupravleniya dlya komandnovo sostava Glavsevmorputi: Ekonomgeografiya Krainevo Severa* [Courses in Political Administration for Executive Personnel of Glavsevmorput': Economic Geography of the Extreme North], Moscow-Leningrad, Glavsevmorput', 1940, p. 17. In 1926 the indigenous population numbered 366,000, or 56 per cent of the total population of the region. The subsequent influx of settlers, who are concentrated in the towns and workers' settlements, has reduced this percentage. Margolin, A. B., "Goroda Zapolyar'ya" [Cities Above the Arctic Circle], *Sovetskaya Arktika* [Soviet Arctic], Moscow, No. 7, 1937, pp. 82-96.

[3] From the organizational structure of the railroad it is evident that the Soviet government attached great hopes to operations in the Barents Sea. The administration of the railroad, originally called the Transport-Industrial-Colonization Combine, included five departments: (a) railroad management, (b) forest industries, (c) fisheries, (d) colonization, and (e) the Murmansk port. The last three were directly concerned with Barents Sea operations. Chirkin, G. F., *Transportno-promyshlenno-kolonizatsionnyi kombinat Murmanskoi zheleznoi dorogi* [The Transport-Industrial-Colonization Combine of the Murmansk Railroad], Moscow-Leningrad, NKPS, 1928 (*Trudy gosudarstvennovo nauchno-issledovatel'skovo instituta zemleustroistva i pereseleniya* [Works of the State Scientific Research Institute for Land Use and Resettlement], Vol. IX).

[4] See "Komitet sodeistviya narodnostyam severnykh okrain" [Committee for Assistance to the Nationalities of the Northern Borderlands], *Bol'shaya Sovetskaya entsiklopediya* [Large Soviet Encyclopedia], Moscow, Vol. XXXIII, 1938, col. 631.

[5] *Ibid.*, cols. 631-33. On the northern nationalities see Skachko, A., *Narody Krainevo Severa i rekonstruktsiya severnovo khozyaistva* [The

Rationale of Soviet Work in the Arctic

Peoples of the Extreme North and the Reconstruction of the Northern Economy], Leningrad, Institut narodov Severa, 1934; and Lappo, S. D., *Spravochnaya knizhka polyarnika* [Manual for Polar Personnel], Moscow-Leningrad, Glavsevmorput', 1945, Chs. 10 and 11.

[6] At a conference of inhabitants of the Nenets National Okrug in 1930 delegate Lantander declared: "I have children of school age, but I will not send them to the school; they have to shoot me before they can take them." Ustyugov, P., "Samokritika na suglanakh" [Self-Criticism at Meetings], *Sovetskii Sever* [The Soviet North], Moscow, No. 7-8, 1930, p. 54. Similarly frank complaints were made at this meeting concerning the inadequate supply of occupational equipment and other goods. *Ibid.*, pp. 40-41, 46-47. The arrival of the "Red Tents" (mobile propaganda units) in northern communities was greeted with remarks such as: "You've come for nothing; we have no use for the Red Tent. Neither our fathers nor our grandfathers knew anything about Red Tents, and yet they lived better than we do." "Ocherednye zadachi kul'turnovo stroitel'stva na Krainem Severe: Po dokladu T. Davydova na IX Plenume Komiteta Severa" [The Next Tasks of Cultural Construction in the Extreme North: From the Report of Comrade Davydov at the Ninth Plenum of the Committee of the North], *Sovetskii Sever*, No. 4, 1932, p. 94.

[7] For a compilation of some of the decrees of the All-Russian Central Executive Committee and the Council of People's Commissars regulating the disposition of furs in the North, see Kruglov, A., "Severnoye zakonodatel'stvo" [Northern Legislation], *Sovetskii Sever*, No. 1, 1931, pp. 194-96, 198. These decrees forbid the purchase by, or sale to, private citizens of northern furs, as well as the removal of any furs however acquired, by private citizens across the borders of the extreme North.

[8] Archives of the Committee for Assistance to the Nationalities of the Northern Borderlands. *Snabzheniye severnovo promyslovovo naseleniya posle grazhdanskoi voiny* [Supplying the Northern Trading Population After the Civil War], Official Memorandum, File for 1927. See also the various resolutions and decrees of central government bodies and the Party on the necessity of delivering foodstuffs and industrial goods to the extreme North, reprinted in *Sovetskii Sever*, No. 4, 1930, pp. 116-68; No. 6, 1931, pp. 132-34; No. 5, 1932, pp. 149-51; and "Postanovleniya TsK partii i SNK v ikh primenenii k Severu" [Decrees of the Central Committee of the Party and of the Council of People's Commissars and Their Application to the North], *Sovetskii Sever*, No. 3, 1932, p. 11.

[9] Archives of the Committee for Assistance to the Nationalities of the Northern Borderlands. *Klassovaya bor'ba na Chukotskom poluostrove* [The Class Struggle on the Chukotsk Peninsula], Official Memorandum, File for 1929.

[10] "Vestiges of the chauvinism of the national majority, with its kulaklike tendencies to view the nationalities of the North as 'forest creatures' and 'real Asiatics' fit for unbridled exploitation, were more tenacious among the Siberian peasants than anywhere else, since they

17

had been accustomed to a colonial situation." Skachko, *op. cit.*, p. 46. "The shameful heritage of the past was liquidated during the Soviet period. On the basis of Lenin's nationality policy the territorial organization of the small nationalities of the North was carried out, and the Northern Sea Route became an active seaway from the estuaries of the Ob' and the Yenisei in the west to the estuaries of the Kolyma and the Lena in the east. . . ." Baranski, N. N., *Ekonomicheskaya geografiya SSSR* [Economic Geography of the U.S.S.R.], Moscow, Uchpedgiz, 1936, p. 402.

[11] See "Komitet sodeistviya," *op. cit.*

[12] *Sovetskaya Arktika: Obzor nauchno-issledovatel'skoi raboty Vsesoyuznovo arkticheskovo instituta v Sovetskom sektore Arktiki* [The Soviet Arctic: A Survey of the Scientific Research of the All-Union Arctic Institute in the Soviet Sector of the Arctic], Leningrad, Vsesoyuznyi Arkticheskii Institut, 1934, p. 12.

[13] For the development of navigation in northern waters, see Krypton, Constantine, *The Northern Sea Route: Its Place in Russian Economic History Before 1917*, New York, Research Program on the U.S.S.R., 1953.

[14] See Waultrin, René, "La question de la souveraineté des terres arctiques," *Revue générale de droit international public*, Paris, Vol. XV, 1908, pp. 78-125, 185-209. See also his "Le problème de la souveraineté des pôles," *ibid.*, Vol. XVI, 1909, pp. 649-60.

[15] The text of the note is as follows: "New achievements have been added to the considerable number of discoveries and geographic explorations made in the course of centuries by the efforts of Russian navigators and merchants in the region of the polar lands situated north of the Asiatic coast of the Russian Empire: the work of Captain Second Class Vil'kitski, aide-de-camp to His Imperial Highness and director of the hydrographic expedition, who was entrusted during the period 1913-14 with the exploration of the Arctic Ocean has been completed. In 1913 this officer of the Imperial Russian Fleet made a survey of several vast areas along the northern coast of Siberia and discovered at 74°45′ N. lat. an island later named General Vil'kitski Island. Then moving north from the Taimyr Peninsula he discovered lands which have been named Emperor Nicholas II Land [Severnaya Zemlya], Tsesarevich Aleksei Island [Malyi Taimyr Island] and Starokadomski Island.

"During 1914 Captain Vil'kitski, having made important new explorations, discovered a new island near Bennett Island; it has been named Novopashennyi Island [Zhokhov Island].

"The Imperial Russian Government has the honor herewith to inform the governments of allied and friendly powers that these lands have been incorporated in the territory of the Russian Empire.

"The Imperial Government takes this opportunity to note that it considers an indivisible part of the Empire the Henrietta, Jeannette, Bennett, Herald, and Uyedineniye Islands, which, together with the New Siberian, Wrangel and other islands situated near the Asiatic coast of the Empire, constitute a northern continuation of the con-

Rationale of Soviet Work in the Arctic

tinental territory of Siberia. The Imperial Government has not considered it necessary to include in the present note Novaya Zemlya, Vaigach and other islands of various sizes situated near the European coast of the Empire, since they have been generally recognized for centuries as part of the territory of the Empire." Quoted in Mineyev, A. I., *Ostrov Vrangelya* [Wrangel Island], Moscow, Glavsevmorput', 1946, pp. 35-36.

[16] Stefansson, Vilhjalmur, *The Adventure of Wrangel Island*, New York, Macmillan, 1925, p. 119. See also Ushakov, A., "Ostrov Vrangelya" [Wrangel Island], *Sovetskaya Arktika*, No. 8, 1936, pp. 23-24.

[17] Stefansson, *op. cit.*, p. 125.

[18] See Ushakov, *op. cit.*, p. 29.

[19] "Ostrov Vrangelya" [Wrangel Island], *Izvestiya*, November 4, 1924. On the expeditions, see Mineyev, *op. cit.*, pp. 36-38.

[20] See Mineyev, *op. cit.*, Ch. 3. A permanent Soviet settlement was established on the island.

[21] *Sovetskaya Arktika: Obzor nauchno-issledovatel'skoi raboty*, p. 33.

[22] Quoted in Klyuchnikov, Yu. V., and A. V. Sabanin, eds., *Mezhdunarodnaya politika noveishevo vremeni v dogovorakh, notakh i deklaratsiyakh* [Recent International Politics in Agreements, Notes and Declarations], Moscow, NKID, 1928, Part 3, *fasc.* 1, Document No. 166.

[23] *Izvestiya*, April 16, 1926. The claim to lands "which at the time of publication of this decree are not recognized by the [U.S.S.R.] as territories of any foreign states" is applicable to the eastern islands of the Spitsbergen archipelago lying between 32^0 E. long. and 35^0 E.

[24] Abbreviation for *Glavnoye upravleniye Severnovo morskovo puti* (Main Administration for the Northern Sea Route).

[25] "Political Rights in the Arctic," *Foreign Affairs*, New York, Vol. IV, No. 1, October 1925, pp. 46-70.

[26] See, for example, Lakhtin, V. L., *Prava na severnye polyarnye prostranstva* [Rights to North Pole Areas], Moscow, NKID, 1928.

[27] "*Aktivist O. A. Kh.*" was the pseudonym of Andrei V. Sabanin, at one time the head of the juridical department of the People's Commissariat of Foreign Affairs. Sabanin later fell victim to the Yezhov purges.

[28] *Aktivist O. A. Kh.*, "Imperializm na polyarnom Severe i interesy SSSR" [Imperialism in the Polar North and the Interests of the U.S.S.R.], *Sovetskii Sever*, No. 1-2, 1932, p. 39.

[29] *Ibid.*, p. 20.

[30] *Ibid.*, pp. 39-40.

[31] [Editor's note: The 1926 decree is generally regarded, however, as being based on the sector principle. See Smedal, Gustav, *Acquisition of Sovereignty Over Polar Areas*, Oslo, Dybwad, 1931, p. 69; Hyde, Charles Cheney, "Acquisition of Sovereignty Over Polar Areas," *Iowa Law Review*, Vol. XIX, 1934, p. 289. On the general subject of the sector principle, see Hackworth, Green H., *Digest of International Law*, Washington, D.C., 1940, pp. 449-76 (U.S. Department of State Publication No. 1506, Vol. I).]

19

[32] Decrees of the Council of People's Commissars May 20, 1930, and of the Presidium of the Central Executive Committee November 1931. See Orlovski, P., "2-oi mezhdunarodnyi polyarnyi god (1 avg. 1932 g.—31 avg. 1933 g.)" [The Second International Polar Year (August 1, 1932—August 31, 1933)], *Sovetskii Sever*, No. 1-2, 1932, pp. 85-86.

[33] "Arktika" [The Arctic], *Kratkaya Sovetskaya entsiklopediya*, Moscow, OGIZ, 1943, col. 68.

[34] "Arktika," *Bol'shaya Sovetskaya entsiklopediya*, 2d ed., Vol. III, 1950, p. 30.

[35] *Ibid.*, p. 32.

[36] Korovin, E., ed., *Mezhdunarodnoye pravo* [International Law], Moscow, Institut prava Akademii Nauk SSSR, 1951, p. 269. See also Durdenevski, V. N., "Problemy pravovovo rezhima pripolyarnykh oblastei" [Problems of the Legal Status of the Arctic Regions], *Vestnik Moskovskovo universiteta* [The Moscow University Herald], Moscow, No. 7, 1950.

[37] "Arktika," *Bol'shaya Sovetskaya entsiklopediya*, 2d ed., Vol. III, 1950, p. 33.

[38] *Ibid.*, p. 32.

[39] Special Instructions of Glavsevmorput', issued in 1933.

[40] See Frieden, K. K., "Sowjetische Hoheitsansprueche im noerdlichen Eismeer," *Svenska Dagbladt*, Stockholm, August 25, 1952, reprinted in *Ost-Probleme*, Bad Godesberg, No. 37, September 13, 1952, p. 1214.

[41] "K voprosu o rezhime Antarktiki" [On the Problem of the Status of the Antarctic], *Sovetskoye gosudarstvo i pravo* [Soviet State and Law], Moscow, No. 3, March 1951, pp. 38-43.

[42] Vyshnepol'ski, S. A., "K probleme pravovovo rezhima arkticheskoi oblasti" [On the Problem of the Legal Status of the Arctic Region], *Sovetskoye gosudarstvo i pravo*, No. 7, July 1952, p. 36.

[43] *Ibid.*, p. 45.

[44] At the beginning of the 1930's submarines were also proposed for exploring the Arctic. See Sverdrup, von, H., and K. Wagener, *Polarbuch. Neue Forschungsfahrten in Arktis und Antarktis mit Luftschiff, U-Boot, Schlitten and Forschungsschiff*, Berlin, 1933; and Sverdrup, Kh. [Sverdrup, von, H.] *Vo l'dy na podvodnoi lodke* [In the Ice with a Submarine], Leningrad, Vsesoyuznyi Arkticheskii Institut, 1932.

[45] The nine countries represented were: England, Germany, Norway, Spain, U.S.S.R., Finland, France, Japan, and Estonia. See Internationale Studiengesellschaft zur Erforschung der Arktis mit dem Luftschiff "Aeroarktik," *Verhandlung der 1. ordentlichen Versammlung in Berlin, 9-13. November, 1926*, Supplement to *Petermans Mitteilungen*, Gotha, 1927.

[46] See Vittenburg, P. V., ed., *Trudy vtoroi polyarnoi konferentsii 18-23 iyunya 1928 g.* [Transactions of the Second Polar Conference of June 18-23, 1928], Leningrad, Aeroarktik, 1930.

Rationale of Soviet Work in the Arctic

[47] See Assberg, F. F., and E. T. Krenkel', *Dirizhabl' v Arktike* [The Dirigible in the Arctic], Moscow-Leningrad, Gosmashmetizdat, 1933; Baschin, O., "Die Arktiksfahrt des Luftschiffes 'Graf Zeppelin,'" *Naturwissenschaften*, Berlin, Vol. XX, No. 1, 1932, pp. 6-13; and Ellsworth, L., and F. H. Smith, "Reports of the Preliminary Results of the Aeroarctic Expedition with the 'Graf Zeppelin,'" *Geographical Review*, New York, Vol. XXII, No. 1, 1932, pp. 61-82.

[48] Karavayev, A., "Narodnoye khozyaistvo: Sel'skoye khozyaistvo" [The National Economy: Agriculture], *Bol'shaya Sovetskaya entsiklopediya: SSSR* [Large Soviet Encyclopedia: The U.S.S.R.], Moscow, 1947, col. 852.

[49] Bruns, Walter, "Doklad o rezul'tatakh poyezdki na Kol'skii poluostrov v Murmansk" [Report on the Results of the Expedition to Murmansk on the Kola Peninsula], *Trudy vtoroi polyarnoi konferentsii,* pp. 14-21.

[50] *Ibid.*, p. xv. It is interesting that the proceedings of the Leningrad conference of Aeroarctic were published first in German and only later in Russian.

[51] The lecture, which the present writer attended, was given in the fall of 1931 in the Vyborg House of Culture and was sponsored by the Leningrad Presidium of Osoaviakhim (*Soyuz obshchestv sodeistviya oborone i aviatsionno-khimicheskomu stroitel'stvu SSSR* [Union of Societies for the Promotion of Defense and Aero-Chemical Development of the U.S.S.R.]).

[52] Zarzar, V. A., "Noveisheye v sovremennom aeronautizme" [The Latest in Contemporary Aeronautism], *Voprosy vozdushnovo prava* [Problems of Air Rights], ed. by V. I. Baranov *et al.*, Moscow-Leningrad, Osoaviakhim, No. 2, 1930, p. 7-28; Zarzar, V. A., and V. L. Lakhtin, *Bor'ba za vozdukh* [Struggle for the Air], Moscow, Osoaviakhim, 1927.

[53] See, for example, *Aktivist* O. A. Kh., *op. cit.*, pp. 30, 35-37, *passim.* It should be noted that England, a member of the organization, did not participate in the Leningrad conference of Aeroarctic in 1928.

[54] See Anvel't, Ya. Ya., *et al.*, eds., *Vozdushnye puti Severa* [Air Routes of the North], Moscow, Sovetskaya Aziya, 1933, pp. 8-9.

[55] The Soviet Government nevertheless invited Walter Bruns in the late twenties to carry out an assignment related to Soviet attempts to set up air lines in the Arctic Ocean. This author was so informed by a prominent Soviet authority on the Arctic.

[56] Yermashov, I. I., *Polyarnaya strategiya i polyarnaya ekspansiya* [Polar Strategy and Polar Expansion], Moscow, Izdatel'stvo "Pravda," 1947.

[57] Golant, V., "Polyarnaya likhoradka v Amerike" [Polar Fever in America], *Zvezda* [The Star], Leningrad, No. 11, November 1947, pp. 173-79.

[58] *Amerikanskii Sever* [The American North], Moscow, Izdatel'stvo inostrannoi literatury, 1950.

[59] "Alyaska v planakh amerikanskikh agressorov" [Alaska in the Plans of the American Aggressors], *Izvestiya*, September 8, 1950.

II. THE ORIGINAL SERVICE AREAS OF THE NORTHERN SEA ROUTE

1. The Shipping Lanes

From Murmansk or Archangel vessels plying the Northern Sea Route pass through the Barents Sea and, depending upon ice conditions, either through one of the straits of Yugorski Shar, Karskiye Vorota and Matochkin Shar or around Cape Zhelaniye to enter the area of the Northern Sea Route. The shortest course from Archangel to Dickson, through Matochkin Shar, is 1,994 kilometers; the distance through Yugorski Shar is 2,128 kilometers, and through Karskiye Vorota about the same; and around Cape Zhelaniye it is 2,319 kilometers. The lower reaches of the Yenisei are deep enough to permit maritime vessels to put in at Igarka, 873 kilometers up river from Dickson. The lane runs from the Kara Sea through Vil'kitski Strait into the Laptev Sea. From Tiksi the lane goes through Dmitri Laptev Strait or through Sannikov Strait to Ambarchik in the East Siberian Sea, then eastward through Long Strait, the Chukotsk Sea and the Bering Strait, the eastern limit of the Route proper. Southward from Providentiya Bay, vessels proceed to Petropavlovsk (Kamchatka) and Vladivostok, the terminal port for vessels operating in the eastern sector of the Northern Sea Route.

Strictly defined, the Northern Sea Route is bounded on the west by the passages between the Kara and Barents Seas and on the east by the Bering Strait. Maritime shipping or voyages which do not enter this area are not subsumed in the discussion of shipping on the Northern Sea Route.[1] On the other hand, voyages on the Northern Sea Route do not necessarily terminate within these geographical limits, and the area which the Route serves may lie completely beyond its formal boundaries. Thus an economic study of the Route requires that the discussion should range to other areas as well.

The commercial sea runs which make use of the Northern Sea Route include the following:[2]

1. Through runs between Murmansk and Vladivostok. The physical practicability of making this voyage in one navigation season was first demonstrated in 1932.

2. Runs between Murmansk or Archangel and the estuaries of the Ob' or the Yenesei (conventionally called Kara Sea runs). Ports in Western Europe sometimes function as the western terminus for these runs. The Kara Sea runs were established in tsarist times.

3. Runs between Vladivostok and the Chukotsk Peninsula or the estuaries of the Lena and Kolyma rivers. These runs were also established before the Revolution.

4. Runs between Murmansk or Archangel and the estuaries of the Lena or Kolyma Rivers. Beginning with 1935, these runs supplemented freight shipments originating at Vladivostok.

5. Local coastwise shipping which originates and terminates within the area of the Northern Sea Route. The year 1935 marked the beginning of systematic use of such shipping lines.

These shipping runs, and consequently the Northern Sea Route as a whole, can have an economic value only if there is a basis for an economic interchange of sizable proportions between the areas in the vicinity of their eastern and western termini. These regions, in Russian parlance called "areas of attraction," are the service areas of the Northern Sea Route.

2. *The Kara Sea Commercial Runs*

The Kara commercial runs, begun in the last quarter of the nineteenth century, were the first to be developed in northern seas. A result of radical economic changes in Siberia, their establishment is an interesting illustration of economic demands hastening the solution of extremely complicated technological problems.[3] The Soviet government regarded the economic usefulness of the Kara Sea route as a foregone conclusion and devoted much attention to it. Later the same attitude was automatically adopted toward all other Arctic sea lines, including the Murmansk-Vladivostok run. Soviet specialists were obliged to take this view, and foreign writers also have accepted it.

For example, in his comprehensive work on the Soviet conquest of the Arctic, Taracouzio, although he recognizes the role of other factors, emphasizes that maritime transportation in the Arctic is the very foundation of the Soviet program for development of the North.[4] A similar opinion was expressed by another commentator in an article which appeared in England after World War II:

> It had long been clear that a reliably operating Northern Sea Route would permit the delivery of freight to the mouths of all the rivers tributary to the Arctic and its southward despatch up these into most parts of the interior with only one transshipment. As the economic development of the northern half would be contingent on the growth of Arctic marine transport, it was decided to charge the organization responsible for the development of the Northern Sea Route with the economic control of this part of the sub-Arctic.[5]

Whether these judgments are valid will be indicated by a survey of the economic history of the Kara Sea runs, which formed the basis of the Northern Sea Route, as well as by an evaluation of the economic usefulness of the other shipping runs on the Route.

The original service areas of the Kara Sea transportation

line were (a) southwestern Siberia and (b) the central European countries and England. In the development of Russian agriculture there was a noticeable "shifting," long before World War I, of certain production zones away from western Russia and the outlets to the accessible seas toward the Siberian interior as a result of railroad construction and population movement.[6] The Kara Sea route, at the estuaries of the western Siberian rivers, offered the means of overcoming, to some degree, the disadvantages of this trend. England and the central European countries were potential consumers of Siberian agricultural and lumber exports. The Kara Sea route brought Siberia into closer transport relations with those countries than with most other parts of Russia. The run from the mouth of the Yenisei to London or Hamburg is shorter than from the same point to Leningrad via the Baltic route. The European countries offered a large market for Siberian agricultural products as well as a potential source of supply of industrial goods for Siberia.

Despite these favorable factors the Kara Sea lines could not be fully developed until the two obstacles of a short navigation season and high shipping costs were overcome. The Kara Sea route, with an average of only 90 navigation days a year, offered even less opportunity for commercial use than the river routes, which in the European part of the U.S.S.R. have a navigation season approximately two and one half to three times as long.[7] Although this situation raised the question of the economic expediency, and even the possibility, of developing the Kara Sea route, the foreign demand for Siberian agricultural products prevented its relinquishment, particularly since the short navigation period occurs right after the harvest, from August through late October. High shipping costs result from the necessity of servicing the route both from the air and on the water. Without icebreakers there can be no navigation in northern waters. In 1933 the steamer "Chelyushkin" was lost when it was abandoned by its icebreaker almost at the end of its eastbound passage along the Northern Sea Route. The 1940 feat of the German auxiliary cruiser "Komet," bound for the Pacific Ocean, was a rare exception.[8]

The use of icebreakers has provided a reliable transportation line in the Kara Sea. The decreased hazards are reflected in the sharp drop in insurance rates on the world market for Kara Sea shipping. In 1914 the rate for ships was 8 per cent, and in 1939, 2.25 per cent; the cargo rates were respectively 6 and 0.8 per cent.[9] The fact remains, however, that the large capital investments required for icebreakers can be justified only by a large volume of cargo shipments. This condition appeared realizable in the case of the Kara Sea line.

During the period of the New Economic Policy (1921-1928) the Soviet government, aiming at rapid restoration of the economy, decided to make full use of the possibilities presented by the Kara Sea route. In 1925 it was stated in the journal *Severnaya Aziya* [Northern Asia]:

> Until now the immense latent resources of Siberia have been lost to the world economy, although the need for these resources is tremendous.[10]

In 1923 Komseverput',[11] formed in 1920 by the Siberian Revolutionary Committee and at first placed under the jurisdiction of several commissariats, was transferred to the U.S.-S.R. People's Commissariat of Foreign Trade and became a transportation as well as trade organization; later it became a "transportation-trade-industrial" organization. Originally Komseverput' was made responsible for export-import operations through the estuaries of the western Siberian rivers. It was to provide facilities for the maximum volume of exports possible from localities served by the Northern Sea Route, that is, of export commodities that could not be shipped to outside markets by any other route or would be subject to undue price increase if sent by other carriers. Later Komseverput' was given control of industrial enterprises exploiting the region's natural resources for export, particularly those engaged in the timber industry, sea-animal hunting, mining, and fish preserving. The main offices of Komseverput' were in Novosibirsk; field offices for the Ob' and Irtysh rivers were in Omsk, and for the Yenisei in Krasnoyarsk. The organization also maintained representatives abroad, in London, Berlin and Hamburg.

In 1928 Komseverput' was reorganized as the North Siberian State Stock Company with the same functions of trade, industry and transportation. It remained under the jurisdiction of the Commissariat of Foreign Trade, which, jointly with the Siberian Krai Executive Committee, had set up the new company. Its capital was fixed at 10 million rubles.[12]

Goods produced by enterprises in Siberia, the Urals and Kazakhstan were shipped to the Siberian bases of Komseverput', where they were loaded on river boats. Such bases were located on the Ob' River at Kamen', Novosibirsk, Tomsk, and Mogochin; on the Irtysh River at Omsk, Tara and Ust'-Ishim; and on the Yenisei River at Krasnoyarsk and Maklakovo. Industrial goods for Siberia, which were bought in European markets by Soviet trade representatives, including those of Komseverput', were usually shipped to the port of Hamburg or London. It was arranged that the river boats with export goods from Siberian bases and the ships with import goods from Hamburg and London should depart so as to arrive in the ports of the Kara Sea at the same time and thus complete the exchange of cargoes with a minimum of delay.

The volume of the shipping operations of Komseverput' from 1920 to 1932 is shown in Table I. The marked increase in cargo shipments via the Kara Sea during this period is to be attributed to the early Soviet policies of permitting Kom-

Table I. Freight Turnover on the Kara Sea (tons) [13]

	On the Ob'			On the Yenisei			Total by sea			Percentage of total by sea	
	From Siberia	To Siberia	Total	From Siberia	To Siberia	Total	From Siberia	To Siberia	Total	From Siberia	To Siberia
1920	9,589	.....	9,589	722	.....	722	10,311	.....	10,311	.....	.....
1921	10,561	5,581	16,142	3,153	4,782	7,935	13,714	10,363	24,077	.....	.....
1922	5,837	7,790	13,627	.....	.....	.....	5,837	7,790	13,627	.....	.....
1923	.....	.....	.....	24	1,076	1,100	24	1,076	1,100	.....	.....
1924	2,102	5,368	7,470	2,046	1,205	3,251	4,148	6,573	10,721	.....	.....
Total	28,089	18,739	46,828	5,945	7,063	13,008	34,034	25,802	59,836	56.9	43.1
Per cent	82.5	72.8	78.3	17.5	27.2	21.7	100.0	100.0	100.0		
1925	3,122	5,868	8,990	2,460	1,734	4,194	5,582	7,602	13,184	.....	.....
1926	5,981	6,453	12,434	4,089	2,644	6,733	10,070	9,097	19,167	.....	.....
1927	6,188	9,050	15,238	4,926	4,264	9,190	11,114	13,314	24,428	.....	.....
1928	6,613	7,706	14,319	10,494	4,565	15,059	17,107	12,271	29,378	.....	.....
Total	21,904	29,077	50,981	21,969	13,207	35,176	43,873	42,284	86,157	50.9	49.1
Per cent	49.9	68.8	59.2	50.1	31.2	40.8	100.0	100.0	100.0		
				First Five-Year Plan							
1929	26,299	8,185	34,484	33,761	4,957	38,718	60,060	13,142	73,202	.....	.....
1930	44,497	11,928	56,425	87,844	10,743	98,587	132,341	22,671	155,012	.....	.....
1931	10,851	8,572	19,423	38,163	9,531	47,694	49,014	18,103	67,117	.....	.....
1932	8,486	6,497	14,983	71,620	10,667	82,287	80,106	17,164	97,270	.....	.....
Total	90,133	35,182	125,315	231,388	35,898	267,286	321,521	71,080	392,601	81.9	18.1
Per cent	28.0	49.5	31.9	80.0	50.5	68.1	100.0	100.0	100.0		

severput' to import foreign goods into Siberia and to export agricultural products and raw materials. Furthermore, for several years imports were allowed into the North duty-free.[14]

Siberia was in need of everything—consumer goods, medical supplies, agricultural machines, electrical equipment, motor vehicles, unfinished products, and industrial raw materials —and at the same time had agricultural products, lumber, and furs for export. So long as the policy of the Soviet Government favored Siberian foreign trade, the Kara Sea route continued to develop despite the difficult conditions of polar waters and the inadequacy of available equipment. Even the troublesome problem encountered by many transportation lines of providing ships with cargo on both outgoing and return trips was successfully solved during the years 1921-1928, as Table I indicates.

Imports into Siberia showed a steady increase during the twenties. During 1920-1932 the volume of foreign imports

Table II. *Siberian Imports from Europe via the Kara Sea (tons)*[15]

Product	1920-24	1925-28	First Five-Year Plan (1929-32)
Industrial raw materials, primarily nonferrous metals	2,364	11,454	33,063
Unfinished products	3,739	15,764	59
Equipment	3,468	2,530	12,229
Motor vehicles	2	45	———
Electrical equipment	42	266	———
Agricultural supplies	6,634	9,030	2,000
Medical preparations	251	1,013	———
Consumer goods	7,883	2,182	3,575
Total	24,383	42,284	50,926

going to Siberia by the Kara Sea far exceeded the volume of Soviet goods. From 1920 through 1924, only 1,419 tons of domestic goods went to Siberia through the Kara Sea; from 1925 through 1928 there were no such shipments; and during the First Five-Year Plan (1929-1932) Soviet goods accounted

29

for 20,154 tons out of the total of 71,080 shipped into Siberia.[16]

From 1920 throughout the NEP period Kara Sea shipments to and from Siberia remained nearly in balance. During the First Plan, however, the correlation changed drastically. Outgoing shipments, almost entirely to Western Europe, which had constituted 50.9 per cent of the Kara Sea turnover from 1925 to 1928, rose to 81.9 per cent during the period 1929 to 1932 (see Table I).

Despite the fact that the tonnage of cargoes leaving Siberian ports during the First Plan was almost ten times greater than that during the period 1920-1924, the export of agricultural products declined sharply, as is shown in Table III. Lumber from the Igarka sawmills, built at the beginning of the First Plan period, became the main, and virtually the only, export cargo shipped via the Kara Sea route. (Furs were sent to industrial centers of western U.S.S.R. before shipment abroad.)

Table III. *Exports of Siberian Agricultural Products via the Kara Sea (tons)*[17]

Product	1920-24	1925-28	First Five-Year Plan (1929-32)
Wheat	17,463	5,351	———
Raw cotton	415	4,493	540
Fiber	2,055	3,516	4,466
Hair, bristle, raw leather, wool	8,793	2,961	2,513
Butter, cheese	92		
Miscellaneous	119	118	430
Total	28,937	16,439	7,949

The launching of the First Five-Year Plan was proclaimed as the beginning of a new era which would bring "deliverance from foreign dependence"—still a principle of Soviet economic policy. "The most important task of socialist planning of the national economy is to assure the independence of our country and freedom from capitalist encirclement," it was reiterated in 1950.[18] Instead of encouraging the import of foreign goods and the export of agricultural products through the Kara route, the plans ultimately eliminated both.

The interests of individual regions of the country, in this case Siberia, were no longer the decisive factor. In the explanation of 1950, "Comrade Stalin teaches us that the supreme criterion of socialist planning is the general interests of the state."[19]

With the beginning of the Second Five-Year Plan, despite Siberia's exceptionally favorable position for trading with the markets of Western Europe via the Kara Sea route, foreign imports into Siberia ceased entirely, a situation still obtaining at the present time. The ban was so complete that the government even ignored the possibility of importing goods on the foreign ships calling at Igarka for Siberian lumber. Sending these ships light not only increased navigation costs but also made more difficult their voyages in the icy waters of the Kara Sea.[20]

At the same time the export of Siberian agricultural products came to an end. Still earlier the shipment of grain, Siberia's most advantageous export even before the Revolution, had been deflected from foreign ports to various regions of the U.S.S.R., in preparation for the new role assigned to Siberia in the Soviet drive for economic independence.

In 1930 construction of the Turkestan-Siberian Railroad (Turksib), one of the earliest and largest Soviet engineering projects, was completed. Siberia and Central Asia had been connected only by the Chelyabinsk-Chkalov (formerly Orenburg) line. The Turksib now reduced the rail distance between these regions by 2,000 kilometers. During the First Five-Year Plan it was pointed out at the Fifth Siberian Party Congress that

> completion of the Turkestan-Siberian Railroad opens tremendous prospects for economic relations of the [West] Siberian

Krai, particularly the Kuznetsk industrial area, with the richest areas of Kazakhstan and Central Asia. Siberian industry and the organs managing it must make it their first and most important task to prepare for the demands made by [this] direct connection. . . .[21]

The purpose in planning to supply western Siberian grain to Kazakhstan and Central Asia was to free irrigable land in the latter areas for the planting of cotton, rice, orchards and vineyards.

At the same time the food resources of western Siberia were reserved also for other regions of the U.S.S.R. A decree of the Congress of Soviets of the West Siberian Krai announced the following "basic aim":

West Siberia must become a main wheat region of the Soviet Union, supplying grain for the most important industrial districts of the country and Central Asia.[22]

This policy remains unchanged. To improve the transportation of Siberian products to the European U.S.S.R. the electrification of the railroad line Novokuznetsk-Inskaya-Omsk-Chelyabinsk-Dyoma, a distance of 2,350 kilometers, was begun after World War II. Wheat was to be one of the main products shipped on this road.[23]

The policy of looking upon Siberian products as a food reserve for Central Asia and "the most important industrial districts" led to absurdities. The Yakut Republic, for example, could not meet all of its food requirements by shipments from western Siberia and sometimes obtained grain by rail or via the Northern Sea Route all the way from the Volga and the old Russian "black soil" regions—an economically unsound practice of the kind which, according to Soviet economists, can occur only in a capitalist economy. But a plan is a plan, and administrative authorities of the Yakut Republic did not dare to object, in spite of the high prices they were forced to pay when the heavy shipping charges were added.

All they could attempt to obtain were such minor concessions as better packing of the freight consigned to them in order to reduce losses and damage en route and proper grading of commodities so that after being hauled across vast distances they might conform to the bill of lading.[24]

Whatever the economic or political validity of this policy, the cessation of exports of agricultural products and imports of foreign goods via the Kara Sea effectively deprived the Kara sector of the Northern Sea Route of its logical service areas—the southwestern regions of Siberia and Western Europe. The service areas remaining to the Route after the curtailment of its functions were the extreme North, the old industrial centers of the U.S.S.R., and the southern regions of the Far East, which were being industrialized.

3. The Role of Glavsevmorput'

Despite the elimination of two service areas of the Northern Sea Route, the Soviet government enlarged the scope of its plans for the Route as a whole. Soon after the successful voyage of the iceforcer "Sibiryakov" from the White Sea to the Pacific Ocean during the 1932 navigation season, the Council of People's Commissars organized Glavsevmorput', which absorbed Komseverput' several months later. The new organization was

> . . . charged with developing the Northern Sea Route from the White Sea to the Bering Strait, completely equipping it, maintaining it in proper condition, and procuring the means to ensure the safety of navigation over the same.[25]

In addition to its transportation functions, responsibilities for the development of industry and trade were assigned to Glavsevmorput'.[26] It was organized not as a stock company but as a government agency directly subordinated to the Council of People's Commissars and vested with broad authority.[27]

33

The functions of Glavsevmorput' included:

1. Organization of geological work, prospecting for useful minerals, and establishment of mining enterprises

2. Location of schools of fish and sea animal stations and organization of government fisheries and kolkhozes for fishing and hunting

3. Organization and management of sovkhozes for raising reindeer and other animals and a network of experimental agricultural farms; and the promotion of agriculture in the extreme North

4. Development of the fur industry

5. Organization of state trade in the extreme North.

Scientific research institutions, schools and industrial enterprises were also transferred to Glavsevmorput', which at first was in charge of most of the Siberian extreme North, including the activities of other Soviet institutions in the region.[28]

In 1935 O. Yu. Shmidt, the first head of Glavsevmorput', announced that the Northern Sea Route had been converted into a normally functioning seaway.[29] The 1937 navigation season, however, was a marked failure. Plans for the volume of freight shipments were unfulfilled, and many vessels locked in the ice were forced to winter at sea. Apart from natural conditions, which Glavsevmorput' cited in explanation, causes of the debacle clearly lay within that organization itself. The Council of People's Commissars ordered that Shmidt submit a full report on operations.[30] The Council then declared that, while Glavsevmorput' had broadened its functions, it had failed to discharge its responsibilities for the economic activities assigned to it and had slighted its prime objective, the conquest and development of the Northern Sea Route. Other charges were poor management and organization, laxity in inspection and selection of executive personnel, questionable financial practices, and even outright embezzlement. On the basis of its findings, the Council of People's Commissars in

1938 drastically reorganized Glavsevmorput'.[31] The earlier optimistic reports on the development of Arctic enterprises were asserted to bear no relation to reality. At a meeting of Glavsevmorput' personnel in fall 1938 in the House of the Red Army in Leningrad, Shirshov, speaking for the new *de facto* chief of Glavsevmorput', I. D. Papanin, labeled Shmidt's reports "downright lies." Papanin officially replaced Shmidt in 1939.

In the reorganization the territorial administrations were abolished, and their functions relating to maritime and river transport, local trade and hydrographic research were transferred to the appropriate central divisions of Glavsevmorput'. Representatives were left in Igarka, Yakutsk and Anadyr'. New measures were adopted which were intended to improve facilities of maritime and river transportation lines, polar aviation and polar stations, to increase the number of fuel bases, and to promote general study of the Northern Sea Route.

The decree took from the control of Glavsevmorput' the tremendous territories north of the 62nd parallel, excluding the littoral areas. The government recognized that the "auxiliary" bureaucratic apparatus of Glavsevmorput' did not stimulate, but rather paralyzed, the development of this territory. The decree of August 29, 1938, stated:

> With the creation in recent years of new oblasts in the northern regions and the consolidation of the [local] soviet agencies there, Glavsevmorput' can be relieved of the responsibility for economic and cultural services in those regions.[32]

All enterprises not directly connected with its basic function of developing the Route were transferred from Glavsevmorput' to the appropriate government bureaus. In its administrative overhaul of the North the Council of People's Commissars overlooked the interests of the native economy, which, because of its peculiar character and relationship with the

Soviet government, requires the attention and guidance of a specialized organization. The predecessor of Glavsevmorput', the Committee of the North, attached to the All-Union Central Executive Committee, had been such an organization. Now that Glavsevmorput' was restricted to the Arctic coastal areas, the northern natives became the responsibility of local government, or, in other words, they were left to themselves. The government later transferred responsibility for the northern economy to the Administration of the Districts of the Extreme North, attached to the R.S.F.S.R. Ministry of Agriculture,[33] and from this action it seems clear that the local government bodies were unable to cope with the problem.

Finally in 1953 Glavsevmorput' was attached to the newly-created Ministry of the Maritime and River Fleet.[34]

Bureaucratic methods of management had left their imprint on all activities connected with the Route, and in response to government demands Glavsevmorput' had produced not success but reports of success. But administrative changes with respect to Glavsevmorput' did not alter the basic economic situation, which alone could provide a *raison d'être* for the Northern Sea Route.

NOTES

[1] Voyages in the White and Barents Seas which do not enter the area of the Northern Sea Route are conventionally called Northern Basin runs. Analogous trips in the area between Vladivostok and the Bering Strait are called Far East Basin voyages. The cargo turnover in these two basins is computed separately from the cargo turnover on the Northern Sea Route in Soviet statistics, and therefore it is essential to keep these distinctions in mind.

[2] For details on the opening of the lines established before the Revolution, see Krypton, Constantine, *The Northern Sea Route: Its Place in Russian Economic History Before 1917*, New York, Research Program on the U.S.S.R., 1953; and Armstrong, Terence, *The Northern Sea Route: Soviet Exploitation of the North East Passage*, Cambridge, Cambridge University Press, 1952 (Scott Polar Research Institute, Special Publication No. 1).

[3] See Krypton, *op. cit.*

Original Service Areas of the Route

[4] Taracouzio, T. A., *Soviets in the Arctic: An Historical, Economic and Political Study of the Soviet Advance into the Arctic*, New York, Macmillan, 1938, pp. 141-43.

[5] Webster, C. J., "The Economic Development of the Soviet Arctic and Sub-Arctic," *The Slavonic and East European Review*, London, Vol. XXIX, No. 72, December 1950, p. 197.

[6] See Bernshtein-Kogan, S. V., *Ocherki geografii transporta* [Outlines of the Geography of Transport], Moscow-Leningrad, Gosizdat, 1930.

[7] The western Dvina is navigable 236 days a year, the Dnepr at Kiev 267 days, the upper Volga 224 days, and the Volga at Astrakhan' 264 days. *Ibid.*, p. 21.

[8] For details on the voyage of the "Komet," see p. 167.

[9] Data from Glavsevmorput'.

[10] Notkin, A. I., "Severnyi morskoi put' " [The Northern Sea Route], *Severnaya Aziya* [Northern Asia], Moscow, No. 1-2, 1925, p. 28.

[11] Abbreviation for *Komitet Severnovo morskovo puti* [Committee for the Northern Sea Route].

[12] See "Komitet Severnovo morskovo puti," *Sibirskaya Sovetskaya entsiklopediya* [Siberian Soviet Encyclopedia], Vol. II, Novosibirsk, 1931, cols. 872-73; "Karskaya ekspeditsiya" [The Kara Run], *ibid.*, col. 543.

[13] Based on data of the Moscow Scientific Research Institute for the Economy of the North, quoted without specifying source by Sibirtsev, N. and V. Itin, *Severnyi morskoi put' i Karskiye ekspeditsii* [The Northern Sea Route and the Kara Runs], Novosibirsk, Zap.-Sib. izdat., 1936, p. 110. Unless otherwise stated all tonnage figures given in the present work refer to metric tons.

[14] See decrees in Kruglov, A., "Severnoye zakonodatel'stvo" [Northern Legislation], *Sovetskii Sever* [Soviet North], Moscow, No. 1, 1931, 209-10, 212.

[15] Sibirtsev and Itin, *op. cit.*, p. 111.

[16] *Ibid.*

[17] *Ibid.*, p. 109.

[18] Perov, G., "Stalin i sotsialisticheskoye planirovaniye narodnovo khozyaistva" [Stalin and Socialist Planning of the National Economy], *Narodnoye khozyaistvo SSSR* [The National Economy of the U.S.S.R.], Sbornik [Symposium], No. 3, ed. by B. I. Eidel'man, Moscow, Gosplanizdat, 1950, p. 52.

[19] *Ibid.*

[20] These disadvantages have been pointed out in annual reports of Glavsevmorput'.

[21] Baranski, N. N., and B. Kaminski, *Sotsialisticheskaya rekonstruktsiya oblastei, kraev i respublik SSSR v postanovleniyakh partiinykh i sovetskikh organov* [Socialist Reconstruction of Oblasts, Krais and Republics of the U.S.S.R. in Decrees of Party and Soviet Organs], Moscow, Sotsial'no-ekonomicheskoye izdatel'stvo, 1932, Part 1, p. 366.

[22] *Ibid.*, p. 372. On the shipment of grain into Central Asia, see "Turkestano-Sibirskaya zheleznaya doroga" [The Turkestan-Siberian Rail-

road], *Bol'shaya Sovetskaya entsiklopediya* [Large Soviet Encyclopedia], Vol. LV, 1947, cols. 238-40.

23 "Siberian wheat, iron, steel, timber, fish, salt, and other freight will be transported at high speed on the improved road." "Elektrifikatsiya Omskoi zheleznoi dorogi" [The Electrification of the Omsk Railroad], *Pravda*, July 16, 1948.

24 See Yankin, V., "Ob otgruzke tovarov raionam Krainevo Severa" [On Freight Shipments to the Extreme North], *Izvestiya*, June 29, 1948; and Lyapin, N. [Minister of Food Supply of the Yakut A.S.S.R.], "Vopros zhdyot resheniya Ministerstva" [The Question Awaits Decision by the Ministry], *Izvestiya*, December 8, 1950. That such mistakes still occur is indicated by a speech of L. M. Kaganovich at a session of the Supreme Soviet of the U.S.S.R. in 1954, in which he said: "From October 1953 to March 1954 the Ministry of Procurements shipped 296,000 tons of wheat from the Volga region, the Bashkir A.S.S.R. and Chkalov Oblast to the Urals and Siberia, and in April 1954 is hauling the same wheat from Siberia and the Urals to the center [of European Russia]." "Zasedaniya Verkhovnovo Soveta SSSR: Rech' deputata L. M. Kaganovicha" [Sessions of the Supreme Soviet of the U.S.S.R.: Speech of Deputy L. M. Kaganovich], *Izvestiya*, April 27, 1954.

25 *Sobraniye zakonov i rasporyazhenii pravitel'stva SSSR* [Collection of Laws and Ordinances of the Government of the U.S.S.R.], Moscow, 1932, I, No. 84, Par. 522 (English translation in Taracouzio, *op. cit.*, p. 383).

26 *Sobraniye zakonov*, 1933, I, No. 21, Par. 124 (English translation in Taracouzio, *op. cit.*, pp. 385-87); and *Izvestiya*, August 3, 1934 (English translation in Taracouzio, *op. cit.*, pp. 389-91).

27 *Sobraniye zakonov*, 1935, No. 7, Par. 59 (English translation in Taracouzio, *op. cit., pp.* 393-94).

28 See decrees of 1932, 1933, 1934, and 1935, *supra;* also statute of Glavsevmorput' in *Sobraniye zakonov*, 1936, I, No. 36, Par. 317 (English translation in Taracouzio, *op. cit.*, pp. 395-400).

29 "Na stupen' vyshe" [A Step Up], *Sovetskaya Arktika* [Soviet Arctic], Moscow, No. 5, 1935, p. 3.

30 "V Sovete Narodnykh Komissarov Soyuza SSR: O rabote Glavsevmorputi za 1937 g." [In the Council of People's Commissars of the U.S.S.R.: On the Work of Glavsevmorput' for 1937], *Izvestiya*, March 29, 1938.

31 "Postanovleniye Sovnarkoma SSSR ob uluchshenii raboty Glavnovo upravleniya Severnovo morskovo puti ot 29 avgusta 1938 g." [Decree of August 29, 1938, of the Council of People's Commissars of the U.S.S.R. on Improving the Work of Glavsevmorput'], *Pravda*, August 30, 1938. Despite the clear language of the decree, as well as subsequent articles in *Sovetskaya Arktika* (listed below) criticizing the disgraceful record of Glavsevmorput', C. J. Webster gives the following explanation of the reorganization of Glavsevmorput': "The drafting and inauguration of the Third Five-Year Plan of the U.S.S.R. was dominated by the lengthening shadow of war. . . . The GUSMP [Glav-

Original Service Areas of the Route

sevmorput'] was ordered to devote all its attention to completing the complex construction required to transform the Arctic into a useful ocean basin and make the entire length of the northern sea route a reliable waterway. *To assist in this task* [italics mine—C. K.], the government relieved the GUSMP of all its continental enterprises. . . ." "The Economic Development of the Soviet Arctic and Sub-Arctic," *The Slavonic and East European Review*, London, Vol. XXIX, No. 72, December 1950, p. 206. If the war had been the government's major concern, it would have been expedient to retain Glavsevmorput' as a powerful transportation and industrial organization (a "northern empire"), uniting the vast regions of the Asiatic North under a single jurisdiction. Among the articles in *Sovetskaya Arktika* on the failures of Glavsevmorput' were: Gakkel', Ya. Ya., "Oshibki v arkticheskoi navigatsii 1937 g." [Mistakes of the 1937 Navigation Season], No. 3, 1938, pp. 28-40; Savin, V., "Protiv povtoreniya oshibok navigatsii 1938 g." [Against the Repetition of the Mistakes of the 1938 Navigation Season], No. 2, 1939, pp. 80-82; Makhotkin, V., "Ob oshibkakh navigatsii 1938 g." [On the Mistakes of the 1938 Navigation Season], No. 4, 1939, pp. 95-101; Meshcherin, V., "Za chotkuyu organizovannuyu rabotu" [For the Efficient Organization of Work], No. 5, 1939, pp. 55-57; Khrapal', A., "K navigatsii 1940 goda gotovitsya seichas" [Preparations for the 1940 Navigation Season Are Now Being Made], No. 10, 1939, pp. 9-18; Annin, N., and K. Yevtyukhov, "Vazhneisheye zveno v podgotovke k navigatsii 1940 goda: O sudoremonte" [The Most Important Part of the Preparations for the 1940 Navigation Season: Concerning Ship Repair], No. 11, 1939, pp. 65-70.

[32] "Postanovleniye Sovnarkoma SSSR ob uluchshenii raboty Glavnovo upravleniya Severnovo morskovo puti ot 29 avgusta 1938 g.," *op. cit.*

[33] The date of the change is not known, but that it took place is evidenced by press reports of the 1949 session of the R.S.F.S.R. Supreme Soviet. At this session, the work of the Administration was described as unsatisfactory, and it was recommended that a special committee for the North be organized directly under the R.S.F.S.R. Council of Ministers. "Rech' deputata S. A. Nemtseva ot Krasnoyarskovo Kraya" [Address by Deputy S. A. Nemtsev of Krasnoyarsk Krai], *Izvestiya*, May 31, 1949.

[34] "Zakon o preobrazovanii ministerstv SSSR" [Law on the Reorganization of the Ministries of the U.S.S.R.], *Vedomosti Verkhovnovo Soveta SSSR* [News of the Supreme Soviet of the U.S.S.R.], March 20, 1953, Par. 14. In August 1954 the Ministry of the Maritime and River Fleet was divided into a Ministry of the Maritime Fleet (headed by Viktor A. Bakayev) and a Ministry of the River Fleet (headed by Zosima A. Shashkov, the former head of the combined ministry). "V Prezidiume Verkhovnovo Soveta SSSR" [In the Presidium of the Supreme Soviet of the U.S.S.R.], *Pravda*, August 29, 1954. Presumably Glavsevmorput' is under the jurisdiction of the Ministry of the Maritime Fleet, although no information on this point has been published in the Soviet press.

III. THE ECONOMIC POTENTIAL OF THE SERVICE AREAS OF THE NORTHERN SEA ROUTE

When Glavsevmorput' was first organized, the purpose of the Northern Sea Route, as defined in treatises and administrative instructions concerned with the northern economy, was to assure regular economic relations between the various regions of the extreme North and the more developed regions of the country,[1] that is, to promote an interregional division of labor as well as to help populate the extreme North and develop its natural resources. The North was to receive food and manufactured goods and ship out raw materials and semifinished products.

The question whether economic interchange between the reduced service areas of the Northern Sea Route would provide a sound economic basis for the operation of the Route depended on a number of factors: the level of development and prospects of individual industries in the North whose output and supplies would in some measure be shipped via the Route; the overall economic development of the North, which determines the potential level of economic demand and output on which the Route might rely; the emergence of alternate sources of supply for goods to be shipped to and from the North via the Route; and the state of navigation, equipment and facilities on the Route and complementary or competing means of transportation. These factors will be discussed individually before an attempt is made to analyze their combined effect on the Northern Sea Route.

Economic Potential of the Service Areas

1. *Industries of the North*

   a. The Northern Coal Industry

   (1) Sources of Coal in the Western Sector

The westernmost of the coal sources which are of importance to the Northern Sea Route is the Pechora Basin. Its deposits are concentrated in the northeast section of the Komi A.S.S.R. and in adjacent parts of the Nenets Okrug, particularly around the Vorkuta River area, where mining was begun in 1931. According to the analysis of Soviet specialists, including those of Glavsevmorput', the quality of Vorkuta coal equals that of Donets, which has a caloric content of about 7,500. Vorkuta coal is suitable for metallurgic use and meets the standards of the fleet,[2] although some of the coal in the area is apparently of very poor quality.[3] The coal reserves in the Pechora Basin have been estimated at 60 billion tons.[4]

Before the war Pechora coal was supplied to the industrial enterprises of the Kola Peninsula as well as to the ships of the White and Barents seas. Mining in the Pechora Basin was limited, however, by the inadequacy of transportation facilities. From the mine area on the non-navigable Vorkuta River, coal had to be hauled 63 kilometers by narrow-gauge railroad to the Usa River, shipped by barge down the Usa and Pechora rivers, and at Nar'yan-Mar reloaded to vessels bound for Murmansk. The Usa is shallow—its depth in summer is only .5 to to .6 meter—and the sand bar at the mouth of the Pechora hinders navigation of ships with deep draft. For these reasons the annual shipment of Vorkuta coal in the prewar years amounted to only 150,000 or 200,000 tons.[5]

When the German invasion cut off the southern coal regions, the Soviet government was compelled to undertake intensive development of the Pechora Basin to supply Leningrad, the industries of the northern European U.S.S.R. and the northern naval fleet. Measures were taken to speed up construction of the Pechora Railroad, which at the end of December 1941 had reached Vorkuta.[6] "Distinguished leaders in military uniform" arrived on the scene.[7] The builders were given ample means and were instructed to disregard the difficulties of polar conditions in the use of "human material." A sum of 617 million rubles was invested in the development of the Pechora coal basin, of which 518 million were spent during the war.[8]

Vorkuta is the main city of the Pechora Basin. Of the eighteen working mines and twenty under construction in the Pechora Basin at the end of the war, Vorkuta alone had eleven working mines and fourteen under construction. The Vorkutugol' Trust, which operates the mines, had become a large organization.[9]

The following data show the wartime increase in Pechora coal output:[10]

1940	100% (225,000 tons)[11]
1941	118%
1942	271%
1943	603%
1944	871%
1945	1,110%

The first postwar Five-Year Plan (1946-1950) projected development of new mines to bring total annual output of the Pechora Basin to 7.7 million tons;[12] it is not known whether this goal was attained.[13] The coal is transported by the Pechora Railroad and, in the summer, also by the river routes to the coast and then by freighter to Murmansk and Archangel.[14] The easy availability of these vast coal supplies has made the Pechora Basin into the new coal base of the northern European U.S.S.R., including Leningrad,[15] and has eliminated the necessity of shipping coal supplies to the northwestern industries from the remote deposits of Siberia,[16] particularly Noril'sk.

The development of the Pechora coal basin revived an old

plan for building a railroad line from Vorkuta to Yugorski Shar. Surveys of the route had been made in 1932 by the Main Administration for Railroad Construction of the People's Commissariat of Transportation.[17] Construction of this line may be currently underway.[18] If so, Pechora coal is certain to become an even greater competitor of Noril'sk coal, even in supplying fuel for ships on the Northern Sea Route.[19]

Farther east is the Tunguska Basin, with reserves estimated at billions of tons.[20] The Noril'sk coal fields, which have been extensively prospected, are a northern branch of the Tunguska Basin. These deposits were first worked in order to supply the Noril'sk Polymetal Combine.[21] From Noril'sk the coal was dispatched by the 112-km. rail line to Dudinka[22] on the Yenisei, which is only a short run from Dickson. The Noril'sk-Dudinka railroad, the first above the Arctic Circle in the Asiatic part of the U.S.S.R., was built during the 1930's to aid in the construction of the combine and to provide transportation for its output. Since the lower Yenisei is so deep that seagoing vessels call at Igarka, south of Dudinka, for lumber, Noril'sk coal can be taken on at Dudinka at very low transportation cost to these freighters. Later, because of the great quantity and high quality of the coal here, the Noril'sk fields began to send coal to Dickson to supply also the merchant fleet of the Northern Sea Route. The first shipments of Noril'sk coal for the merchant fleet of Glavsevmorput' took place in 1939 and amounted to about 50,000 tons.[23] It was planned to ship Noril'sk coal to industrial areas of the northern European U.S.S.R. in 1941-42; preliminary estimates of the volume of shipments ran into hundreds of thousands of tons.[24] In this connection Dudinka was made a coaling base, and the narrow-gauge rail line connecting it with Noril'sk was rebuilt as a broad-gauge road. During World War II the Noril'sk mines supplied fuel for the northern naval fleet.

Farther north there is an extension of the Tunguska Basin

on the Taimyr Peninsula in the area of the Pyasina River and around the Gulf of Yenisei, which contains anthracite and other coal deposits.[25] According to Glavsevmorput' this coal is suitable for ship bunkers as well as for use by industry. However, nothing can be found in Soviet literature to indicate that work in this area has progressed beyond the prospecting stage.

(2) Sources of Coal in the Eastern Sector

The expansion of coal mining on the Nordvik Peninsula beyond its modest beginnings in the early thirties was stimulated by the need of the salt industry in that area for local sources of fuel and power. Three years before World War II a coal mine in this area was turned over to Glavsevmorput' for development; its output amounted in 1938 to 8,150 tons.[26] The Third Five-Year Plan (1938-1942) called for an increase in the production of Nordvik coal from the working mines, proving of other deposits and the opening of a new mine near the coast so that, in addition to supplying all local construction operations, Nordvik mines could also bunker vessels that put in for salt.[27]

In the Lena Basin coal is mined at Sangar and Kangalasskiye Kopi.[28] The city of Yakutsk and its industries rely on the latter source. The Sangar mines, frequently referred to in Glavsevmorput' reports as the most important coal base for vessels in the eastern sector of the Arctic, are located on the right bank of the Lena River, 1,332 kilometers south of Tiksi Bay and 339 kilometers north of Yakutsk. The total reserves of Sangar coal were at first estimated at about 7.5 million tons, but were later ascertained to be only 807,000 tons. The coal occurs in wide seams and has a caloric content of from 6,000 to 7,000 and a small ash-moisture content. It can be used by maritime and river vessels. In the mid-thirties, however, the tonnage of coal extracted from the Sangar and Kangalasskiye mines was negligible, as the following annual production figures show:[29]

	1933	1934	1935	1936	1937
Sangar	11,600	9,000	17,700	22,800	22,100
Kangalasskiye	8,700	9,500	11,000	13,000	10,400

Although the Third Five-Year Plan of Glavsevmorput' required the construction of new mines, mechanization of labor and improved technical equipment, which were to increase production in the Sangar mines to 120,000 tons a year,[30] in 1940 output had not yet reached 40,000 tons.[31] The Soviet press indicates that intensive efforts have been applied in the postwar years:

> In 1936 in Sangar there were only seventeen little houses; now it is one of the liveliest places on the Lena River. From early spring to late autumn, boats and barges with heavy cargoes stand at the moorings and the coal pier.[32]

The fact remains that the Sangar mines are an unsatisfactory source of fuel for vessels operating in the eastern sector of the Northern Sea Route. The quality of the coal is too low to justify the haul of 1,332 kilometers from the mines to Tiksi Bay. In the late 1930's, however, Glavsevmorput', for want of working mines in the vicinity of the Route, recommended that the production of Sangar coal be increased to the maximum despite the excessive costs.[33]

At the same time prospecting for coal in the lower reaches of the Lena had been in progress for several years.[34] A prewar report of Glavsevmorput' stated that coal had been discovered in the Tiksi Bay area, near the Lena, in sufficient quantities to serve as a future source of supply for vessels engaged in cabotage.[35]

East of the Lena lie the Zyryanka deposits. The coal has a heating capacity of 6,000 to 7,800 calories with a low ash-moisture content, and is a good fuel for ships. These deposits are extensive, being estimated at about 150 million tons, but have been little explored. The Zyryanka mines are 61 kilometers from Zyryanka on the Kolyma River. Until the late thirties these mines, which were run by Dal'stroi, the NKVD (later MVD) Far Eastern development project, filled only the needs of Kolyma River vessels. In 1939 the mines were transferred to the jurisdiction of Glavsevmorput' and began to supply bunkers to vessels entering Ambarchik Bay with freight for transshipment by river craft. The annual output of the Zyryanka mines was increased to 40,000 tons, and the loading of coal at the Zyryanka pier was mechanized.[36] After the war the area became well populated.[37] Simultaneously with the development of the Zyryanka deposits, exploratory work in the lower reaches of the Kolyma was planned.

In the eastern part of the Chukotsk Peninsula a coal deposit about three to six miles from Ugol'naya Bay has been found and partly proved. The quality of the coal is suitable for the merchant fleet. The reserves surveyed, estimated at 30 million tons, were considered adequate to supply ships and also local industry, mainly fish canning. Before World War II a Glavsevmorput' publication stated:

> The needs of ships sailing in the [northern] Far Eastern seas and of Kamchatka's industries are met with Sakhalin coal. With the development in the near future of coal production in Ugol'naya Bay, Sakhalin coal for the northern fleet will be replaced.[38]

However, up to World War II the output of coal from the Ugol'naya Bay deposits amounted to only about seven or eight thousand tons annually.[39] Since there has been no reference to them in recent Soviet literature, there probably has been no substantial increase in their output.

The search for coal on Kamchatka was stimulated by the economic needs of the peninsula itself as well as by the need of local coal for ships plying the Northern Sea Route. Brown coal was found in northern Kamchatka and mining begun in the vicinity of the Gulf of Korf. Since the coal was not of sufficiently high quality for fueling ships, the search for new fields as well as better deposits in the Korf area continued.[40]

Thus, before World War II the main source of fuel for ships in the eastern section of the Northern Sea Route was the high quality coal on Sakhalin Island, which was also used for the Soviet Far Eastern merchant fleet and industry. According to official Soviet data, the output of coal on the island, even before the southern part was annexed, amounted to 2 million tons annually.[41]

The war disrupted any plans to develop a substitute for Sakhalin coal. The coal supply for ships and industry in the entire northeastern sector lies, as before, in Sakhalin, although this situation contradicts the principles of a rational economy. A deputy from the Khabarovsk Krai pointed out at a session of the Supreme Soviet in the summer of 1950:

> Hundreds of thousands of tons of coal are brought in annually to the shores of Kamchatka and Okhotsk, but the difficulty of shipping and the shortage of bottoms often hamper the work of various enterprises. At the same time coal that is available on the Kamchatka and Okhotsk shores is mined in insignificant quantities. We consider it advisable to transfer the working coal mines to the Ministry of the Coal Industry so that the output of coal may be increased considerably in 1951. It is also necessary to instruct the Ministry of the Coal Industry to begin the exploitation of coal on the coasts of Kamchatka and Okhotsk.[42]

It is obvious that, for at least five years after the war, development of coal mining in the remote districts of the northeast remained in the hands of local authorities, while the Ministry of the Coal Industry disclaimed responsibility.

(3) The Need of Local Sources of Coal for the Northern Sea Route

Economically efficient use of the Northern Sea Route required the development of coal mining along the Arctic coast for the fueling of ships plying the coastal waters. The Soviet government also regarded local coal production as a spur to the general economic development of the Arctic and subarctic regions.[43] Furthermore, the transportation system of

47

the U.S.S.R. consumes about one-third of the country's total output of coal,[44] and supplying the Northern Sea Route from the old coal districts (the Donets and Kuznetsk basins and the Urals) would constitute an additional drain on their resources.

Until the middle thirties coal from Soviet sources for the Northern Sea Route came from Barentsburg and Grumant on Spitsbergen Island,[45] Suchan, Sakhalin, and the Donets, Kuznetsk and Minusinsk basins. Spitsbergen coal, because of its geographic location, can be utilized only in the extreme western ports of the northern route, Murmansk and Archangel. The distance between Spitsbergen and Murmansk is over 1,000 kilometers; for Spitsbergen coal transshipped to Dickson Island, the main base in the western sector of the Northern Sea Route, another 2,000 kilometers is added. The use of Spitsbergen coal becomes even less practical for ports farther east. The mines of Suchan and Sakhalin, as well as those along the coast that have been worked recently, are also of limited usefulness to the Route. Although Suchan coal, for instance, can be used advantageously for fueling ships for the first lap of the run from Vladivostok, it can no longer be considered local coal when shipped to the northeast, as it has been for many years, to provide bunkers at Petropavlovsk and the Chukotsk Peninsula.[46]

Equally unsatisfactory as sources of fuel for northern navigation are the Donets, Kuznetsk and Minusinsk basins. Although Komseverput' experimented with the use of Kuznetsk coal for the purpose—beginning in 1932, when 525 tons were shipped to Novyi Port on the Ob' Bay for the westbound return trip of several foreign vessels—the Kuznetsk Basin, because of its great distance from the northern coast, could not be relied upon as a regular source of fuel. The Ob', which still does not have an adequate number of craft, is over 3,500 kilometers long. The river vessels transporting coal north had to haul their own fuel supply because of the poor bunkering facilities en route. As a result the cost of using Kuznetsk coal for northern coastal shipping was high.[47] Shipping coal down the Yenisei River from the Chernogorsk mines located in the Minusinsk Basin, 2,500 kilometers from the Arctic Ocean, was also economically unsound.

It was likewise clear that coal from the Donets Basin could not solve the fuel problem. It had to be transported either by railroad, across the entire European part of the U.S.S.R., or via the long water route around Western Europe (from the Black Sea to Murmansk), a distance of 11,500 kilometers. From Murmansk to Dickson, through Arctic waters, vessels required special servicing. Nevertheless, for many years up to the mid-1930's Donets coal was hauled via the long inland route to Dickson.[48] The former head of Soviet heavy industry, Ordzhonikidze, said at the Seventeenth Party Conference in 1932:

> The Donets Basin has been, and still is, supplying coal for Moscow and Leningrad. Coal from the Donets Basin goes even to Berezniki and Perm'. . . . This folly must not be continued —we haul coal from one region of our Union to another, and then we ourselves complain that we are short of rolling stock.[49]

During 1935 Glavsevmorput' had to pay the following prices for coal at the main ports of the Northern Sea Route:[50]

Port	Rubles per ton of bunker coal
Murmansk	65
Spitsbergen	50
Dickson	126
Igarka	80
Novyi Port	80
Tiksi	190
Kolyma	190
Provideniya Bay	100
Petropavlovsk (Kamchatka)	80
Vladivostok	50

Because of shipping charges, coal in Murmansk cost twice as much as on the Black Sea, and at Dickson four times as much.

49

In the eastern sector similar price increases occurred for coal shipped from Vladivostok north to Petropavlovsk, Provideniya Bay and the mouth of the Kolyma River.

Until 1934 vessels plying the Northern Sea Route were sometimes supplied with English and German coal—a practice which contravened the policy of "liberation from foreign dependence" and drained off foreign currency reserves.[51] In the early developmental stage of the North Sea Route, however, coal was obtained where most readily available.

(4) Distribution of Coaling Stations

Undoubtedly the northern coal industry has been largely successful in freeing the ships of the Northern Sea Route from dependence on fuel shipped from great distances. Furthermore, distribution of mining operations and, even more important, of coal reserves along the Route promised to render it possible to provide a well-spaced series of coaling stations and thus to assure the most efficient use of deadweight tonnage. The fewer opportunities for bunkering en route, the higher the percentage of deadweight tonnage occupied by fuel reserves, and the lower the percentage occupied by the ship's commercial cargo. The result is increased cost of transportation. Because of the great distances and difficulties that have to be overcome in the polar seas the rational utilization of capacity is especially urgent.

Before World War II the coaling bases along the Northern Sea Route were Murmansk or Archangel, Dickson, Tiksi, Provideniya Bay, Petropavlovsk (Kamchatka), and Vladivostok, with distances of 2,000 kilometers or more between bases. Part of the run between Provideniya Bay and Tiksi is heavily covered with ice and therefore requires additional refueling for ships somewhere along the way. For this reason it was planned before World War II to construct a coal base at the mouth of the Kolyma. The further development of individual lines of the Northern Sea Route, such as between Murmansk and Igarka, Murmansk and Tiksi, Murmansk and the Kolyma, and Vladivostok and the Kolyma, would require additional bases supplied with local fuel as well as storage facilities.

There is evidence that the fueling of northern shipping with local coal has been more successful in the western sector of the Northern Sea Route than in the eastern. The port of Murmansk receives coal from the Pechora Basin deposits, which were actively developed during the war, and Dickson receives coal from Noril'sk. In the eastern sector, however, the Sangar mines do not solve the bunkering problem at Tiksi, and although closer to the Route, Zyryanka is still too far for economical feeding of a coaling base at the mouth of the Kolyma. In the northeast, production at Ugol'naya Bay is low, and the Korf deposits yield coal of poor quality.

b. Oil and Minerals

(1) General Survey

Geologic explorations have been conducted in the extreme North by a number of organizations, including the Arctic Institute, the Department of Mining and Geology of Glavsevmorput', the U.S.S.R. Academy of Sciences, and various industrial enterprises.[52]

In a survey of the area from west to east, the first point to be noted is the Kola Peninsula, where there are large apatite and nephelite reserves in the Khibiny Mountains[53] near the new city of Kirovsk. The apatite has a higher calcium phosphate content than that of the average Soviet deposit and withstands long-distance transportation. Mining developed to the point where the U.S.S.R. has been able to export apatite concentrates.[54] In the southwest part of the peninsula there are copper and nickel deposits in the Monche tundra and sizable deposits of iron near Lake Imandra.[55] According to postwar Soviet data, Monchegorsk ranks third in copper production in the U.S.S.R., following the Urals and Noril'sk.[56] In the Pechenga area there is an important nickel mine, around which has grown the industrial settlement Nikel'.[57]

The Kola Peninsula, although geographically part of the extreme North and at least nominally a service area of the Northern Sea Route, is economically in close relations with the southerly industrial areas and contributes little or nothing to the development of the Route. Its mining industry is geared to the needs of the old industrial districts, principally Leningrad, and like other industries on the peninsula, depends for transportation on the Kirov Railroad.[58]

Southwest of the Vorkuta coal deposits in the Komi A.S.-S.R., oil deposits have been found in the Ukhta River region. Near the strait of Matochkin Shar mineral deposits have been found containing zinc sulphide, lead and copper pyrites, but their industrial value has not been ascertained. On Vaigach Island and the Yugorski Peninsula about 350 discoveries have been officially registered, among them copper, lead, zinc, manganese, and fluorspar. There are several known deposits of fluorspar on the Yugorski Peninsula, the largest of which, in Amderma, constitutes a substantial part of the total Soviet reserves of the mineral.

The Noril'sk area contains extensive mineral deposits, including copper, nickel and platinum. Since the second half of the nineteenth century, coal and copper have been known to exist there, and nickel and platinum were found in 1922. It is believed that there are other useful mineral deposits southwest of Noril'sk.[59]

The graphite deposits at Kureika near Igarka are among the largest in the U.S.S.R.[60] Mining here started before the Revolution.[61] Although some additional equipment was installed in the 1920's,[62] the author was informed by Kureika residents in 1940 that the exploitation of the graphite deposits had ceased and that the equipment had been abandoned and

52

allowed to deteriorate. Mining of the Iceland spar deposits along the Lower Tunguska River was also discontinued by 1940.[63] Since 1930 deposits of nonferrous metals have been known to exist along the Severnaya River, a right tributary of the Lower Tunguska.

There are oil fields along the lower reaches of the Yenisei in the area of Ust'-Port, as well as a natural-gas field measuring 2,000 square kilometers and containing more than twenty outlets. Farther up the Yenisei, in the Turukhansk area, signs of oil have been found.

On the Nordvik Peninsula, between the estuaries of the Khatanga and the Anabar Rivers, it is believed there are oil and minerals (salt, gypsum and coal). Oil was indicated by the findings of a Glavsevmorput' expedition which in 1933 explored the coast of Nordvik Bay, the Yuryung-Tumus Peninsula and Begichev Island.[64]

The geologic importance of the Khatanga region was emphasized by N. N. Urvantsev, formerly one of the administrators of the Arctic Institute and a prominent Arctic geologist and petroleum specialist.[65] In 1935, referring to the region as a new mining area, he indicated that oil was the largest of its deposits.[66] In the same year Urvantsev recommended geologic and geophysical surveys of the Yenisei River,[67] and described the location and methods of exploration in the Asiatic part of the Arctic, particularly the Khatanga oil region.[68] The existence of oil and salt deposits in the Khatanga region was confirmed by a Glavsevmorput' expedition of 1935-1936, which selected the following places for exploratory drilling: the Kozhevnikovo dome, the Yuryung-Tumus Peninsula, the Anabar cupola, the Chaidak and Belaya domes, the cupolas on the Pashka Peninsula and Begichev Island, the Kheta River region, and Mount Balakhna.[69] During this period many engineers participated in oil prospecting along the shores of the Khatanga and Yenisei and other parts of the North, and a special literature on Arctic oil made its appearance.[70]

However, actually finding and extracting oil was not a simple task. When Glavsevmorput' failed to show any progress in this matter at the end of the Second and beginning of the Third Five-Year Plan, Urvantsev was arrested in 1938 and, along with Samoilovich, the former head of the Arctic Institute, was accused of having located Arctic oil deposits but of having deliberately concealed them and belittled their industrial value.[71] The accused were charged with having aimed at the overthrow of the Soviet government with the help of foreign interventionists and at the seizure of Soviet oil deposits for themselves. Soviet geologic literature itself refutes these charges. A. G. Vologdin declared in 1938 that the industrial value of the oil deposits of the Krasnoyarsk area was still undetermined.[72] G. Ye. Ryabukhin stressed the need for further oil prospecting in the lower Yenisei.[73] Other writers declared that too few points on the Taimyr Peninsula had been explored for oil.[74]

In its continued search for oil in the Khatanga region Glavsevmorput' started drilling around Kozhevnikovo Gulf before World War II and year after year sent large expeditions there as well as to the lower reaches of the Yenisei.[75]

In 1939 a Glavsevmorput' expedition noted signs of oil in the lower reaches of the Olenyok River.[76] Indications of oil have also been found near the lower Tuolba.[77]

The first reports of minerals in the Verkhoyansk Mountains appeared during the second half of the eighteenth century. However, the mountains remained relatively unexplored until 1931, when a systematic study of the area was begun. Six years of work uncovered several hundred ore deposits containing precious and nonferrous metals in the western and northern parts of the mountains. The minerals discovered in the area include lead, zinc, arsenic, silver, and tin.

Economic Potential of the Service Areas

The Chukotsk-Anadyr' region, one of the least studied areas of the Soviet Union, has substantial mineral deposits, including gold, platinum, nickel, silver, zinc, lead, copper, antimony, arsenic, mercury, molybdenum, tin, iron, manganese, titanium, fluorite, graphite, mica, Iceland spar, semi-precious stones, and mineral springs. There are more than forty known gold deposits and fourteen tin deposits, four of which are of major size. Geologic conditions indicate that there are large quantities of gold and tin. Quartz has been found on Wrangel Island, and gold on the upper Kolyma.

The mining area in the upper reaches of the Kolyma River is noted for its gold mining industry, which is under the jurisdiction of the MVD. The industry receives most of its supplies from and ships most of its output to the southern ports of the Soviet Far East via the Sea of Okhotsk. Before World War II the Kolyma area led the U.S.S.R. in gold production.[78]

Other mineral deposits are known to exist in the extreme North. Before World War II it was reckoned that in this region there were some 1,500 or 1,600 localities with signs of mineral resources.[79]

The North also possesses tremendous deposits of peat which can be used as fuel, in the manufacture of construction materials (building blocks, insulating materials and so on), and in agriculture. Exploitation of the peat bogs would further the general development of the North, improve transportation by clearing impassable areas and transform the bogs into pastures and meadowlands.[80]

The Soviet Arctic is still relatively unknown; at the beginning of World War II detailed maps had been made for only 8.3 per cent of the area.[81] Although intensive and successful geologic research in the North has been conducted for many years, the industrial value of the minerals uncovered has yet to be determined.

(2) Oil

Oil prospecting and drilling in the North were stimulated mainly by the need of fuel for ships plying the Northern Sea Route as well as for northern aviation, motor transport, industrial plants, and river craft.

The use of oil, which takes up less of the carrying capacity and has a greater heating capacity than coal, makes it possible to increase the commercial cargo and cruising radius of the ship, factors that are particularly important under the adverse conditions of the Northern Sea Route. Another advantage of liquid fuel over coal is that it is more quickly loaded. Bunkering delays increase the already inflated costs of Arctic navigation. Nevertheless, most vessels of the merchant fleet plying the Northern Sea Route, as well as the old icebreakers, are still using coal.[82]

Should substantial oil deposits be found in northern Siberia, the southern districts of central Siberia, which also have to obtain oil from fields to the west and from the Far East, would share the benefits. Although a long and costly haul is involved for both regions, the extreme North is at a much greater disadvantage with the existing situation. The following table shows a comparison of the prices of oil and oil products in 1937 in Irkutsk in the south, and Yakutsk in the north:[83]

	Price per ton (rubles)	
Product	*Irkutsk*	*Yakutsk*
Fuel Oil	97	1,115
Kerosene	700	1,736
Ligroine	900	2,110
Gasoline	1,200	2,483

Although the price differential between the two cities is enormous, it is still not so great as it is farther north, at Tiksi, for example. This prohibitive cost explains why the Soviet Union has put so much effort into developing northern oil production.

Economic Potential of the Service Areas

Drilling in Ukhta began in 1931, and before World War II the production of oil there reached 100,000 tons, according to official materials on file in the Leningrad Institute for the Peoples of the North. The output of the oil refinery built at Ukhta is shipped to the surrounding districts and to distant areas of the country.[84] According to off-the-record views of some officials of Gosplan, however, the prewar estimate of 100,000 tons was an exaggeration, and the quality of the oil questionable. The construction of the Ukhta-Pechora Railroad during the war should have stimulated oil production; although no figures have appeared in Soviet literature to confirm this supposition, heightened activity in the area is suggested in a postwar description of the Soviet North:

> [As] we approach Ukhta, we find oil refineries, laboratories and storage tanks.[85] On the Yarega River, where a deposit of heavy oil has been discovered, a mine for the extraction of oil without the drilling of deep wells—the first in the Soviet Union—has been constructed.[86] [This oil mine] at Ukhta is the largest [of its kind] in the world. In the course of the postwar Five-Year Plan new oil mines will be developed. Extracting heavy oil on the Yarega by the mine method is the major goal of the Ukhta oil industry. At the same time the new deposits of light oil in the area of the upper Izhma River will be worked.[87]

Even this enthusiastic account, published in the third year of the postwar Plan, refers to only one operating oil mine in Ukhta. It is unlikely that the goals mentioned could have been reached by 1950.

After World War II Soviet scientists continued to study the oil deposits at Nordvik, Ust'-Port and elsewhere in the vicinity,[88] where signs of oil had previously been found. According to the postwar work of Professor Suslov, however, the Nordvik oil deposits have been found to have no industrial value.[89] There is no information in postwar Soviet literature concerning the industrial value of the other oil deposits in this area. It had been planned, in case efforts to find deposits were successful, to ship the fuel to the southern districts of

Siberia and to the northern European U.S.S.R., and even the Far East via the Northern Sea Route.[90]

The development of a synthetic oil industry, at one time considered by the Soviet government to meet the need of liquid fuel in the North, may be a realistic solution, since the coal in the extreme North is suitable for liquefaction. As early as 1932 Komseverput' had designated the lower reaches of the Yenisei for development with this possibility in mind. As consumers of the fuel Komseverput' had in view the synthetic industry itself, the port of Igarka, the enterprises along the Yenisei and its tributaries, and the industry of the city of Krasnoyarsk.[91]

The question of building a synthetic oil industry for the U.S.S.R. as a whole has been frequently discussed,[92] without specific allocation of any of the planned output to the extreme North. As the result of the occupation of East Germany by Soviet troops after World War II, the Soviet Union obtained German equipment for producing synthetic oil, plants necessary to produce the equipment, and a number of experienced specialists, so that the creation of a Soviet synthetic oil industry became an immediate possibility.

(3) Fluorspar, Polymetallic Ores,[93] Salt, and Tin

The mining of industrial fluorite, used particularly by munitions plants, began in Amderma in 1933, but its annual output had not exceeded 20,000 tons at the beginning of World War II.[94] Production in this area, as well as at the lead and zinc mines of Vaigach, has been hampered by the absence of reduction plants and local fuel. Construction of the planned railroad from Amderma, now an industrial settlement,[95] to the Vorkuta coal deposits would solve the fuel problem.

The construction of the Noril'sk Polymetal Combine, of great importance to the national economy, was probably com-

58

pleted after World War II. Although the Noril'sk-Dudinka railroad was built originally to serve the transportation needs of the Combine, platinum shipments have been made by plane for many years.[96] The city of Noril'sk is a restricted area which cannot be entered without a pass from the MVD. A fairly large city even before the war, Noril'sk has made many improvements in the course of its rapid growth afterwards.[97]

Before World War II the organizations in charge of the northern economy hoped for an extensive development of the Nordvik salt deposits to supply the fishing industry in the North and Far East and to provide freight for the Northern Sea Route.[98] Prewar plans for an annual output of up to 150,000 tons[99] are, however, evidently far from realization. In April 1954 a Supreme Soviet deputy from the Yakut A.S.-S.R. placed emphasis on the construction of a salt mining combine at Olekminsk to supply salt to the Soviet Far East and made no mention of the Nordvik deposits.[100]

In 1940, in preparation for the establishment of a tin mining combine in the Verkhoyansk area, various construction materials were shipped to a point along the Yana River,[101] but it is not known how far the work has advanced.

c. The Fishing and Sea Animal Industries

Before the Revolution there was no well-developed fishing industry in the seas off the northern coast, either in the European or Asiatic part of Russia. Instead of exporting fish from the Barents and White Seas, northern European Russia imported fish from Norway. Fishing had been developed to some extent in the Far East, but the processing methods in use there were defective.

This situation changed radically after 1917. The process of rebasing the fishing industry from the inland waters in the South to the open seas in the North and Far East, which had begun in the 1930's, proceeded rapidly after World War II.

While the catch of fish from the southern waters decreased 50 per cent between the late 1940's and the beginning of the 1950's it increased steadily in the open sea fisheries. By the end of the second postwar Five-Year Plan (1951-1955) the output of the fish and sea-animal industries in the open seas is expected to increase to 75 per cent of the U.S.S.R. total.[102]

Before World War II a number of motor-fishing stations had been set up in the open-sea fisheries of the North. These stations service fishing kolkhozes in accordance with individual agreements similar to those made by the MTS (machine-tractor stations) with the kolkhozes in grain districts. The motor-fishing stations are set up to perform the following funtions: rent motor vessels with complete fishing equipment to the kolkhozes; maintain the vessels and supply them with oil, grease and spare parts; carry out reconnaissance for schools of fish; tow fishing boats back and forth to the fishing grounds; and train engineers, crews, and master mechanics to operate mechanical net hoists, seines and so forth. Larger, deep-water vessels are being added to the motor fleet. In addition, the motor-fishing stations provide mechanized shore installations for seining to the kolkhoz fishermen and train them in the use of such equipment. In 1952 it was stated that 90 per cent of the fishing operations of kolkhozes serviced by polar motor-fishing stations were done mechanically.[103] Finally, the stations are expected to take partial responsibility in providing for the cultural, housing, and food needs of the kolkhoz population.[104] In short, the motor-fishing station is the agency charged with modernization of the fishing industry.

(1) The Northern European U.S.S.R.

The Barents Sea, where the warm currents of the Gulf Stream encourage the growth of plankton, a major source of nourishment for the larger marine organisms, is one of the richest fishing grounds in the North. The greater part of the catch here before World War II consisted of cod (200,000 tons annually) and herring (about 100,000 tons annually),[105] and the catch of salmon has steadily increased. The fisheries in Murmansk Oblast, concentrating their activities almost exclusively in the Barents Sea, accounted for about 20 per cent of the total fish catch in the U.S.S.R. in the 1950's.[106] Fishing and fish processing are the major occupations in the region, making up 55 per cent of its gross industrial production in 1952; for the city of Murmansk the corresponding figure was 64.1 per cent in 1940 and 80.1 per cent in 1951.[107] The Murmansk fish processing industry puts out fresh-frozen, canned and smoked fish; salted fish constituted 53.3 per cent of the region's fish products in 1952.[108] The city of Murmansk is the home base of the trawler fleet, and located there are a large fishing combine,[109] a cooperage, a ship repair yard and other facilities for the fishing industry. Murmansel'd, the government administration for open-sea herring fishing, was organized in 1949, and its fleet approaches the Murmansk trawler fleet in size.[110]

Fish processing plants are also located in northern Archangel Oblast—at Shoina, Indiga and Nar'yan-Mar as well as in the city of Archangel. The trawler fleet in the Archangel area is not very large, and the fishing kolkhozes account for most of the catch.

Both Murmansk and Archangel, being part of the extreme North, are nominally service areas of the Northern Sea Route, but the fishing industry in these regions contributes no freight to the Route.

(2) The Coast of the Central Arctic

The only important fisheries in the Arctic are those of the Barents and White seas. The fish resources of waters along the Northern Sea Route (the Kara, Laptev, East Siberian, and Chukotsk seas) are still relatively untapped. Glavsevmorput' has been trying to develop fisheries in Novaya Zemlya, Gyda

Bay, the lower reaches of the Yenisei and the Pyasina River, and the estuary of the Anadyr'. Capital equipment, labor, transportation, and so forth, were allocated for this purpose during the Second Five-Year Plan (1933-1937). However, the inadequacy of the resources allocated and the other difficulties encountered by Glavsevmorput' are reflected in the small output of these Arctic fishing districts:[111]

	1933	1934	1935	1936	1937
Number of fishing districts	7	9	18	20	42
Catch of raw fish (centners)[112]	85,900	99,200	84,900	89,700	100,600

Despite a large increase in the number of fisheries, their combined output increased only a little over 17 per cent. In its report at the close of the Second Five-Year Plan Glavsevmorput' was forced to admit: "The vast expanses of the northern seas are still undeveloped. The fish resources of most of the northern rivers and lakes are unexploited."[113] Even in the Third Five-Year Plan period Glavsevmorput' could report no significant progress. In 1940 it declared:

Fishing [in the Asiatic north] is becoming more important commercially. The fishermen of Novaya Zemlya have been catching and delivering 4,000 centners of fish a year, while in the lower reaches of the Yenisei between 18,000 and 25,000 centners of marketable fish are caught annually.[114]

These figures indicated no large-scale development. Furthermore, the same report acknowledged that "in many areas, because of insufficient processing and storage facilities, fishing serves local needs only." A postwar statement shows that the situation has not improved materially: "The seas of northern Asia (Siberia)—the Kara, Laptev, East Siberian, and Chukotsk . . . are hardly utilized by the fishing industry."[115] In 1949 at state enterprises in the central and eastern Arctic the average catch of fish and sea mammals per man was less than one-sixth of the average catch in all other Soviet areas and less than one twentieth of that in the Kamchatka waters.[116]

Before World War II fish caught in the central Arctic were canned in two plants; one at Ust'-Port on the lower Yenisei and the other at Anadyr' in the Chukotsk National Okrug. According to Glavsevmorput' data, these plants, the output of which was exported, had a good production record. One third of the output of the Anadyr' plant was classified as superior in quality. However, before the war at least, only a small part of the catch of Glavsevmorput' fisheries in the central Arctic reached these plants; the greater part was salted. Both the central and eastern Arctic, especially in the lower reaches of the Yenisei and Lena, needed more processing plants, including facilities for preliminary processing, such as salting barns, refrigerators and freezers, and warehouses.[117]

(3) The Far East

The fishing industry of the northern part of the Far East is based not only on the Arctic seas, but also on the Pacific, Bering and Okhotsk. The Bering Sea, an expanse of 2.27 million square kilometers, is inhabited by a rich variety of northern species (280) such as gobies, which constitute 22 per cent of the fish fauna, salmon—dog, blueback, humpback, and *kizhuch (oncorhynchus kisutch)*—cod, pollack, and *navaga (eleginus navaga)* as well as a number of unique types.[118] The Sea of Okhotsk, of 1.53 million square kilometers, has an abundance of humpback, dog, *kizhuch,* and other salmon, which come in great masses to the estuaries of the small rivers, mainly those of Kamtchatka, to spawn. The Sea of Okhotsk also has northern and Pacific herring, *ivasi (sardinops sagax melanosticta), navaga,* cod, bass and others.[119] These seas combined provide the following proportions of the total U.S.S.R. catch: salmon, 85.3 per cent; flatfish, 60.4 per cent; *navaga,* 69.3 per cent; and herring, 44.9 per cent.[120]

Just before World War II the Far Eastern fishermen were

63

bringing in 3,800 centners of crabs yearly from the Bering Sea and 165,900 centners from the Sea of Okhotsk.[121] By 1949 the crab catch in the Far East was twice that of the prewar period.[122] The crab fishermen work the Sea of Okhotsk for about five or six months a year, canning their catch aboard ship.[123]

Fishing on Kamchatka, the fishing center in the East, is done by both state organizations and kolkhozes.[124] In 1951 the kolkhozes accounted for 41.5 per cent of the catch. In 1952 there were seven motor-fishing stations, tin-can factories, fifty canneries, and forty-six cold storage buildings on the peninsula. The largest enterprises are the Mikoyan, Kirov, Ust'-Kamchatskii, Ozernovskii, and Kikhchikskii Combines. Each has the use of a power fleet.[125] A branch of the Pacific Ocean Institute of the Fishing Industry and Oceanography is located on Kamchatka.[126] The institute makes studies of fish biology, the crab catching and sea-mammal industries, and the effectiveness of fishing equipment and processing methods.

Before World War II a large shipyard producing iron welded cutters, welded barges, and its own ("Kamchadal") motors for sea cutters was built in Petropavlovsk. The Klyu-chevski Lumber Combine, which manufactures barrels and boxes for the fishing industry, builds houses and makes furniture, is located on a tributary of the Kamchatka River. During the war the combine increased its output of freight barges and began to produce small fishing boats. The production of pre-fabricated houses for the peninsula has been started in Ust'-Kamchatsk, and small service shops have been opened.[127]

After the war, in line with its heightened interest in the Far East, the Soviet government paid greater attention to the fisheries of the Bering and Okhotsk seas, where resources had not been fully exploited.[128] The first postwar Five-Year Plan (1946-1950) gave the same priority to the improvement of Kamchatka's fishing industry as to the development of the highly important areas of southern Sakhalin and the Kurile Islands.[129] To build up the Kamchatka labor force, the same incentives as for Arctic personnel—above-scale wages and special privileges—were offered.[130] The fishing industry, the "most important branch" of the peninsula's economy, was furnished with "hundreds of cod and crab fishing vessels and freighters."[131] As a result, in 1949 Kamchatka's fish catch, which had reached 900,000 to 950,000 centners in 1940,[132] was more than two and one half times that of prewar years;[133] and the output of processed fish, 400,000 to 425,000 cases in 1940,[134] had increased at almost the same rate.[135] With more equipment at its disposal the peninsula's fishing industry expanded into new areas and set up new enterprises and kolkhozes.[136]

The Koryak National Okrug, immediately to the north, almost tripled its catch from 1944 to 1949.[137]

Second in importance to Kamchatka are the fisheries of the Sea of Okhotsk, where after 1948 fishing facilities were being expanded.[138]

(4) River Fishing

Part of the output of the northern fishing industry is provided by the inland waters, especially the rivers. The average yearly catch in centners before World War II from the Siberian rivers was as follows:[139]

	Ob'	*Yenisei*	*Lena*
Sturgeon	11,500	1,800	300
Salmon	6,700	1,100	900
Whitefish	86,100	13,900	17,500
Carp	104,900	600	1,200
Perch	12,300	300	————
Pike	56,700	2,600	19,000
Eel	13,500	2,200	————
Smelt	500	1,100	500
Others	56,900	8,800	1,500
Total	349,100	32,400	40,900

Although the catch from the Siberian rivers was increased during the war to ease the food shortage, there are still large untapped resources in the northern inland waters.[140]

In addition to the fisheries on the Ob', the Yenisei and the Lena, fishing is carried on in the numerous small rivers and lakes. On the Yenisei there are processing plants at Ust'-Port and elsewhere (eight in all),[141] and on the Ob' at Salekhard and Samarovo, as well as seasonal floating facilities and other minor plants for processing fish on the major rivers and some of the smaller ones. Often workers from the processing plants participate in fishing,[142] which is one of the main occupations of the indigenous population.[143]

Since the northern fisheries are generally located in remote and sparsely populated regions, the Soviet government has devised appropriate methods of bringing ideology and education to the personnel of the industry.

> The Ob'-Irtysh Fish Trust has equipped three floating culture bases to service the fishermen. These are large craft towed by cutters, each with a hall accommodating 100 to 150 persons, an assortment of films and a library. The Samarovo culture base has visited more than thirty fishermen's settlements.[144]

(5) Sea Hunting

Before World War II the only large-scale hunting in the northern seas was done in the neck of the White Sea and in the Bering Sea off the eastern coast of the Chukotsk Peninsula.[145] Sea hunting in the White Sea had become a well established industry using icebreakers and air reconnaissance for locating seal rookeries. In the Chukotsk National Okrug, where about one third of the native population takes part in sea hunting, during the late thirties the industry acquired new equipment, including mechanized whaling vessels. Ship repair shops were built in Lavrentiya and Providenical bays, and fat rendering furnaces were set up on the Bering coast. A motor-fishing station was established at Providenical Bay to help the kolkhozes. The yearly catch of true seals (*Phoca Pusa Hispida*) off the Chukotsk Peninsula was between 40,000 and 70,000 head, and of walrus between 4,000 and 6,000 head.[146]

As a food, sea animals are eaten fresh and pickled by the northern population. They also provide shoe leather and warm fur clothing, tent covers and canoes. The animal fats are used for lighting and heating.

The Bering and Okhotsk seas are rich in sea mammals. After the war there were four flotillas in the Far East engaged in whaling, animal hunting, crab catching, and refrigeration. The whalers, which are based at Morzhova Bay near Petropavlovsk (Kamchatka), operate around Capes Dezhnyov and Serdtse-Kamen'.[147] The Sea of Okhotsk and the Bering Sea have a large seal population. The yearly kill in centners during 1936-1939 was as follows:[148]

	Seals	Whales
Barents	1,300	——
White	30,900	——
Bering	9,800	113,100
Okhotsk	5,600	——

Shortages of equipment and labor have retarded exploitation of the sea animal resources of the North. Fuller development of the industry in the Far Eastern seas depends upon the availability of additional vessels.[149]

(6) The Labor Shortage

A perennial problem of the fishing industry in the North has been labor shortages, due primarily to the seasonal nature of the work.[150] Most of the workers brought in for the fishing season are completely unfamiliar with fishing techniques. Because of northern transportation conditions, seasonal laborers may arrive late for the spring season, and because of the autumn storms they must leave the North in the middle of September. The result is that as much as three months of the fishing season may be wasted because the requisite labor is not on hand. Another drawback in bringing in seasonal labor is the large expense involved relative to the amount of work done. Workers must travel for three or four months in order to work for two or three months in the fisheries, and this expense greatly increases the unit cost of production. In the Chukotsk Fish Trust in 1936, 25 per cent of the cost of the total output of preserved fish was chargeable to the cost of transporting 550 workers and paying their wages while en route.[151] Despite the disadvantages involved, the use of seasonal labor is still one of the chief methods of meeting the labor shortage during the fishing season.[152]

d. The Lumber Industry

Timber is one of the great natural resources of the Soviet Union. The U.S.S.R. share of world forest reserves in 1949, following the Soviet acquisitions of territory during World War II, has been estimated as follows: 27 per cent of the forest lands (against 24 per cent before the war), 24 per cent of the total timber reserves, and 54 per cent of the coniferous reserves.[153] The northern regions contain the greater part of the Soviet forest lands, substantial tracts of which are found in the extreme North. Of the total forest lands, 78 per cent are in the Asiatic part of the country.[154] The largest sawmill centers are the Archangel and Vologda Oblasts and the Komi A.S.S.R., the combined output of which was one quarter of the U.S.S.R. total before World War II.[155]

The lumber industry of the northern European U.S.S.R. is favorably located for trade with the markets of Europe. During the 1930's when the Soviet Union needed foreign exchange and when the railroad connections between the North and the interior were inadequate, the Soviet government exported lumber from Archangel Oblast and other northern parts of the European U.S.S.R..[156] Just before World War II, however, these areas began to send more lumber to the domestic market, and after the war the number of Soviet enterprises being supplied with Archangel lumber was 1,540.[157] Production in the area is evidently still on the increase.[158] Like the mining and fishing industries of the northern European U.S.S.R., the lumber industry of Archangel Oblast, the southern part of the Kola Peninsula and Karelia furnishes no freight for the Northern Sea Route.

The location of many forest lands of Siberia near the rivers flowing north has made it possible to establish lumber industries on these rivers. Thus the lumber combine at Igarka, which consists of three sawmills, containing nine frames (saw gates), and a woodworking shop, receives, via the Angara and Yenisei rivers, the superior timber from logging operations in the areas along the Angara. Igarka, which owes its development to the lumber industry, had a population of 10,000 to 12,000 just before World War II.[159]

Although Igarka's various wood products, including furniture and equipment for schools and homes, supply both producer and consumer needs of the northern Yenisei area,[160] the bulk of its lumber has been exported since 1924. Neither the difficult ice conditions nor the poor shipping facilities available in the twenties in the Kara Sea greatly hampered the profitable operation of the Igarka enterprises. By the beginning of World War II the export of Igarka lumber, which has been rated as among the best in the Soviet Union,[161] had risen to tens of thousands of standards.[162]

Other lumber enterprises in the extreme North are the Salekhard mill on the lower Ob' and two mills in the city Yakutsk.[163] Near the Ob'-Irtysh confluence is the Samarovo mill and the Belogor'ye Combine which was still under construction in the late thirties. The plans called for the construction of sawmills and wood-chemical plants, and the enterprise was to process several hundred thousand cubic meters annually.[164] The Samarovo, Salekhard and Yakutsk mills produced exclusively for local consumption before World War II; they were described as insignificant and their equipment as badly worn.[165]

Apart from the Igarka mills and its suppliers the only lumber enterprises of any importance in the extreme North before World War II were in the Kolyma region, where the MVD-administered gold mines are located. The other vast forest lands east of the Urals were still *terra incognita* up to 1940: not more than 5 per cent of the forest lands of the Asiatic part of the U.S.S.R. had been explored.[166] In 1937 the neglect and deterioration of these forest reserves caused Glavsevmorput' to declare:

> The development of the northern lumber industry demands from Narkomles [People's Commissariat of the Lumber Industry] not only the reconstruction of existing enterprises and increase of their productive capacity but also the construction of new enterprises in the lower reaches of the Ob', Yenisei and Lena rivers and their tributaries.[167]

A lecturer of the Siberian Lumber Technical Institute speaking of the Siberian lumber industry before the Fourth Five-Year Plan (1946-1950) said that the forests had "hardly been exploited" north of the Trans-Siberian Railroad and in the Angara Basin. Interestingly enough, he cited as one reason for this lack of development the fact that the "main Siberian rivers, as is known, flow to the north, into the Arctic Ocean."[168] This statement is obviously based on the assumption that the export of lumber over the Northern Sea Route was not a significant factor in the exploitation of the Siberian forests.

It is very difficult to evaluate the postwar state of the lumber industry in the extreme North. The available evidence indicates that Igarka continues to be the only major sawmill center.[169] There is evidence that by the 1950's Salekhard had developed into an important sawmill center; its output, however, apparently is shipped to the southwest, possibly over a new rail line running west from the Ob' River to the Pechora Railroad.[170] There are no other indications in published Soviet sources that the prewar state of the lumber industry has changed significantly since the end of World War II.

The factors hindering the expansion of logging operations in the extreme North are the primitive organization of production methods, the low quality of available equipment, and the inadequate and unstable labor force. The postwar plan "to convert logging operations, in which manual labor predominates, into a well-developed, mechanized industry with a skilled and stable body of workers,"[171] which was to have been fulfilled by 1950, was very far from realization in Siberia in 1949:

> The newest machinery is in operation in Siberian forests; yet at the same time . . . the obsolete methods of our grandfathers are still in use. . . . Trimmers spend almost an entire week cleaning trees that were felled by electric saws in a day. . . . There is not one loading mechanism at places where timber of all assortments has to be loaded on trucks. . . . Hours pass before a truck is loaded. . . . As in Upper Kamenka, all timber centers experience great difficulties with materials and spare parts for caterpillar tractors, motor vehicles and winches.[172]

The lumber industry is keenly affected by the general labor shortage in the North. The Chairman of the Archangel Oblast Executive Committee, speaking before the R.S.F.S.R. Supreme Soviet in 1946, called on the Council of Ministers of the R.S.F.S.R. to provide a remedy:

> At the end of the [first postwar] Five-Year Plan there must be 40,000 permanent workers in the enterprises of the Ministry of the Lumber Industry and 12,000 in the forest enterprises of the Ministry of Communications. This does not include the requirements of lumber enterprises on the republic and local level. At present only 18,900 permanent workers have been made available. . . . Reliance solely on a seasonal labor force is incompatible with the maximum mechanization of logging operations. A permanent, skilled body of workers is needed to operate the machines. In the course of the five-year plan

Archangel Oblast can provide the lumber industry with thirteen to fifteen thousand seasonal workers from the kolkhozes and four to five thousand permanent workers; that is, the rest of the labor force, up to 30,000 workers, must be recruited in other regions of the country.[173]

In 1952 the Minister of the Lumber Industry stated that the recruitment of a permanent labor force was lagging behind the growth of mechanization and therefore seasonal labor still played an important role. In 1951 the Ministry's lumbering enterprises performed 75 per cent of their work with their own labor and 25 per cent with seasonal workers.[174]

The lumber industry, like other branches of the northern economy, also suffers from a lack of highly-qualified personnel. Southern Siberia and Khabarovsk Krai also suffer from a shortage of specialized managerial personnel, engineers and technicians in the lumber industry.[175]

e. Other Industries

(1) The Fur Trade

The basic occupations of the northern aborigines are fishing, reindeer farming, and most important of all, the hunting and breeding of fur-bearing animals. The fur trade makes the greatest contribution to national income, while the marketable production of the other occupations is small.

The fur catch of northern hunters has been restricted largely to two varieties, the Arctic fox (92 per cent of the total catch in the tundra) and the squirrel (98 per cent of the catch in the taiga).[176] The need is to expand the catch of the more valuable varieties such as ermine and the silver fox, which are particularly good for export. The problem of developing the hunting industry in the extreme North permits of no quick and easy solution. In 1941 there were only 40,000 hunters in the huge expanses of the extreme North,[177] and there is no evidence that the number has been increased significantly since that time. Furthermore, the depletion of fur-bearing animals may be affecting the development of the industry.[178]

For the purpose of developing the fur trade, state Industrial-Hunting Stations were set up beginning in 1933. By 1941 there were fifteen such stations in operation: two in Archangel Oblast, one in the Komi A.S.S.R., six in the Ob' Basin, three in Novosibirsk Oblast, two in Krasnoyarsk Krai, and one in the Yakut A.S.S.R.[179] The stations were to organize hunting in areas where it had been neglected and to guide the further development of the already-existing hunting industry.[180] It was hoped that the stations would serve as a means of reconstructing the hunting industry on the basis of their studies and conservation measures.[181] It is not known how successful the stations have been. A significant pointer, however, is that they have been praised by the Soviet press for overfulfillment of their own hunting quotas rather than for their part in achieving the more fundamental objectives.[182]

(2) Animal Breeding

The animal-breeding farms of the extreme North, first set up in 1928, provide pelts from the silver fox, the blue Arctic fox, the seal, and other fur-bearing animals. In 1936 the government began to devote more attention to the development of the industry. By 1941 there were twenty-two kolkhozes, four cooperatives, and one large sovkhoz in the extreme North which were devoted to the breeding of fur-bearing animals. In this year planning agencies referred to the animal-breeding industry as one of the underdeveloped branches of the northern economy.[183]

A network of reindeer sovkhozes was set up in the extreme North in the early thirties to help increase the supply of draft animals as well as reindeer meat and hides by developing improved techniques and otherwise aiding reindeer farmers. By

1941 northern sovkhozes had 270,000 head of reindeer. The total number of reindeer in the extreme North during the 1930's was as follows: 1,456,500 in 1933; 1,676,600 in 1936; 1,770,400 in 1937; 1,970,000 planned in 1938; and about 2,000,000 in 1940.[184] The increases, which were in any case unspectacular, were robbed of any significance to the Northern Sea Route because the prewar plans for establishing enterprises to process reindeer products were not carried out.[185] In 1948 it was acknowledged that the reindeer industry had not as yet taken on any commercial significance.[186] Nevertheless the reindeer is important to the inhabitants of the extreme North because it provides them with food and hides as well as a means of overland transport.[187]

(3) Northern Agriculture

The growth of new settlements and cities in the extreme North brought with it the need for local sources of food. The earliest measures to develop northern agriculture were taken on the Kola Peninsula with the establishment in 1923 of the Khibiny experimental agricultural station (67°N.). Others followed in the town of Kola (68°N.) near Murmansk and in Loukhi (about 66°N.) in Karelia.[188] Subsequently agricultural stations appeared elsewhere in the North, and sovkhozes producing vegetables, meat, and grains were established. Individual kolkhozes also began to produce some of their own food, on a limited scale. According to a report in 1953, the more hardy crops can be grown in the open between the 68th and 69th parallels in the European U.S.S.R. and between the 70th and 71st parallels in areas east of the Urals.[189] Soviet scientific institutions are working intensively on the scientific problems of moving agriculture northward, prominent among them being the Timiryazev Institute of Plant Physiology and the Institute of Frost Study of the Academy of Sciences of the

U.S.S.R.[190] But the scientific effort to overcome the climatic obstacles will not by itself ensure the success of northern agriculture. A Soviet postwar geographic study specifically cited the general underdevelopment of the Siberian North as the major obstacle.[191] Another hindrance is that the indigenous population, from which most northern kolkhoz members are drawn, cannot successfully develop agriculture, a new occupation, without substantial guidance and material assistance, which are often not received.[192]

Hothouse vegetable growing is an important branch of northern agriculture. In 1932 the area under hothouse cultivation was 8,300 square meters, and in 1940 the area had risen to 34,300 square meters.[193] The northern kolkhozes share in this activity, but more important are the large vegetable-growing sovkhozes near some of the more heavily populated settlements. The same overall problems pertain to hothouse growing as to other forms of northern agriculture. World War II had the effect of halting the expansion of hothouse vegetable growing in the North, especially among the kolkhozes.

(4) Local Industry and Producers' Cooperatives

The extreme North has made only a beginning in developing enterprises which are classified in Soviet terminology under the headings of local industry and producers' cooperatives.[194] Products of the kind produced by such industries are in the main shipped from distant parts of the U.S.S.R., including the central industrial regions. In addition to the transportation costs involved, the products received are often ill-adapted to the needs of the northern population—for example, traps sent to northern hunters from the Volga region. Some change in the situation is in sight if the extreme North is to share in the planned build-up of local industry and producers' cooperatives in the Urals, Siberia and the Far East.[195]

2. Limiting Factors

a. Manpower Problems

The inadequacy of the labor force, which has been mentioned several times previously as a handicap to individual industries, imposes severe limitations upon the economic development of the North in general. One of the primary purposes of the Soviet Arctic program, as outlined in Chapter I, was the "regeneration" of the northern national minorities. Employment in industry was, axiomatically, regarded as the most effective means toward this end as well as toward the political aims of the Soviet regime. Stalin stated in 1923:

> The trouble is that some nationalities have no proletarians of their own, they have had no industrial experience, nor have they begun to acquire any; they are terribly backward culturally and are unable to take advantage of the rights granted them by the Revolution. . . .
>
> It is necessary that, in addition to the measures respecting schools and language, the Russian proletariat take all measures to establish centers of industry in the distant reaches of our country, in culturally backward republics. . . .
>
> [This is necessary] so that in these centers there may be groups of local proletarians to serve as a transmission bridge from the Russian proletarians and peasants to the working masses of those republics.[196]

In pursuance of this policy, Siberian governmental administrative offices, Komseverput' and later Glavsevmorput' attempted to draw the native indigenous population into northern industry. Statistics issued on the composition of the labor force of various Siberian organizations were designed to demonstrate progress particularly toward employment of the native inhabitants. For instance, workers in the enterprises of the fish industry of the Yamal region in 1935 were categorized as indicated in the table opposite.[197]

At the time Glavsevmorput' was reorganized in 1938, however, such figures were declared to have been falsified. In actual fact, there were few representatives of the local popula-

Economic Potential of the Service Areas

Organization	Local workers	Resettled workers	Seasonal workers	Total
Omsk Territorial Administration of Glavsevmorput'	36	——	58	94
Ob' Fish Trust	920	1,483	1,326	3,729
Cooperatives	709	——	——	709
Total	1,665	1,483	1,384	4,532

tion in the state fisheries and state reindeer farms. The physical and psychological make-up of the vast majority of the indigenous population is such that even the transition from a nomadic to a sedentary life—to say nothing of work in an industrial enterprise—has frequently had an adverse effect on health.[198] Accounts in the Soviet press of the emergence of machine tool operators, skilled mechanics, tractor drivers, and even aviators among these peoples are highly exaggerated for propaganda purposes. A more accurate impression is obtained from a prewar Glavsevmorput' report:

> About six hundred seasonal workers are recruited yearly for the Chukotsk Fish Trust. The total number of workers during the fishing season amounts to over one thousand men. Among them are only a few from the local population [the Luoravet-lany].[199]

From his own observations, the author can testify to the fact that before World War II no representatives of the indigenous population were employed at the Noril'sk Polymetal Combine, Igarka's lumber enterprises, the Ust'-Yeniseisk fishery, or the two state farms on the lower Yenisei (vegetable and stock-raising in Igarka and reindeer breeding in Potapovo). The situation is the same elsewhere in the extreme North. In the southern part of the Yakut A.S.S.R., however, Yakuts work in the gold mining industry.

It has also been difficult to build up the labor force by bringing in workers from other parts of the country. The housing shortage prevalent throughout the U.S.S.R. has its effect in the extreme North, as the Chairman of the Archangel Oblast Executive Committee pointed out:

> It is not enough to bring in workers; it is necessary to create conditions that would encourage them to stay permanently. . . . At present the workers live in temporary barracks which are not suitable for family life. . . .[200]

The usual type of home, when available, is in any event not much improvement over barracks life. Overcrowding is the rule in the settlements of the extreme North. In Dudinka, for example, the average floor space in 1939 was two square meters per person.[201]

In order to compensate for the poor living conditions and the unpleasantness of life in general in the North—caused by the isolation, the cold and the long winter night—workers were for a time paid higher wages and received special privileges such as increased pension benefits, liberal vacations and travel allowances, and certain tax exemptions.[202] During World War II, however, these benefits were revoked, except for Glavsevmorput' personnel working above the Arctic Circle. As a result, it became impossible to recruit new personnel and the efficiency of workers already in the extreme North declined. After the war, therefore, the Presidium of the Supreme Soviet of the U.S.S.R. restored most of the privileges for employees of state, cooperative, cultural and other enterprises in the extreme North.[203] Although this measure succeeded in attracting some manpower to the North, an acute shortage of labor has been felt throughout the entire country as an aftermath of the war casualties. The shortage is most severe in the less densely populated areas such as Siberia, where most of the workers for the extreme North are recruited. Of Krasnoyarsk Krai, for example, it was said in 1948 that it had "tremendous land expanses which make it possible to expand the area of cultivation, but the density of population is too low."[204]

To satisfy the heavy demands for additional personnel in the northern districts of the Khabarovsk Krai after World War

II, a campaign was conducted for resettling of former border security troops in the sparsely inhabited Northeast. The newspaper *Kamchatskaya Pravda,* for example, published the following letter from a group of such settlers:

> We [are] demobilized border soldiers, participants in battles with aggressors [and we] have decided to remain in Kamchatka forever. . . . We want to help the people of Kamchatka in the development of their resources and to raise still higher the economy of the peninsula. With pride we say: "Our Kamchatka, our beloved country!" [205]

The use of seasonal labor, with all its disadvantages, must be continued on a large scale as a makeshift solution for the labor shortage in the North.

Forced labor is an important source of manpower for the Kolyma gold mining area, the Pechora coal basin, the Noril'sk Polymetal Combine and other enterprises in the extreme North. Human values and political considerations aside, forced labor is no final solution to the labor problem. In the first place, the range of tasks which can be performed by forced labor is generally limited to those which do not require skills, high productivity, initiative, freedom of movement, and so forth. The rapid physical deterioration of forced laborers also calls into question the economic expediency of the system. For example, in three Kuznetsk prisoner-of-war labor camps in 1944, 60 per cent of the prisoners were in good health and 40 per cent were at least fit for work; by 1947, 10 per cent were fit for work and 90 per cent were exhausted and invalid.[206] The situation in the labor camps of the extreme North is worse: the climate is more rigorous than that of Kuznetsk, and Soviet citizens in the northerly camps do not have the protection, however slight, enjoyed by prisoners of war. A stable and balanced economic development of the extreme North cannot be based upon forced labor alone. Even in the Soviet government's view, "voluntary settlement and voluntary labor" are also required.[207]

b.   Permafrost

Construction work in the extreme North is seriously hampered by the permafrost:

> Experience has shown that structures build on perpetually frozen soil according to the old technical principles have become deformed and ruined. It is enough to remove the sod, pull out a bush, make a hole or bank, put up a fence, or build a house to disturb the thermal and water balance between the air and the soil and between the ground under the foundation and the next layers of earth, to cause the surface of the frozen ground to sink or rise, or to cause the frost under the structure to melt. As a result, the foundation of the building sinks, cracks appear in the walls, doors and windows warp, water seeps into the cellar, bridge piles protrude, water pipes burst. . . . We need a deeper understanding of this eternal frost and its effect upon buildings. . . . This would help . . . to find the correct way to build frost-resistant structures.[208]

The problem of construction in regions of permafrost is under constant study. In Vorkuta the Scientific Frost Research Station of the Academy of Sciences of the U.S.S.R. works in collaboration with the geologists of the coal trust.[209] Although there is still much to learn about the subject, great success has been attained in building suitable structures in Vorkuta, Noril'sk and elsewhere. The cost of such construction in labor and material is, however, very high.

The frost also interferes with the water supply. In the winter the small rivers freeze to the bottom. It is almost impossible to dig wells for what little ground water there is, and water pipes require complicated warming devices.[210] In 1944 efforts were first made to drill for water through the permafrost at Yakutsk. The permafrost was found to extend for a depth of 231 meters. A study published in 1947 described how the population of Yakutsk was still forced to resort to primitive makeshifts in order to obtain water:

> Yakutsk stands on the bank of the Lena. Around the city there are abundant lakes of various sizes; nevertheless, the

water problem there is no less acute than in torrid Ashkhabad, which stands at the edge of a waterless, sandy desert. . . . In the summer, on the northern road of Yakutsk, one can observe the inhabitants carrying pails, shovels and pitchers to the large, dry sand cliffs of the Lena Valley to fetch water . . . that accumulates there from the melting ice. In the summer one can see in the yards of many Yakutsk buildings large piles of ice covered with straw, sawdust or other insulating material. These are the . . . storehouses where the water supply is kept for the summer. In the winter they rely on snow and ice for water.[211]

A report in 1949 said that construction of a water main in the industrial part of the city had been started,[212] and in 1953 it was reported that the system was being expanded.[213]

c. Power Sources

Because of the sparseness of population in the extreme North a higher degree of mechanization was required there than in the rest of the country. But natural conditions in the extreme North made it unfeasible to rely on conventional methods of providing the power needed for this purpose. Some of the suggested power projects were farfetched when measured against the actual availability of technical equipment. For example, Glavsevmorput' called attention to the following source:

We should remember the ingenious project of the French Professor Claude. . . . In both the southern and northern waters there are natural differences in temperature. In the tropics there is a difference between the deep, cold level of the water and the upper, warm level. In the Arctic the difference is between the water under the ice and the air above the ice. The latter difference . . . is between thirty and forty, sometimes fifty, degrees. This difference can become the source of great power. Claude's work was not completed because of a lack of means. In the Soviet Union, however, the possibilities for applying new technical achievements are quite different. In this respect the extreme North is wide open with possibilities. Preliminary estimates show that capital expenditures for construction of a [power station utilizing this temperature differential] are one sixth or one seventh the cost of a hydroelectric station.[214]

The low cost of this type of power, it was thought, would make it possible to supply it to homes.

Considerable attention has also been paid to a more practical source of cheap power, the winds that occur everywhere in the North.[215] In April 1935 the Council of Labor and Defense decided to start production of wind generators for use in watering cattle on livestock farms. It was reported that an inexpensive D-5 generator, working eight hours a day, supplied water for at least 200 to 300 head of cattle and saved from 1,200 to 1,700 labor days a year. More powerful wind generators, such as the D-8, were also produced. At the Eighteenth Congress of the Communist Party in 1939 it was decided to begin mass production of wind generators and the construction of wind-generated power stations.[216]

Up to World War II, however, the use of wind generators in the North was not extensive. The wind had been harnessed for a radio installation and lighting purposes on Severnaya Zemlya as well as at Yugorski Shar and Uyedineniye Island, where the polar stations had in 1936 received wind generators from the Administration of Polar Stations of Glavsevmorput'. The Agricultural Administration of Glavsevmorput' had sent generators to Dickson, Salekhard and Igarka to be used in Arctic hothouses. Another had been sent to a machine shop in Provideniya Bay by the Administration for the Economic and Cultural Development of the Peoples of the North. Other generators had been installed at polar stations as follows: in 1938, six D-3's and four D-12's; in 1939, five D-5's and one powerful D-30; and in 1940, seven of miscellaneous power. Plans in 1941 and 1942 called for installation of twenty-eight more generators at polar stations.[217] It is clear from the use made of the prewar generators that they did not play a significant role in the northern economy. The basic source of power in industry was still coal and, in lumber enterprises, sawdust and other waste.[218]

Additional wind generators may have been installed subsequently at polar stations and elsewhere in the Arctic districts. Postwar information indicates, however, that the industrial utilization of wind power is still to be attained. Academician A. V. Vinter wrote in 1953:

> At times wind power installations may be the only practical source of energy available in the Arctic. The powerful winds prevailing there make it possible to build wind power stations of over 50 and 100 kilowatts. Our scientists have worked out a scheme of joining several wind generators into one group that will produce 400 to 500 kilowatts of electricity. Atmospheric and climatic peculiarities of the Arctic are most unfavorable for erecting extensive electric transmission lines. The wind power installations, which can be constructed near the consumer, do not require transmission of power over long distances and thus effect a great saving in copper wire.[219]

The harnessing of wind power is the responsibility of the Ministry of Agriculture of the U.S.S.R. In 1951, according to the head of the Ministry's Department of Wind Power Installation, the plan for installing wind generators was fulfilled only 37 per cent.[220] In 1953 the production of wind generators in the Ukraine was stopped entirely.[221]

d.   Other Factors

One of the overall factors retarding the development of the North is the general management policy in the Soviet economy which eliminates individual initiative and concentrates the power to make investment and managerial decisions in officials at the apex of the bureaucracy and therefore not always in touch with the realities below. This policy is especially injurious to the extreme North, where, because of geographical and economic conditions, every undertaking is exceedingly complex and where mistakes and inaction bring swift and drastic consequences.

The special difficulties encountered in the North may be illustrated by the following example. Storage facilities are especially important to the northern economy because much of the freight going to and from the North is shipped during the relatively short navigation season on the Siberian rivers and the Northern Sea Route. Goods destined for transport from the North must be stored in warehouses until the navigation season opens, and incoming supplies must be stored for distribution throughout the year. Thus extra foresight and unusually sound management are required here; furthermore, any capital investment in northern industry must include an additional expenditure for storage facilities which would not be required in areas with year-round transportation.

3. Southern Siberia in the Regional Pattern

The economy of southern Siberia, especially west of the upper Angara, must be considered in estimating the economic prospects of the Northern Sea Route. On the one hand, southern Siberia is a potential supplier of cargo, chiefly agricultural, for shipment via the Northern Sea Route; on the other hand, it is a potential base for supplying the needs of the North via inland waterways and land routes, thus decreasing or eliminating the east-west flow of goods to the Arctic coast via the Route.

a. Grain

Siberia ranks as one of the major agricultural regions of the U.S.S.R. Not including the Urals and the Far East, the sown area of Siberia made up almost 10 per cent of the U.S.S.R. total in 1937 (ranking higher than the Urals or the central chernozem regions),[222] and the area sown to spring wheat was 23.4 per cent of the total for the whole country.[223] Most of the sown area was concentrated in southern Siberia west of the upper Angara.[224] According to the 1941 state plan, kolkhoz sowings of all summer grain crops in the Altai and Krasnoyarsk Krais and the Omsk and Novosibirsk Oblasts were to be over 15 per cent of the U.S.S.R. total,[225] and the yield was expected to be better than the average for these crops throughout the country.[226]

Agricultural measures introduced by the post-Stalin regime may increase the importance of southern Siberia west of the upper Angara as a grain producer. On March 2, 1954, the Plenum of the Central Committee of the CPSU adopted a resolution which called for increases in grain production and other agricultural produce by "developing idle and virgin lands in Kazakhstan, Siberia, the Urals, the Volga area, and partly in regions of the Northern Caucasus." The resolution called for bringing at least 13 million hectares of new land under cultivation in 1954-1955, from which over 1 billion poods of grain were to be obtained.[227] In August 1954, the goal was revised upward to 28-30 million hectares.[228] The Soviet press subsequently reported that up to November 5, 1954, 17.4 million hectares of such lands had actually been plowed up. In areas of southern Siberia west of the upper Angara, the increase was nearly 5.3 million hectares, that is, over 30 per cent of the total.[229] Although allowance must be made for exaggeration, it may be assumed that the area of plowed land in this region has expanded significantly. There is no definite information on how much of the newly-plowed land has actually been planted, nor is it certain that all of the new tracts will be sown to grain, although it is clear that the whole emphasis of the program is on expanding grain production.[230] If the increase in plowed area results in a corresponding increase in the grain lands and if the yields approach the nation-wide average, the share of this region in total grain production will be greater than in the past.[231]

b. Industry

The heaviest concentration of industry in southern Siberia is in the region west of the Yenisei. The industries in the area include coal mining, ferrous and nonferrous metallurgy and machine construction as well as plants producing chemicals, war equipment, and consumer goods. The coal fields of the Kuzbass rank second in importance in the Soviet Union (after the Donbass) and have the largest reserves of high quality coal. The large-scale expansion of textile mills is a relatively new development. The planned output of the Barnaul textile combine, 200 million meters annually, will supply the needs of the population of Siberia, the Soviet Far East and Kazakhstan for various types of cotton materials.[232] Altai textiles are now being distributed in various parts of the Soviet Union.[233] Farther east, in Kansk, construction has begun on a worsted combine which is to be one of the largest such enterprises in the U.S.S.R..[234]

Even before World War II the Kuzbass served as a supply base for the industrialization of regions east of the Urals and in 1938 provided 84.5 per cent of all metal shipments for Siberia and the Soviet Far East.[235]

During and after World War II there was a flow of equipment, skilled and unskilled labor, engineers and technicians from the European U.S.S.R. to southwestern Siberia and other regions east of the Urals. Large numbers of engineers, office supervisory personnel and skilled workers were transferred on administrative order after October 19, 1940, when the Presidium of the Supreme Soviet of the U.S.S.R. issued a decree on the obligatory transfer of specialist personnel.[236] In the course of three months in the second half of 1941 (after the German invasion), more than 1,360 large-scale enterprises were evacuated eastward from the European U.S.-S.R.; of these, 210 were sent to western Siberia.[237] After the war most of the plants were left in their new locations or only partially moved back to European U.S.S.R.

Further stimulation to the industrial development of southern Siberia, particularly the Kuzbass, may be expected from the completion of the railroad now under construction from the Urals to Abakan.[238]

Novosibirsk, which has grown in population from 120,000 in 1926 to 405,600 in 1939, and to 1,000,000 in 1952,[239] has become a "powerful industrial center" and supplies capital equipment to development projects and industrial enterprises in Siberia, the Soviet Far East and other regions of the U.S.S.R.[240]

Since the twenties, especially beginning with World War II, Krasnoyarsk has developed industrially until it is "on a par with such large industrial centers as Chelyabinsk, Sverdlovsk, Omsk and Novosibirsk."[241] Krasnoyarsk enterprises, which include plants for producing agricultural combines, metal constructions, and mining and lumbering equipment, a heavy machine building plant, and shipbuilding yards,[242] employ tens of thousands of skilled workers, engineers and technicians.[243]

Farther east in southern Siberia, Irkutsk and Chita Oblasts and Ulan-Ude have a small number of industrial enterprises, and in the southern part of the Soviet Far East, Khabarovsk, Komsomol'sk and the Vladivostok area are industrial centers.[244]

A weak point in Siberia's economy has been the underdevelopment of local industry and producers' cooperatives, which produce building materials, carts and various occupational implements, furniture, kitchen equipment and other household articles, artistic wood and iron work, clothing, footwear and a wide variety of other items. From 1946 to 1947 the value of the output of such enterprises increased by 33 per cent throughout the R.S.F.S.R., while the corresponding increase in Siberia was only 1.5 per cent.[245] In 1949 the head of R.S.F.S.R. administration for producers' cooperatives "confessed" that "the administration . . . recognizes its responsibility for the status of producers' cooperatives in the Urals, Siberia, and the Far East" and promised that in the future more assistance would be given to these co-operatives in the form of equipment and funds for new industrial construction and housing.[246] The next year at a conference of chairmen of planning commissions of oblasts, krais and autonomous republics, the Chairman of the R.S.F.-S.R. Gosplan demanded that the planning chairmen carry out the government's instructions on speeding up the plans for local and cooperative industries in the Urals, Siberia and the Far East.[247]

The campaign of the Soviet government for increasing the production of consumer goods, which began in fall 1953, placed the greatest emphasis on the development of local industries and producers' cooperatives in Siberia and the Far East.[248] In order to effect "a more rational use of the profits of industry and to concentrate them on the construction and expansion of enterprises producing consumer goods, especially in regions such as the Urals, Siberia, and the Far East, where local and cooperative industry is underdeveloped," authorities on the raion, oblast, krai, city and autonomous republic level were empowered to re-invest 60 per cent of the profits of enterprises under their jurisdiction for expansion over and above the planned capital investments.[249]

In November 1953 the head of the Department of Local Industry and Producers' Cooperatives of the U.S.S.R. Gosplan stated that the development of these branches of the economy in Siberia and the Far East (as well as in the Urals, Kazakhstan and Central Asia) would "assure the soundest distribution of consumer goods manufacture and the reduction of long-distance transportation of such goods."[250]

In early 1955 the Soviet government restored the emphasis to the development of heavy industry.[251] The reversal in policy does not necessarily mean the abandonment of plans for the development of local industries and producers' cooperatives in Siberia and the Soviet Far East; a shift in the geographic distribution of consumer goods industries without an expansion of this branch of the economy at the expense of heavy industry need not be incompatible with the plans for developing heavy industry.

NOTES

[1] *Kursy politupravleniya dlya komandnovo sostava Glavsevmorputi: Ekonomgeografiya Krainevo Severa* [Courses in Political Administration for Executive Personnel of Glavsevmorput': Economic Geography of the Extreme North], Moscow-Leningrad, Glavsevmorput', 1940, p. 33.

[2] *Ibid.*, p. 14.

[3] During World War II, when the northern naval fleet was supplied with poor-quality Pechora coal, the sailors called it "grade SK" [*Smert' kochegaru* (Death to the stoker)].

[4] *Kursy politupravleniya,* p. 14. As of January 1, 1945, the Pechora coal deposits constituted 3.2 per cent of the total exploitable resources of the U.S.S.R., as against the following percentages for other deposits: Donets, 13; Kuznetsk, 13; Karaganda, 4. Bykhover, N., and M. Rozin, "Priroda: Toplivno-energeticheskiye resursy" [Nature: Fuel and Power Resources], *Bol'shaya Sovetskaya entsiklopediya: SSSR* [Large Soviet Encyclopedia: The U.S.S.R.], Moscow, OGIZ, 1947, col. 245.

[5] Annual reports of Glavsevmorput' for 1938, 1939 and 1940.

[6] Garf, A. L., and V. V. Pokshishevski, *Sever* [The North], ed. by N. N. Mikhailov, Moscow, Molodaya gvardiya, 1948, p. 176.

[7] Velichko, V., *Siyaniye Severa* [Northern Lights], Moscow, Izdatel'stvo "Pravda," 1946, p. 17.

[8] *Ibid.*, p. 29.

[9] *Ibid.*, p. 30. The trust had its own aviation facilities, health resorts and clinics, and large-scale reindeer farming facilities. *Ibid.* Vorkuta has plants producing mining equipment, bricks and tile, a mining technical school, a trade school, four secondary schools, six seven-year schools, and eight elementary schools. "Vorkuta," *Bol'shaya Sovetskaya entsiklopediya,* 2d ed., Vol. IX, 1951, p. 96.

[10] Unless otherwise indicated, data from Velichko, *op. cit.*, p. 29.

[11] Absolute figure for 1940 from Department of the North, R.S.F.S.R. Gosplan.

[12] *Zakon o pyatiletnem plane vosstanovleniya i razvitiya narodnovo khozyaistva SSSR na 1946-1950 g.g.* [Law on the Five-Year Plan for the Reconstruction and Development of the National Economy of the U.S.S.R. for 1946-1950], Moscow, OGIZ, 1946, p. 18.

[13] Official information speaks only of an "important enlargement of the new coal base in the Pechora Basin" without any specific details.

*Soobshcheniye gosudarstvennovo planovovo komiteta SSSR i Tsentral'-
novo Statisticheskovo Upravleniya SSSR: Ob itogakh vypolneniya chetvyortovo (pervovo poslevoyennovo) pyatiletnevo plana SSSR na 1946-
1950 g.g.* [Statement of the State Planning Committee of the U.S.S.R.
and the Central Statistical Administration of the U.S.S.R.: On the
Results of the Fulfillment of the Fourth (First Postwar) Five-Year
Plan of the U.S.S.R. for 1946-1950], Moscow, Gospolitizdat, 1951,
p. 5.

[14] "Na Severe otkrylas' navigatsiya" [Navigation Has Begun in the
North], *Morskoi Flot* [Maritime Fleet], Moscow, May 1949. Pechora
coal is being shipped to Leningrad through Nar'yan-Mar via the
Pechora River. This route received special attention in the second
postwar Five-Year Plan because it would "relieve the pressure on the
Pechora Railroad and substantially reduce the transportation of coal
by railroad." Solomin, V., "Ratsionalizatsiya perevozok—krupnyi
reserv transporta" [The Rationalization of Shipping—a Large Transport Reserve], *Izvestiya*, April 19, 1953.

[15] *Zakon o pyatiletnem plane*, p. 18.

[16] Velichko, *op. cit.*, p. 37.

[17] "Zheleznodorozhnaya magistral' v polyarnoi tundre" [The Railroad
Trunk Line in the Polar Tundra], *Byulleten' Arkticheskovo Instituta*
[Bulletin of the Arctic Institute], Leningrad, No. 6-7, 1933, p. 167.

[18] In 1948 this line was still being referred to as a "project." Garf and
Pokshishevski, *op. cit.*, p. 23.

[19] In the early planning stages it was estimated that about one million
tons would be shipped north on the new line. "Zheleznodorozhnaya
magistral'," *op. cit.*

[20] "The Tunguska coal-bearing region, with an area of nearly one million square kilometers, is situated in the northern part of Krasnoyarsk Krai between the Yenisei and Lena rivers. . . . Huge areas of the
district remain almost unexplored. Estimates of the coal resources in
the Tunguska Basin are tentative. At the Seventeenth International
Geologic Congress [in 1937] they were estimated at 440 billion tons."
"Tunguskii uglenosnyi bassein" [The Tunguska Coal Basin], *Bol'shaya
Sovetskaya entsiklopediya*, Vol. LV, 1947, cols. 151-52. See also Suslov, S. P., *Fizicheskaya geografiya SSSR: Zapadnaya Sibir', Vostochnaya Sibir', Dal'nii Vostok, Srednyaya Aziya* [Physical Geography of
the U.S.S.R.: Western Siberia, Eastern Siberia, the Far East, Central
Asia], Moscow-Leningrad, Uchpedgiz, 1947; Obruchev, S. B., "Problema Tunguskovo basseina" [The Problem of the Tunguska Basin],
Angaro-Yeniseiskaya problema [The Angara-Yenisei Problem], Moscow, Gosplanizdat, 1932, pp. 122-25 (*Trudy I konferentsii po razmeshcheniyu proizvoditel'nykh sil SSSR* [Transactions of the First
Conference on the Geographic Distribution of the Productive Forces
of the U.S.S.R.], Vol. XVI); "Tunguskii uglenosnyi bassein" [The
Tunguska Coal Basin], *Za industrializatsiyu Sovetskovo Vostoka* [For
the Industrialization of the Soviet East], Moscow, No. 2, 1932, pp. 12-
20; Shorokhov, L., "Tunguskii uglenosnyi bassein" [The Tunguska
Coal Basin], *Atlas energeticheskikh resursov SSSR: Vostochno-*

Economic Potential of the Service Areas

Sibirskii krai [Atlas of the Power Resources of the U.S.S.R.: The Eastern Siberian Region], Moscow-Leningrad, Vol. II, No. 13, 1934, pp. 32-37; Popov, V. S., "Tunguskii uglenosnyi bassein" [The Tunguska Coal Basin], *Poleznye iskopayemye Krasnoyarskovo kraya* [Useful Minerals of Krasnoyarsk Krai], Tomsk, 1938, pp. 204-28.

[21] A group of enterprises producing several different metals.

[22] Dudinka, a town above the Arctic Circle, is the administrative and economic center of the Taimyr National Okrug. It has a quay, built during World War II, which is accessible to seagoing vessels. Dudinka also plays an important cultural role in the sovietization of the northern indigenous population. In 1952 there were in the city four clubs, two secondary schools, one seven-year school, two elementary schools, a school for training kolkhoz administrative personnel, a library, and a museum. "Dudinka," *Bol'shaya Sovetskaya entsiklopediya*, 2d ed., Vol. XV, 1952, pp. 274-75.

[23] Annual Report of Glavsevmorput' for 1939.

[24] *Kursy politupravleniya*, p. 22.

[25] Lyutkevich, Ye. M., "Yeniseisko-Pyasinskaya geologicheskaya ekspeditsiya" [The Yenisei-Pyasina Geologic Expedition], *Problemy Arktiki* [Problems of the Arctic], Leningrad, No. 3, 1938, pp. 106-8. See also Mutafi, N. N., "Pyasinskoye mestorozhdeniye uglei v obshchem komplekse Yeniseiskovo uglenosnovo polya" [The Pyasina Coal Deposit in the General Complex of the Yenisei Coal Field], *ibid.*, No. 2, 1938, pp. 43-61.

[26] Annual Report of Glavsevmorput' for 1938.

[27] Data from Glavsevmorput'.

[28] See Monastyrski, A. S., "Ugol'nye resursy Yakutska" [Coal Resources of Yakutsk], *Sovetskaya Arktika* [Soviet Arctic], Moscow, No. 7, 1937, pp. 67-68.

[29] Data from Glavsevmorput'.

[30] *Ibid.*

[31] Annual Report of Glavsevmorput' for 1940.

[32] "Novye goroda Yakutii" [New Cities of Yakutiya], *Izvestiya*, October 7, 1948.

[33] Annual Reports of Glavsevmorput' for 1938 and 1939.

[34] Gusev, A. I., "Bulunskii uglenosnyi raion" [The Bulun Coal District], *Tezisy dokladov sessii Uchonovo Soveta VAI* [Theses of Reports at the Session of the Learned Council of the All-Union Arctic Institute], Moscow-Leningrad, Glavsevmorput', 1935, pp. 42-45. See also his *Bulunskii uglenosnyi raion Yakutskoi ASSR* [The Bulun Coal District of the Yakut A.S.S.R.], Leningrad, Glavsevmorput', 1936, pp. 7-46 (*Trudy ANII* [Works of the Arctic Scientific Research Institute], Vol. LIX).

[35] Annual Report of Glavsevmorput' for 1938.

[36] Data from Glavsevmorput'.

[37] "On the Kolyma the transport workers and miners have built a city for themselves—Zyryanka." "Novye goroda Yakutii," *op. cit.*

[38] *Kursy politupravleniya*, p. 22.

[39] Data from Glavsevmorput'.

[40] *Ibid.*

[41] Lutski, S. L., *Ostrov Sakhalin* [Sakhalin Island], Moscow, Glavsevmorput', 1946.

[42] "Zasedaniya Verkhovnovo Soveta SSSR: Rech' deputata A. P. Yefimova" [Sessions of the Supreme Soviet of the U.S.S.R.: Address by Deputy A. P. Yefimov], *Pravda,* June 18, 1950.

[43] Molodetski, K. G., "Kamennougol'nye bazy Severnovo morskovo puti" [Coal Bases of the Northern Sea Route], *Izvestiya Vsesoyuznovo geograficheskovo obshchestva* [News of the All-Union Geographic Society], Moscow, Vol. LXXIII, No. 1, 1941, pp. 113-17; "Postanovleniye Sovnarkoma SSSR ob uluchshenii raboty Glavnovo upravleniya Severnovo morskovo puti ot 29 avgusta 1938 g." [Decree of the Council of People's Commissars of the U.S.S.R. of August 29, 1938, on Improving the Work of Glavsevmorput'], *Pravda,* August 30, 1938.

[44] Galitski, A., *Planirovaniye sotsialisticheskovo transporta* [The Planning of Socialist Transport], Moscow, Gosplanizdat, 1950, p. 5.

[45] The Grumant mine began operations early in 1932, the Barentsburg mine in December 1932 under concession to the U.S.S.R. Grumant, where 200 Soviet nationals were employed, produced 70,000 tons a year; and Barentsburg, with 815 Soviet workers, produced 250,000 tons. Data from Glavsevmorput'. By 1941 the population of Barentsburg had reached 1,500. During World War II the settlement and mine were destroyed by German air and sea bombardment. Restoration work began immediately after the war. "Barentsburg," *Bol'shaya Sovetskaya entsiklopediya,* 2d ed., Vol. IV, 1950, p. 240. According to Norwegian data, in 1948 there were about 2,500 Russians wintering on Spitsbergen. Armstrong, Terence, *The Northern Sea Route: Soviet Exploitation of the North East Passage,* Cambridge, Cambridge University Press, 1952, p. 83 (Scott Polar Research Institute, Special Publication No. 1).

[46] Apparently this practice is still being followed. See "Zasedaniya Verkhovnovo Soveta SSSR: Rech' deputata A. P. Yefimova," *op. cit.*

[47] Annual Report of Komseverput' for 1932.

[48] Annual Reports of Glavsevmorput' for 1934, 1935 and 1936.

[49] *XVII konferentsiya Vsesoyuznoi kommunisticheskoi partii (b): stenograficheskii otchot* [Seventeenth Conference of the All-Union Communist Party (Bolsheviks): Stenographic Report], Moscow, Partizdat, 1932, pp. 23-24.

[50] Annual Report of Glavsevmorput' for 1935.

[51] "All 28 ships participating in the Kara operations of 1934 were bunkered for the first time at Murmansk with Soviet coal, at a saving of 50,000 rubles in foreign exchange." Annual Report of Glavsevmorput' for 1934.

[52] The general survey of the minerals of the North is based mainly on a special memorandum prepared by Glavsevmorput' in 1940 for its courses in political administration given to executive personnel of the organization. See also Suslov, *op. cit.*

Economic Potential of the Service Areas

[53] Fersman, A. Ye., "Apatit, yevo mestorozhdeniya, geokhimiya, zapasy i ekonomika" [Apatite, Its Occurrence, Geochemistry, Reserves and Economics], *Khibinskiye apatity* [Khibiny Apatites], Leningrad, Vol. III, 1931.

[54] Before World War II the underground workings in the Khibiny Mountains were expected to yield 4 million tons of ore a year (not including the output of the opencut mines). The concentration plant had an annual capacity of one million tons of concentrates in the mid-thirties. "Kirovsk," *Malaya Sovetskaya entsiklopediya* [Small Soviet Encyclopedia], 2d ed., Moscow, Vol. V, 1936, col. 461. Mining operations in this area were interrupted during World War II, but they have since been resumed.

[55] See Lutski, S. L., *Kol'skii gornopromyshlennyi raion* [The Kola Mining District], Moscow, 1939 (*Uchonye zapiski Moskovskovo gosudarstvennovo universiteta* [Scientific Notes of the Moscow State University], No. 21).

[56] Bykhover, N., and M. Rozin, "Priroda: Mineral'nye resursy" [Nature: Mineral Resources], *Bol'shaya Sovetskaya entsiklopediya: SSSR*, Moscow, 1947, cols. 256-57.

[57] For a brief description of the settlement, see "Preobrazhonnaya Pechenga" [Transformed Pechenga], *Pravda*, December 21, 1949; also the report of observations by Norwegians in "V Sovetskoi Arktike" [In the Soviet Arctic], *Novoye Russkoye Slovo*, New York, December 24, 1953.

[58] The section of the railroad north of Kandalaksha has been electrified, and construction of a branch line from Belomorsk to Obozyorskaya, connecting the road with the line from Archangel to Vologda, was completed during World War II. The key role of the Kirov Railroad in the economy of the Kola Peninsula is illustrated by the following details on annual freight turnover before World War II: more than 300,000 tons of southbound freight from the city of Murmansk; over one million tons of southbound apatite and timber; over 1.4 million tons of incoming freight (mostly food, coal and oil) from the railroad station Murmanskiye Vorota. Data from the Administration of the Kirov Railroad, 1940. After the war freight turnover on the railroad showed an overall increase, despite the fact that incoming coal shipments decreased because of the development of the Pechora deposits. In 1951 freight turnover on the Kirov Railroad was 114.9 per cent of the turnover in 1940. "Kirovskaya zheleznaya doroga" [The Kirov Railroad], *Bol'shaya Sovetskaya entsiklopediya*, 2d ed., Vol. XXI, 1953, p. 122.

[59] See "Razvedka Noril'skovo medno-nikelevovo mestorozhdeniya" [Exploration of the Noril'sk Copper and Nickel Deposits], *Izvestiya GK (1925)* [News of the Geological Committee (1925)], Leningrad, Vol. XLIV, No. 2, 1927, pp. 190-91; Pletnyov, V., "Medno-nikelevye mestorozhdeniya Norilya" [The Copper and Nickel Deposits of Noril'sk], *Sovetskaya Zoloto-promyshlennost'* [The Soviet Gold Industry], Irkutsk, No. 2-3, 1932, pp. 22-23. Concerning platinum in Noril'sk, see Vysotski, N. K., "O korennykh mestorozhdeniyakh platiny na

Urale i v Sibire" [Basic Deposits of Platinum in the Urals and Siberia], *Izvestiya GK*, Vol. XLII, No. 1, 1923, pp. 15-21; Urvantsev, N. N., *Klimat i usloviya rabot v raione Noril'skovo kamennougol'novo i polimetallicheskovo mestorozhdeniya* [Climate and Working Conditions in the Area of the Noril'sk Coal and Polymetallic Deposits], Leningrad, 1934 *(Trudy Polyarnoi Komissii AN SSSR* [Works of the Polar Commission of the Academy of Sciences of the U.S.S.R.], Vol. XIV).

[60] "Grafit," *Malaya Sovetskaya entsiklopediya*, 2d ed., Vol. III, 1935, col. 465.

[61] Krypton, Constantine, *The Northern Sea Route: Its Place in Russian Economic History Before 1917,* New York, Research Program on the U.S.S.R., 1953, p. 12 ff.

[62] Bubleinikov, F., "Grafit v SSSR" [Graphite in the U.S.S.R.], *Gornyi zhurnal* [Mining Journal], Moscow, No. 1, 1926, pp. 44-47. See also Shapiro, I. O., "O tekhnicheskoi i ekonomicheskoi vozmozhnosti promyshlennovo ispol'zovaniya kureiskovo mestorozhdeniya grafita" [Concerning the Technical and Economic Possibilities for the Industrial Utilization of the Kureika Graphite Deposits], *ibid.,* No. 6, 1926, pp. 444-48.

[63] Information from the Planning Department of the Krasnoyarsk Krai Executive Committee.

[64] Yemel'yantsev, T. M., "Geologicheskiye issledovaniya v raione Nordvika i ostrova Begicheva v 1933 godu" [Geologic Exploration in the Area of Nordvik and Begichev Island in 1933], *Geologicheskiye issledovaniya Nordvik-Khatangskovo raiona i Taimyrskovo poluostrova* [Geologic Explorations of the Nordvik-Khatanga Area and the Taimyr Peninsula], 1939, pp. 5-40.

[65] Before his arrest in 1938 Urvantsev had written over thirty works on northern Siberia.

[66] Urvantsev, N. N., "Khatanga—novyi gornopromyshlennyi raion" [Khatanga—A New Mining District], *Sovetskaya Arktika*, No. 1, 1935, pp. 5-8. See also his earlier works on this subject, "Gde iskat' neft' v Sovetskoi Arktike?" [Where to Prospect for Oil in the Soviet Arctic?], *Problemy Sovetskoi geologii* [Problems of Soviet Geology], Leningrad, No. 3, 1933, pp. 241-42; "Raboty po khozyaistvennomu osvoyeniyu Leno-Taimyrskovo raiona v 1933 godu" [Work During 1933 on the Economic Exploitation of the Lena-Taimyr Area], *Byulleten' ANII* [Bulletin of the Arctic Scientific Research Institute], Leningrad, No. 5, 1933, pp. 113-18.

[67] Urvantsev, N. N., "Geologiya i poleznye iskopayemye Taimyrsko-Vilyuiskoi depressii" [The Geology and Useful Minerals of the Taimyr-Vilyui Depression], *Tezisy dokladov sessii Uchonovo Soveta VAI,* pp. 46-48.

[68] Urvantsev, N. N., "Geofizika na sluzhbe osvoyeniya nedr Arktiki" [Geophysics in the Service of the Development of the Mineral Resources of the Arctic], *Byulleten' ANII,* No. 12, 1935, pp. 425-28. See also his "Geologiya i poleznye iskopayemye Khatangskovo raiona"

Economic Potential of the Service Areas

[The Geology and Useful Minerals of the Khatanga Area], *Problemy Arktiki*, No. 2, 1937, pp. 5-24.

[69] Yeml'yantsev, T. M., "Geologicheskiye issledovaniya v raione rek Khety, Khatangi, Taimyrskovo poluostrova v 1935-36 godakh" [Geologic Explorations in the Areas of the Kheta and Khatanga Rivers and the Taimyr Peninsula During 1935-36], *Geologicheskiye issledovaniya Nordvik-Khatangskovo raiona i Taimyrskovo poluostrova*, 1939, pp. 91-128.

[70] See Shatski, N. S., "Neft' Yakutskoi ASSR" [Oil of the Yakut A.S.S.R.], *Atlas energeticheskikh resursov SSSR: Dal'nevostochnyi krai, Yakutskaya ASSR* [Atlas of the Power Resources of the U.S.S.R.: The Far Eastern Krai, the Yakut A.S.S.R.], Moscow-Leningrad, Vol. II, No. 14, 1934, pp. 95-96; Senyukov, V. M., "Novaya neftenosnaya oblast' kembriiskikh otlozhenii severnovo sklona Aldanskovo massiva" [The New Oil-Bearing Region of the Cambrian Deposits of the Northern Slope of the Aldan Massif], *Neftyanoi Institut* [The Oil Institute], No. 7, 1937, pp. 54-60; "Geologo-s"yomochnye raboty v Olekminskom raione" [Geologic Survey Work in the Olekma District], *Otchot Neftyanovo Instituta za 1934 god* [Report of the Oil Institute for 1934], 1936, pp. 38-39; "Yakutskaya ekspeditsiya" [The Yakut Expedition], *Razvedka nedr* [Exploration for Mineral Resources], Moscow, No. 6, 1938, p. 65. See also Berzin, A. I., "Geologicheskoye issledovaniye neftenosnovo mestorozhdeniya Nordvik v 1934-35 godu" [Geologic Exploration of the Nordvik Oil Deposit During 1934-35], *Geologicheskiye issledovaniya Nordvik-Khatangskovo raiona i Taimyrskovo poluostrova*, pp. 41-74; Ryabukhin, G. Ye., "Novye dannye po geologii nizhnevo techeniya r. Yeniseya" [New Data on the Geology of the Lower Reaches of the Yenisei], *Sovetskaya geologiya* [Soviet Geology], Leningrad, No. 11, 1940, pp. 21-34; Vologdin, A. G., "K poiskam nefti v Turukhanskom raione" [Explorations for Oil in the Turukhansk Area], *Vestnik Zapadno-Sibirskovo geologicheskovo upravleniya* [Courier of the West Siberian Geologic Administration], Novosibirsk, No. 2, 1940, pp. 28-35; Buyalov, N. I., "Poiski nefti v Nordvik-Khatangskom raione" [Prospecting for Oil in the Nordvik-Khatanga Area], *Razvedka Nedr*, No. 12, 1940, pp. 4-10; Tuayev, N. P., "Ocherk geologii i neftenosnosti Zapadno-Sibirskoi nizmennosti" [Outline of the Geology and Oil Resources of the West Siberian Lowland], *Trudy neftyanovo Geologo-razvedochnovo instituta* [Works of the Oil Geologic Exploration Institute], Moscow-Leningrad, New Series, No. 4, 1941; Gedroits, N. A., "Ust'-Yeniseiskii port i perspektivi yevo neftenosnosti" [The Ust'-Yeniseisk Port and Its Oil Bearing Prospects], *Problemy Arktiki*, No. 13, 1940, pp. 100-23; Saks, V. N., "Osnovnye etapy formirovaniya Taimyrskoi depressii" [Principal Stages in the Formation of the Taimyr Depression], *ibid.*, No. 10, 1940, pp. 52-65.

[71] This announcement was made by Papanin, the *de facto* head of Glavsevmorput', at a general meeting of Leningrad personnel of Glavsevmorput' held in the Leningrad House of the Red Army in 1938, at which the author was present.

95

[72] Vologdin, A. G., "Problema nefti v Krasnoyarskom kraye" [The Problem of Oil in the Krasnoyarsk Krai], *Poleznye iskopayemye Krasnoyarskovo kraya* [Useful Minerals of Krasnoyarsk Krai], Tomsk, 1938, pp. 392-414. See also his "Novyi Turukhanskii neftenosnyi raion" [The New Turukhansk Oil Bearing Area], *Sovetskaya geologiya*, No. 12, 1938, pp. 4-13.

[73] Ryabukhin, G. Ye., "Geologicheskoye stroyeniye i neftenosnost' raiona Ust'-Porta na reke Yeniseye" [Geologic Structure and Oil Resources of the Ust'-Port Area on the Yenisei River], *Problemy Arktiki,* No. 3, 1939, pp. 29-40.

[74] Anikeyev, N. P., and G. G. Moor, "Sushchestvuyet li Taimyrskii Shariazh?" [Is There a Taimyr Overthrust Sheet?], *Problemy Arktiki,* No. 4, 1939, pp. 48-59. See also Anikeyev, N. P., and A. I. Gusev, *Geologicheskii ocherk yugo-zapadnoi chasti Taimyrskovo poluostrova* [Geologic Outline of the Southwestern Part of the Taimyr Peninsula], 1939 (*Trudy ANII* [Works of the Arctic Scientific Research Institute], Vol. CXL).

[75] *Kursy politupravleniya,* p. 16.

[76] *Ibid.*

[77] Senyukov, V. M., "Problema neftenosnosti Kembriiskikh otlozhenii Sibiri v basseine r.r. Lena-Aldan" [The Problem of Oil Resources in the Cambrian Deposits of Siberia in the Lena and Aldan River Basin], *Neftyanoye khozyaistvo* [Oil Economy], Moscow, Vol. XXVII, No. 2, 1935, pp. 26-29; and Senyukov, V. M., "Reka Tolba i neftenosnost' severnovo sklona Aldanskovo massiva" [The Tolba (Tuolba) River and the Oil Deposits of the Northern Slope of the Aldan Massif], *Trudy neftyanovo Geologo-razvedochnovo instituta* [Works of the Oil Geologic Exploration Institute], Leningrad, Series A, No. 107, 1938.

[78] *Kursy politupravleniya,* p. 21.

[79] Data from the Arctic Institute of Glavsevmorput'.

[80] See Kazakov, George, *Soviet Peat Resources: A Descriptive Study,* New York, Research Program on the U.S.S.R., 1953, pp. 124-39.

[81] Data from the Arctic Institute of Glavsevmorput'.

[82] The necessity of switching to oil was mentioned before World War II in the annual reports of the Maritime Department of Glavsevmorput'.

[83] Data from the Yakutsk Trade Department of the Yakutsk Executive Committee.

[84] *Kursy politupravleniya,* p. 51.

[85] Garf, A. L., and V. V. Pokhishevski, *op. cit.,* p. 154.

[86] *Ibid.,* p. 156.

[87] *Ibid.,* p. 160.

[88] See Gedroits, N. A., "Perspektivi neftenosnosti severa Sibiri" [Prospects of Oil Deposits in the North of Siberia], *Nedra Arktiki* [Mineral Resources of the Arctic], Moscow-Leningrad, No. 1, 1946, pp. 9-14; Kornilyuk, Yu. I., T. P. Kochetkov and T. M. Yemel'yantsev, "Nordvik-Khatangskii neftenosnyi raion" [The Nordvik-Khatanga Oil Bearing Area], *ibid.,* pp. 15-73; Lappo, V. I., "Neftyanoye mestorozhdeniye Nordvik" [The Nordvik Oil Deposit], *ibid.,* pp. 74-129.

[89] Suslov, *op. cit.*, p. 189.

[90] *Kursy politupravleniya*, p. 16.

[91] Archives of Komseverput'. *Plan Komsevmorputi na 1932 god* [Plan of Komseverput' for 1932].

[92] "The creation of a synthetic liquid fuel industry based on the hydrogenation of solid fuel should be the first task in the East. . . ." *Rezolyutsii XVIII s"yezda VKP(b)* [Resolutions of the Eighteenth Congress of the All-Union Communist Party (Bolsheviks)], Moscow, Gospolitizdat, 1939, p. 17. "We must create an industry for transforming coal and shale into liquid fuel . . . [with an output of] 900,000 tons [by 1950]." *Zakon o pyatiletnem plane . . . na 1946-1950 g.g.*, p. 20.

[93] Polymetallic ores are defined as ores containing several recoverable metals.

[94] *Kursy politupravleniya*, p. 48.

[95] Amderma has a secondary school, a hospital and other institutions. "Amderma," *Bol'shaya Sovetskaya entsiklopediya*, 2d ed., Vol. II, 1950, p. 220.

[96] Data on the shipment of platinum obtained from the Planning Department of the Krasnoyarsk Krai Executive Committee in 1940.

[97] "Novostroiki samovo molodovo goroda v Zapolyar'ye" [New Construction in the Newest City Above the Arctic Circle], *Pravda*, November 22, 1953. See also Shabad, Theodore, "Secret Siberian City Linked to Uranium," *New York Times*, January 16, 1955.

[98] Urvantsev, N. N., "K probleme promyshlennovo osvoyeniya soli v vostochnom sektore polyarnoi zony SSSR" [On the Problem of Industrial Utilization of Salt in the Eastern Sector of the Polar Zone of the U.S.S.R.], *Arktika* [The Arctic], Leningrad, No. 3, 1935, pp. 43-53; Anan'yev, P. M., "Nordvikskaya sol' real'na" [Nordvik Salt is Real], *Sovetskaya Arktika*, No. 4, 1936, pp. 46-51; Kondakov, Zh., "O dobyche soli v raione bukhty Kozhevnikova" [On the Mining of Salt in the Kozhevnikovo Gulf Area], *ibid.*, No. 7, 1940, pp. 22-27.

[99] *Kursy politupravleniya*, pp. 68-69.

[100] "Zasedaniya Verkhovnovo Soveta SSSR: Rech' deputata R. G. Vasil'yeva" [Sessions of the Supreme Soviet of the U.S.S.R.: Address of Deputy R. G. Vasil'yev], *Izvestiya*, April 25, 1954. See also the speech of the representative of the Gosplan of the Yakut A.S.S.R. "Soveshchaniye predsedatelei planovykh komissii oblastei, krayov i avtonomnykh respublik v Gosplane RSFSR" [Conference of Representatives of Planning Commissions of Oblasts, Krais and Autonomous Republics in the R.S.F.S.R. Gosplan], *Planovoye khozyaistvo* [Planned Economy], Moscow, No. 5, 1950, p. 85.

[101] Annual Report of Glavsevmorput' for 1940.

[102] Mikhailov, S. [Senior Scientist of the Institute of Oceanography of the U.S.S.R. Academy of Sciences], "Rybnyi promysel i yevo vozmozhnosti" [The Fishing Industry and Its Potentialities], *Izvestiya*, February 25, 1953. Before the 1954 spring fishing season it was reported that the catch of fish in the open seas made up over two thirds of the total catch. "Nakanune vesennei putiny" [On the Eve of the Spring Fishing Season], *Izvestiya*, March 4, 1954.

[103] Zubrikov, A. F., "Uspekhi Polyarnoi MRS" [Success of the Polar Motor-Fishing Stations], *Rybnoye khozyaistvo* [Fishing Economy], Moscow, No. 8, August 1952, p. 41.

[104] Kurski, V. I., *Ryby v prirode i khozyaistve cheloveka* [Fish in Nature and in the Economy of Man], ed. by L. V. Averintsev, Moscow, Uchpedgiz, 1949, p. 135.

[105] Data from the Accounting Section of the Murmansk Oblast Planning Commission, 1940.

[106] "Murmanskaya oblast' " [Murmansk Oblast], *Bol'shaya Sovetskaya entsiklopediya,* 2d ed., Vol. XXVIII, 1954, p. 572.

[107] *Ibid.,* and "Murmansk," *ibid.,* p. 570.

[108] "Murmanskaya oblast'," *op. cit.,* p. 573.

[109] The combine consists of two salting plants, a freezer, and various shops turning out individual specialties. In addition, the combine controls a number of smaller processing plants in Murmansk.

[110] "Murmansk," *op. cit.,* p. 570. See also "Promysel sel'di na Severe" [The Herring Industry in the North], *Izvestiya,* August 9, 1951.

[111] Data from Glavsevmorput'. Report on the Second Five-Year Plan (1933-1937) of Glavsevmorput'.

[112] A metric centner equals 100 kg. or 220.46 lb.

[113] Data from Glavsevmorput'. Report on the Second Five-Year Plan (1933-1937) of Glavsevmorput'.

[114] *Kursy politupravleniya,* p. 27.

[115] Kurski, *op. cit.,* p. 119. See also Suslov, *op. cit.,* p. 28.

[116] Mikhailov, S., "Puti pod"yoma rybnoi promyshlennosti" [Paths to the Expansion of the Fishing Industry], *Planovoye khozyaistvo* [Planned Economy], Moscow, No. 4, 1953, p. 69.

[117] Data from Glavsevmorput'.

[118] See Suslov, *op. cit.,* p. 227; also "Beringovo more" [The Bering Sea], *Bol'shaya Sovetskaya entsiklopediya,* 2d ed., Vol. V, 1950, pp. 18-20.

[119] Suslov, *op. cit.,* p. 350.

[120] Kurski, *op. cit.,* pp. 119-20.

[121] *Ibid.,* pp. 130-31.

[122] "Vdvoye bol'she konservov chem do voiny" [Twice as Much Canned Food as Before the War], *Pravda,* November 18, 1949.

[123] "A crabbing vessel produces 25,000 cans of crab meat a day." Gerasimov, S. K., *Patrioty Dal'nevo Vostoka* [Patriots of the Far East], Moscow, Pishchepromizdat, 1946, p. 32.

[124] Kurski, *op. cit.,* 133-34.

[125] Mikhailov, S. V., and S. P. Udovenko, "Kamchatskaya oblast' " [Kamchatka Oblast], *Bol'shaya Sovetskaya entsiklopediya,* 2d ed., Vol. XIX, 1953, p. 556.

[126] *Ibid.,* p. 558.

[127] Gerasimov, *op. cit.,* p. 51.

[128] *Ibid.,* pp. 19-21.

[129] *Zakon o pyatiletnem plane . . . na 1946-1950 g.g.,* p. 33.

[130] See *Sbornik po trudovomu zakonodatel'stvu dlya rabotnikov Severnovo morskovo puti* [Collection of Labor Laws for Personnel of the

Economic Potential of the Service Areas

Northern Sea Route], comp. by P. I. Nedzvedski, Moscow-Leningrad, Glavsevmorput', 1948, p. 249; and Gerasimov, *op. cit.,* pp. 102-4.

[131] "Na Kamchatke" [On Kamchatka], *Izvestiya,* December 30, 1949.

[132] Data for 1940, Department of the North, R.S.F.S.R. Gosplan. The figures for 1940 pertain only to Soviet operations and do not include Japanese fishing and canning activities at their concessions in the Kamchatka area before World War II.

[133] Mikhailov and Udovenko, *op. cit.,* p. 556.

[134] Data for 1940, Department of the North, R.S.F.S.R. Gosplan.

[135] Mikhailov and Udovenko, *op. cit.,* p. 556.

[136] For a brief description of the new Yelizov raion, see "V molodom raione Kamchatki" [In a New Raion on Kamchatka], *Pravda,* June 14, 1950.

[137] "Na zapadnom poberezh'i Kamchatki" [On the Western Coast of Kamchatka], *Pravda,* August 20, 1949.

[138] See for example "Rybolovetskaya baza v Gizhiginskoi gube [A Fishing Base in Gizhiga Bay], *Pravda,* August 8, 1948; *Pravda,* April 4, 1948; "Zasedaniya Verkhovnovo Soveta: Rech' deputata A. P. Yefimova," *op. cit.* For examples of shortcomings in the Far Eastern fishing industry, see *ibid;* Mikhailov, S., "Rybnyi promysel," *op. cit.;* and "Sodoklad predsedatelya Byudzhetnoi Komissii Soveta Soyuza, deputata P. L. Korniyetsa" [Co-Report of the Chairman of the Budget Commission of the Soviet of the Union, Deputy P. L. Korniyets], *Izvestiya,* March 12, 1949.

[139] Kurski, *op. cit.,* pp. 130-31. The lower reaches of the Siberian rivers have more fish than the upper. Suslov, *op. cit.,* pp. 22, 174.

[140] Kurski, *op. cit.,* pp. 130-31; and Suslov, *op. cit.,* p. 174.

[141] Butuzov, S. M., "Krasnoyarskii krai," *Bol'shaya Sovetskaya entsiklopediya,* 2d ed., Vol. XXIII, 1953, p. 270.

[142] "U rybakov zapolyar'ya" [With the Fishermen Above the Arctic Circle], *Ivzestiya,* March 10, 1949.

[143] See "Na Taimyre" [On Taimyr], *Izvestiya,* July 19, 1951; "Tyulenskiye rybaki" [Seal Fishermen], *Izvestiya,* February 3, 1953.

[144] "Plovuchiye kul'tbazy" [Floating Culture Bases], *Izvestiya,* August 18, 1951. See also "Plovuchii lektorii" [Floating Lecture Hall], *ibid.,* June 22, 1949; and *Izvestiya,* September 2, 1950.

[145] *Kursy politupravleniya,* p. 27.

[146] *Ibid.,* p. 78.

[147] Gerasimov, *op. cit.,* p. 42.

[148] Kurski, *op. cit.,* pp. 130-31. See also Vinogradov, M. P., *Morskiye mlekopitayushchiye Arktiki* [Sea Mammals of the Arctic], Moscow-Leningrad, 1949; and Chapski, K. K., *Morskiye zveri sovetskoi Arktiki* [Sea Animals of the Soviet Arctic], Moscow-Leningrad, 1941.

[149] Gerasimov, *op. cit.,* p. 36.

[150] Mikhailov, "Rybnyi promysel," *op. cit.*

[151] Data from Glavsevmorput'.

[152] Even the Mikoyan Combine, the largest fishery on Kamchatka, has been unable to work out a satisfactory solution to the problem. Every year, at the beginning of the fishing season, 600 to 800 seasonal work-

ers arrive at the combine, at "no small cost" and at great "inconvenience." Gerasimov, *op. cit.*, pp. 47-48. The Lower Amur Fishing Trust expends four to five million rubles every year to bring in seasonal workers from the central regions of the U.S.S.R. Travel time takes about four months, and the time spent in direct work amounts to two months. A Party official of the Amur region called for a halt to the "irrational" practice. Chaika, Ya., "Neispol'zovannye vozmozhnosti rybnoi promyshlennosti" [Unutilized Potentials of the Fishing Industry], *Pravda,* November 22, 1954. The use of seasonal labor was apparently discontinued in the Ob' basin fishing industry in the 1950's, but a government official of the region subsequently called for a return to the practice to meet the shortage of labor during the fishing season. Cherezov, I., "Polneye ispol'zovat' rybnye bogatstva Sibiri" [Make Fuller Use of the Fish Resources of Siberia], *Izvestiya,* November 23, 1954.

[153] Gurvich, I. Ya., "Poslevoyennye izmeneniya v geografii lesov [Postwar Changes in the Geography of Forests], *Izvestiya Vsesoyuznovo geograficheskovo obshchestva* [News of the All-Union Geographic Society], Leningrad, Vol. LXXXII, No. 4, July-August 1950, p. 378.

[154] Nesterov, V., "Narodnoye khozyaistvo: Lesnoye khozyaistvo" [The National Economy: The Timber Economy], *Bol'shaya Sovetskaya entsiklopediya: SSSR,* col. 944.

[155] Baranski, N. N., *Ekonomicheskaya geografiya SSSR* [Economic Geography of the U.S.S.R.], 14th ed., Moscow, Uchpedgiz, 1953, p. 154. See also Nikitin, N. V., *Lesnaya promyshlennost' Arkhangel'skoi oblasti za 30 let i perspektivy yeyo dal'neishevo razvitiya* [Thirty Years of the Lumber Industry of Archangel Oblast and the Prospects for Its Further Development], Archangel, 1948; and Chernov, A. A., *Mineral'no-syr'yevaya baza severo-vostoka Yevropeiskoi chasti SSSR: Analiz i perspektivy* [The Mineral Raw Material Base of the Northeast Part of the European U.S.S.R.: Analysis and Prospects], Moscow-Leningrad, Akademiya Nauk SSSR, 1948.

[156] Baranski, *op. cit.*, p. 153.

[157] "Pervye ploty v Arkhangel'ske" [The First Rafts in Archangel], *Izvestiya,* May 20, 1948.

[158] "Recently thousands of families of workers who wanted to become loggers were resettled in Archangel Oblast. In the great northern forests new settlements have appeared, with blocks of small houses built by the settlers with means provided them by the government." "V severnykh lesakh" [In the Northern Forests], *Izvestiya,* December 19, 1952.

[159] Data from the Igarka City Soviet, 1940.

[160] For example, Igarka provides lumber for the Dudinka Promkombinat, which manufactures furniture. Kovalkin, I., "Za polyarnym krugom" [Above the Arctic Circle], *Izvestiya,* November 5, 1953.

[161] Annual Report of Komseverput' for 1931.

[162] A standard is equivalent to 165 cu. ft. Soviet foreign exports of lumber via the Kara Sea from 1935 to 1939 averaged about 63,000 standards annually; it may be assumed that virtually all of these ship-

ments went through Igarka. "The Kara Sea Route," *The Polar Record,* Cambridge, Vol. VI, No. 46, July 1953, p. 826.

[163] See Stsepuro, N. V., "Lesnaya promyshlennost' v tret'yem pyatiletii na Krainem Severe" [The Lumber Industry in the Third Five-Year Plan in the Extreme North], *Sovetskaya Arktika,* No. 2, 1937, p. 82.

[164] *Ibid.,* pp. 84-85. An earlier report stated that the combine was to saw as much as 275,000 cu. m. annually. Sokolov, A. A., "Belogorskii lesokombinat" [The Belogor'ye Lumber Combine], *Sovetskaya Arktika,* No. 9, 1936, p. 46.

[165] Stsepuro, *op. cit.,* p. 82.

[166] Only 3 per cent of the forest lands of the Yakut A.S.S.R. had been explored. Data from the Department of the North, R.S.F.S.R. Gosplan.

[167] Materials of Glavsevmorput' on the Third Five-Year Plan, 1937.

[168] Tikhomirov, B., "Sibirskii les—na sluzhbu narodnomu khozyaistvu strany" [Siberian Lumber—In the Service of the National Economy of the Country], *Izvestiya,* April 16, 1953. The lecturer underrated the level of development, for the Igarka enterprise is of some importance; however, his statements are entirely justified if the degree of exploitation is considered in relation to the available lumber resources.

[169] See Baranski, *op. cit.,* p. 46. An article on the sawmill industry published in 1954 named only Igarka and Maklakova as the sites of very important saw milling centers built during the Soviet period. "Lesopil'naya promyshlennost' " [The Sawmill Industry], *Bol'shaya Sovetskaya entsiklopediya,* 2d ed., Vol. XXV, 1954, p. 23.

[170] For the importance of the Salekhard mill and the direction of the shipment of its output, see Baranski, *op. cit.,* Fig. 12, p. 47. Earlier editions of this work do not show the Salekhard mills (see Baranski, *op. cit.,* 9th ed., Moscow, 1948, Fig. 16, p. 38; and *op. cit.,* 12th ed., Moscow, 1951, Fig. 15, p. 48). The new rail line runs from Labytnangi (on the Ob' opposite Salekhard) through Ust'-Vorkuta to Chum on the Pechora Railroad (see map of the Komi A.S.S.R. in *Bol'shaya Sovetskaya entsiklopediya,* 2d ed., Vol. XXII, 1953, facing p. 140).

[171] *Zakon o pyatiletnem plane . . . na 1946-1950 g.g.,* p. 31.

[172] Chornykh, Ye., "O novom i otstalom na lesozagotovkakh Sibiri" [About the New and the Old in Siberian Lumbering], *Izvestiya,* November 16, 1949. See also *Soobshcheniye gosudarstvennovo planovovo komiteta,* p. 9; "Polneye ispol'zovat' lesnye bogatstva Dal'nevo Vostoka" [Make Fuller Use of the Lumber Resources of the Far East], *Izvestiya,* February 24, 1952; and Sudnitsyn, I., "Mekhanizatsiya lesnoi promyshlennosti" [Mechanization of the Lumber Industry], *Planovoye khozyaistvo,* No. 3, 1949. The author was informed by former German prisoners of war who returned from the U.S.S.R. in 1948 and 1949 that lumbering operations in which they participated and which they observed in the southern part of Krasnoyarsk Krai were conducted without the benefit of mechanized equipment.

[173] *Zasedaniya Verkhovnovo Soveta RSFSR 20-25 iyunya 1946 g. (sed'maya sessiya): Stenograficheskii otchot* [Sessions of the Supreme

Soviet of the R.S.F.S.R. of 20-25 June 1946 (Seventh Session): Stenographic Report], Moscow, Izdaniye Verkhovnovo Soveta RSFSR, 1946, pp. 65-66.

[174] "Zasedaniya Verkhovnovo Soveta RSFSR: Rech' ministra lesnoi promyshlennosti RSFSR" [Sessions of the Supreme Soviet of the R.S.F.S.R.: Address of the Minister of the Lumber Industry of the R.S.F.S.R.], *Izvestiya*, March 29, 1952.

[175] See Berzilov, N., "V storone ot nuzhd predpriyatii" [Apart from the Needs of Enterprises], *Pravda*, March 21, 1951; and "Polneye ispol'zovat' lesnye bogatstva," *op. cit.*

[176] Data from the Department of the North, R.S.F.S.R. Gosplan, 1941.

[177] *Ibid.*

[178] A Siberian planning study published in 1930 stated that only 20 per cent of the hunting areas of the North had not been "depleted." *Materialy k general'nomu planu razvitiya narodnovo khozyaistva Sibirskovo kraya* [Materials for the General Plan for the Development of the National Economy of the Siberian Krai], Novosibirsk, Sibkraiizdat, 1930, Ch. 9. Directives of the R.S.F.S.R. Gosplan in 1930 strongly emphasized the need for a complete physical study and description of the North as part of an effort to replenish depleted hunting areas by 1942-1943. "Direktivy Gosplana RSFSR po sostavleniyu perspektivnovo pyatiletnovo plana po sotsialisticheskoi rekonstruktsii i razvitiyu narodnovo khozyaistva Krainevo Severa" [Directives of the R.S.F.S.R. Gosplan on the Drawing Up of a Prospective Five-Year Plan for the Socialist Reconstruction and Development of the National Economy of the Extreme North], *Sovetskii Sever* [Soviet North], Moscow, No. 1, 1930, pp. 186-87, Paragraphs 15a and 15g. A study of this nature is almost prerequisite to any serious effort to restore the hunting areas, and from the speeches of Supreme Soviet deputies in 1949 and 1950 it is clear that this prerequisite has not been met; see the speech by V. K. Shishonkov, deputy of the Komi A.S.S.R. in *Pravda*, July 19, 1950, and by F. N. Shchurov, deputy of Tyumen' Oblast in *Izvestiya*, May 31, 1949.

[179] Data from the Department of the North, R.S.F.S.R. Gosplan, 1941.

[180] For the statute on the Industrial-Hunting Stations, see *Sovetskii Sever*, No. 2, 1933, pp. 133-134. An English translation is given in Taracouzio, T. A., *Soviets in the Arctic: An Historical, Economic and Political Study of the Soviet Advance into the Arctic*, New York, Macmillan, 1938, Appendix XXII, pp. 456-61.

[181] This role was mapped out for the stations in "Plan raboty Komiteta Severa na 1935 g." [Work Plan of the Committee of the North for 1935], *Sovetskii Sever*, No. 1, 1935, p. 108, Section II, Paragraph 3.

[182] See, for example, "Uspekhi okhotnikov Zapolyar'ya" [Successes of the Polar Hunters], *Pravda*, April 16, 1953.

[183] Data from the Department of the North, R.S.F.S.R. Gosplan, 1941.

[184] Data for 1933-1938 from *ibid.* Data for 1940 from Kogan, A., "Narodnoye khozyaisto: Zhivotnovodstvo" [The National Economy:

Animal Breeding], *Bol'shaya Sovetskaya entsiklopediya: SSSR,* col. 930.

[185] For the prewar plans for the development of reindeer-processing enterprises, see "Direktivy Gosplana RSFSR," *op. cit.,* p. 186.

[186] Koshelev, I., "O rukovodstve raionami Krainevo Severa" [On the Management of Regions of the Extreme North], *Izvestiya,* January 17, 1948.

[187] For a general survey of northern reindeer farming and its importance see Titunov, P. S., and F. A. Terent'yev, eds., *Severnoye olenevodstvo* [Northern Reindeer Farming], Moscow, Sel'khozgiz, 1948.

[188] On the twenty-fifth anniversary of the Khibiny station, the Soviet press reported that workers at the station had turned up fifteen early-maturing high-yield grain varieties and other plants more suited to northern climatic conditions. "Michurintsy Severa" [Michurinites of the North], *Pravda,* September 18, 1948.

[189] Dadykin, V. P., "Problema osevereniya zemledeliya" [The Problem of Adapting Agriculture to the North], *Priroda* [Nature], Leningrad, No. 4, October 1953, p. 41. For a cartographic representation of the northern boundaries of agriculture in the U.S.S.R. see *Geograficheskii atlas SSSR* [Geographical Atlas of the U.S.S.R.], Moscow, Glavnoye Upravleniye Geodezii i Kartografii MVD SSSR, 1954, p. 18.

[190] "Vydayushchiyesya nauchnye trudy" [Outstanding Scientific Studies], *Pravda,* May 16, 1953.

[191] Suslov, *op. cit.,* p. 138.

[192] Kovalkin, I., "V raionakh Krainevo Severa" [In Areas of the Extreme North], *Pravda,* October 1, 1952.

[193] Data from Glavsevmorput'.

[194] The types of northern enterprises which fall into these categories are as follows: food processing, wood products (furniture, skis, shovel handles, runners for sleighs, trunks and so forth), household articles (iron stoves, pails, wash basins, teapots, metal containers), occupational equipment (traps, anchors, hunting knives, rings for reindeer harnesses), building materials (bricks), and clothing. Bread bakeries were among the first such enterprises to be developed in the North. In the Khanty-Mansi National Okrug, for example, the number of bakeries grew from nineteen in 1935 to over a hundred in 1940. Data from the Leningrad Institute for the Peoples of the North.

[195] For a discussion of these plans, see p. 87 ff.

[196] Stalin, I. V., *Marksizm i natsional'no-kolonial'nyi vopros* [Marxism and the National and Colonial Question], Moscow, Partizdat, 1937, pp. 117-18, *passim.*

[197] Data from Glavsevmorput'.

[198] Krypton, Constantine, "Soviet Policy in the Northern National Regions After World War II," *The American Slavic and East European Review,* New York, Vol. XIII, No. 3, October 1954, pp. 350-51.

[199] Data from Glavsevmorput'.

[200] *Zasedaniya Verkhovnovo Soveta RSFSR,* p. 66.

[201] Annual Report of the Taimyr Okrug Executive Committee for 1939.

[202] See the Statute on Privileges for Persons Working in the Extreme North of the R.S.F.S.R. of May 10, 1932, in Taracouzio, T. A., *op. cit.*, Appendix XXXIII, pp. 491-95.

[203] *Sbornik po trudovomu zakonodatel'stvu dlya rabotnikov Severnovo morskovo puti*, Ch. 9.

[204] "Zamechatel'naya pobeda krasnoyarskikh kolkhoznikov" [A Remarkable Victory of Krasnoyarsk Kolkhoz Members], *Pravda*, October 2, 1948.

[205] The text of the letter is reprinted in Gerasimov, *op. cit.*, p. 49. Of course military and political considerations also prompted the government to initiate the campaign.

[206] "V kholodnykh prostorakh Sibiri" [In the Cold Expanses of Siberia], *Novoye russkoye slovo*, New York, February 26, 1949.

[207] In the beginning of 1940 the Institute for the Peoples of the North in Leningrad, in conjunction with the Department of the North of the R.S.F.S.R. Gosplan, undertook a special study of geographical areas and occupational categories in the extreme North which were suitable for voluntary settlers from the European R.S.F.S.R. The project was intended to prepare for efficient utilization in the North of an anticipated surplus of labor elsewhere as a result of increasing mechanization of agriculture in the European R.S.F.S.R.

[208] Suslov, *op. cit.*, pp. 156-57.

[209] Velichko, *op. cit.*, pp. 26-27.

[210] Suslov, *op. cit.*, p. 158.

[211] Lutski, S. L., *Geograficheskiye ocherki russkoi taigi* [Geographic Sketches of the Russian Taiga], Moscow, Geografgiz, 1947, pp. 135-36.

[212] "Otovsyudu" [From Everywhere], *Pravda*, August 26, 1949.

[213] "Yakutsk," *Pravda*, June 5, 1953.

[214] Archives of Glavsevmorput'. Report "O moshchnom istochnike energii v Arktike" [On an Abundant Source of Power in the Arctic], 1936.

[215] See Krasovski, N. V., "Vetroenergeticheskiye resursy SSSR i perspektivi ikh ispol'zovaniya" [Wind Power Resources of the U.S.S.R. and the Prospects for Their Utilization], *Atlas energeticheskikh resursov SSSR* [Atlas of the Power Resources of the U.S.S.R.], ed. by A. V. Vinter and G. M. Krzhizhanovski, Moscow-Leningrad, 1935, Vol. I, Part 3. See also Krasovski, N. V., *Kak ispol'zovat' energiyu vetra* [How to Utilize the Power of the Wind], Moscow-Leningrad, 1936. Regarding the use of wind power in the extreme North, see Shekhovtsov, N., "Ob ispol'zovanii energii vetra na Krainem Severe" [On the Utilization of the Wind Power in the Extreme North], *Sovetskaya Arktika*, No. 10, 1939, pp. 75-77; Vasil'yev, P., "Vetrosilovye ustanovki v Arktike" [Wind Power Installations in the Arctic], *ibid.*, No. 6, 1940, pp. 14-17; Khrapal', A., "Vetroenergiya v predpriyatiyakh Glavsevmorputi" [Wind Power in the Enterprises of Glavsevmorput'], *ibid.*, No. 7, 1940, pp. 17-22.

Economic Potential of the Service Areas

216 *Rezolyutsii XVIII s"yezda VKP(b)* [Resolutions of the Eighteenth Congress of the All-Union Communist Party (Bolsheviks)], Moscow, Gosudarstvennoye izdatel'stvo politicheskoi literatury, 1939, p. 27.

217 Data from Glavsevmorput'.

218 Based on the author's observations and conversations with local officials in Turukhansk, Dudinka, Igarka, and Noril'sk.

219 Vinter, A. V., "Ispol'zovaniye energii vetra" [Utilization of Wind Power], *Priroda* [Nature], Leningrad, No. 2, February 1953, p. 27.

220 Karmishin, A., "O vetrodvigatelyakh" [On Wind Generators], *Izvestiya,* October 19, 1951.

221 Shevno, Ye., "Uvelichit' proizvodstvo vetrodvigatelei" [Increase the Production of Wind Generators], *Izvestiya,* May 16, 1953.

222 Computed from Balzak, S. S., *et al.,* eds., *Economic Geography of the U.S.S.R.,* trans. by Robert M. Hankin and Olga A. Titelbaum, New York, Macmillan, 1949, Table 33, p. 375. According to computations from the data in the table, the total sown area in the U.S.S.R. equaled roughly 135.3 million hectares, and Siberia (excluding the Urals and the Far East) accounted for about 13.2 million hectares of this total. Baranski writes that by 1941 western Siberia alone had a sown area of 12.6 million hectares. Baranski, *op. cit.,* 14th ed., p. 242.

223 Balzak, *op. cit.,* p. 375.

224 *Ibid.,* Fig. 53, p. 367.

225 Computed from *Gosudarstvennyi plan razvitiya narodnovo khozyaistva SSSR na 1941 god* [State Plan for the Development of the National Economy of the U.S.S.R. for 1941] (American Council of Learned Societies Reprints: Russian Series No. 30), Photo-Lithoprint by Universal Lithographers, Baltimore, Md., Supplement No. 43, pp. 225-26. The seed acreages are not included in the computation.

226 The average yield anticipated in these areas was around 12.5 centners per hectare, and the average for the U.S.S.R. as a whole was to be 11.7 centners per hectare. See *ibid.,* Supplement No. 58, pp. 256, 258.

227 "O dal'neishem uvelichenii proizvodstva zerna v strane i ob osvoyenii tselinnykh i zalezhnykh zemel': Postanovleniye Plenuma TsK KPSS, prinyatoye 2 marta 1954 g. po dokladu tov. N. S. Khrushchova" [On the Further Increase of the Production of Grain and on the Development of Virgin and Idle Lands: Resolution of the Plenum of the Central Committee of the CPSU, Adopted on March 2, 1954, on the Basis of the Report of N. S. Khrushchov], *Izvestiya,* March 6, 1954.

228 "V Tsentral'nom Komitete Kommunisticheskoi partii Sovetskovo Soyuza i Sovete Ministrov Soyuza SSR: O dal'neishem osvoyenii tselinnykh i zalezhnykh zemel' dlya uvelicheniya proizvodstva zerna" [In the Central Committee of the CPSU and the Council of Ministers of the U.S.S.R.: On the Further Development of Virgin and Idle Lands for Increased Grain Production], *Izvestiya,* August 17, 1954.

229 The Siberian territories included here are Altai Krai, Omsk Oblast, Novosibirsk Oblast, Krasnoyarsk Krai, Kurgan Oblast, Tyumen' Oblast, and Kemerovo Oblast. The increase in the Kazakh S.S.R. ex-

ceeded 7.7 million hectares. "Soobshcheniye Tsentral'novo Komiteta KPSS i Soveta Ministrov SSSR o vypolnenii gosudarstvennovo plana khlebozagotovok kolkhozami i sovkhozami Sovetskovo Soyuza iz urozhaya 1954 goda" [Statement of the Central Committee of the CPSU and the Council of Ministers of the U.S.S.R. on the Fulfillment of the State Plan for Grain Procurements by the Kolkhozes and Sovkhozes of the Soviet Union from the 1954 Harvest], *Pravda,* November 8, 1954.

[230] The Party resolution of March 2, 1954, called for increases in grain and "other agricultural produce," but a later statement by Khrushchov indicated that all of the newly-plowed land is to be planted in grain crops; see "Beseda tov. N. S. Khrushchova s angliiskim uchonym i obshchestvennym deyatelem Dzhonom Bernalom" [Conversation of N. S. Khrushchov with the English Scientist and Public Figure John Bernal], *Pravda,* December 29, 1954.

[231] Khrushchov stated that the minimum yield from the new lands would be 10 centners of grain per hectare. *Ibid.* The average grain yield for the whole U.S.S.R. in 1941, as mentioned before, was planned at 11.7 centners per hectare. For an estimate of the chances of success of the virgin and idle lands program, see Harris, C. D., "Growing Food by Decree in Soviet Russia," *Foreign Affairs,* Vol. XXXIII, No. 2, January 1955, pp. 268-81.

[232] Khrenov, N. I., and M. I. Vilenski, "Novostroiki khlopchatobumazhnoi promyshlennosti" [New Construction in the Cotton Industry], *Nauka i zhizn'* [Science and life], Moscow, No. 4, 1954, p. 8.

[233] "Bol'she dobrotnykh tkanei" [More Good-Quality Textiles], *Pravda,* May 11, 1953.

[234] "Kamvol'no-sukonnyi kombinat v Sibiri" [Worsteds Combine in Siberia], *Pravda,* August 7, 1954.

[235] "Kuznetskii ugol'nyi bassein" [The Kuznetsk Coal Basin], *Bol'shaya Sovetskaya entsiklopediya,* 2d ed., Vol. XXIII, 1953, pp. 602, 604.

[236] For the text of the decree see *Izvestiya,* October 20, 1940.

[237] Voznesenski, N., *Voyennaya ekonomika SSSR v period otechestvennoi voiny* [The War Economy of the U.S.S.R. in the Period of the Patriotic War], Moscow, OGIZ, 1948, p. 41.

[238] The stretch from Akmolinsk to Abakan is scheduled to be completed during the Fifth Five-Year Plan. "Kuznetskii ugol'nyi bassein," *op. cit.,* p. 606.

[239] Data for 1926 and 1939 from "Aziya" [Asia], *Bol'shaya Sovetskaya entsiklopediya,* 2d ed., Vol. I, 1949, p. 514; data for 1952 from Baranski, N. N., "Ob izuchenii raionov Sibiri" [On the Study of the Districts of Siberia], *Geografiya v shkole* [Geography in School], Moscow, No. 5, 1952, p. 55.

[240] Baidakov, B., "Novosibirsk," *Pravda,* December 13, 1954.

[241] Malov, F., "Gorod na Yeniseye" [City on the Yenisei], *Izvestiya,* April 8, 1953.

[242] "Krasnoyarsk," *Bol'shaya Sovetskaya entsiklopediya,* 2d ed., Vol. XXIII, 1953, p. 265.

[243] Malov, *op. cit.*

[244] MVD enterprises in the Soviet Far East produce some of their own equipment. A report from Magadan, for example, states: "In the settlement 'Atka' there are small electrical machine shops of Dal'stroi. Until now they only repaired electrical equipment. Recently these shops have started producing powerful electric motors which, from the smallest screw to the most complicated parts, are built by their own personnel. One can now find motors in the mines marked 'Made in Kolyma.' . . . In November the shops began putting out a special motor adapted for work in conditions of dust and dampness." "Sdelano na Kolyme" [Made in Kolyma], *Kamchatskaya Pravda,* Petropavlovsk, December 7, 1945.

[245] "Neotlozhnye zadachi mestnykh sovetov Urala, Sibiri i Dal'nevo Vostoka" [Urgent Tasks of Local Soviets in the Urals, Siberia and the Far East], *Izvestiya,* September 7, 1948.

[246] "Zasedaniya Verkhovnovo Soveta RSFSR: Rech' nachal'nika upravleniya promkooperatsii pri Sovete ministrov RSFSR P. F. Kravchuka" [Sessions of the Supreme Soviet of the R.S.F.S.R.: Address by P. F. Kravchuk, Head of the Administration for Producers' Cooperatives Under the Council of Ministers of the R.S.F.S.R.], *Izvestiya,* June 1, 1949.

[247] Urinson, M., "Soveshchaniye predsedatelei planovykh komissii oblastei, krayov i avtonomnykh respublik v Gosplane RSFSR" [Conference of Chairmen of Planning Commissions of Oblasts, Krais, and Autonomous Republics in the R.S.F.S.R. Gosplan], *Planovoye khozyaistvo,* No. 5, 1950, p. 82.

[248] "V Sovete Ministrov SSSR i Tsentral'nom Komitete KPSS: O rasshirenii proizvodstva promyshlennykh tovarov shirokovo potrebleniya i uluchshenii ikh kachestva" [In the Council of Ministers of the U.S.S.R. and the Central Committee of the CPSU: On the Expansion of the Production of Industrial Consumer Goods and the Improvement of Their Quality], *Pravda,* October 28, 1953.

[249] Machikhin, V., "Razvitiye proizvodstva predmetov narodnovo potrebleniya po predpriyatiyam mestnoi promyshlennosti i promyslovoi kooperatsii" [The Development of the Production of Consumer Goods at Local Industrial Enterprises and Producers' Cooperatives], *Planovoye khozyaistvo,* No. 1, 1954, pp. 60-61.

[250] Aleksandrov, A., "Nasushchnye zadachi mestnoi promyshlennosti i promyslovoi kooperatsii" [Urgent Tasks of Local Industry and Producers' Cooperatives], *Pravda,* November 21, 1953.

[251] "Ob uvelichenii proizvodstva produktov zhivotnovodstva: Doklad tovarishcha N. S. Khrushchova na Plenume Tsentral'novo Komiteta KPSS 25 yanvarya 1955 goda" [On Increasing the Output of Animal Husbandry Products: Report of N. S. Khrushchov at the Plenum of the Central Committee of the CPSU on January 25, 1955], *Izvestiya,*

February 3, 1955. Khrushchov said in part: "In connection with recent measures for increasing the output of consumer goods some comrades . . . have been trying to prove that the development of heavy industry ceases to be the main task of socialist upbuilding at a certain stage and that it is light industry that can and must outstrip all other industries. These are highly erroneous views, alien to the spirit of Marxism-Leninism and nothing but a slander of the Party. This is a throwback to conceptions hostile to Leninism, to the conceptions once advocated by Rykov, Bukharin and company."

IV. THE NORTHERN SEA ROUTE AND OTHER MODES OF TRANSPORTATION

1. Navigation, Equipment and Facilities of the Northern Sea Route

a. The Ice Barrier

The Kara Sea may be roughly divided into southwestern and northeastern halves by a line running from Cape Zhelaniye to Dickson Island. Navigation is easier in the southwestern half, where there is less ice because of the warm water from the Ob' and Yenisei rivers.[1] The southwestern part of the Kara Sea is also affected by the warm waters of the adjacent Barents Sea. As a result, this area was able to begin maritime trade relations with Western Europe as early as the nineteenth century without the benefit of icebreakers, aviation or radio. In the northeastern half of the Kara Sea, however,

> in certain years the sea may become difficult or impossible to navigate. . . . In general, ice conditions improve only at the end of August or the beginning of September, during the second half of the navigation season; at the end of September new ice begins to form.[2]

The most difficult navigation conditions, however, are found farther east:

> The Laptev and East Siberian seas are notably different from the seas in the western sector with respect to the heaviness of ice formation. Only [in the former], where formation is very rapid, can ships be stopped by newly forming ice. Even in the summer ice forms from the snow cover on the surface. . . . In the coastal zone a combination of low salinity and temperatures, shallowness, and minor variation in the tides leads to a considerable development of ice bars, extending, in the eastern part of

the Laptev Sea and the western part of the Eastern Siberian Sea, for about 300 to 500 kilometers from the mainland. This effect is less marked in the Chukotsk Sea, where, for example, in the Kolyuchin Bay area, the ice extends only for 35 kilometers.[3]

The worst part of the Northern Sea Route is Vil'kitski Strait. Only in the most favorable years can passages easily be forced by icebreakers, while at other times there is only a narrow free channel during August and September directly off Cape Chelyuskin.[4] Measures to improve the situation were considered in the late thirties. During the Third Five-Year Plan (beginning in 1938), and again after the war, efforts were made to find a new lane to the north of Severnaya Zemlya, the New Siberian Islands and Wrangel Island.[5] In 1945 the area between the pole and 85° N. lat. was explored by high altitude aviation.[6] At the same time Glavsevmorput' officials conceived of the almost fantastic plan of by-passing Vil'kitstki Strait to the south by building an inland waterway that would connect the small rivers and lakes of the Byrranga Plateau. In 1947 the Soviet press reported that exploration of the plateau had begun although there was no mention of an inland waterway.[7]

b. Scientific Aids to Navigation

Up to the 1950's the effort to overcome the natural obstacles of the Northern Sea Route had not been adequately supported by studies of ice movements,[8] hydrography,[9] and meteorology.[10] N. N. Zubov, the well-known Arctic specialist, now a rear admiral, wrote in 1948:

Arctic forecasting has developed enormously during the Soviet period, but it is still not adequate to serve fully and reliably the demands of polar navigation. . . . Until we explore the central Arctic basin, we shall not be able to give complete answers to practical questions concerning ice conditions in the northern seas.[11]

The peak of Soviet scientific efforts to study the Arctic in the period up to 1950 is represented by the drifting expedi-

The Route and Other Transportation

tions of the ice-forcing ship "Sedov" and the station North Pole 1 which was set up on an ice floe.[12] The "Sedov" drifted a total of 812 days between 83° N. lat. and 87° N. lat. from 1937 to 1940. The station North Pole 1 drifted for 274 days from 1937 to 1938 between 83°N. lat. and 90° N. lat.[13] The value of the "Sedov's" observations does not correspond to the relatively long time spent in drift. The vessel accidentally found itself in the role of a "scientific institution" when it became trapped in the ice. The crew, except for a student at the Hydrographic Institute of Glavsevmorput', consisted of ordinary seamen. The primary concern of the party was to preserve the ship, which was built not to withstand drifting in the Arctic ice fields but to sail along the coast of Newfoundland and Saint Lawrence Gulf, where there are no powerful ice fields and destructive jammings. Lack of equipment prevented the most effective use of the enforced opportunity for scientific research:

> Since the "Sedov" was not prepared to work in deep waters, it had no special winches or lines for such measurements. It was only while they were drifting that the [crew] constructed an electric damper and, with the thick steel cable that was on board, over 14 kilometers of sounding line. Such work alone, at a temperature of —30° C., is real heroism.[14]

The station North Pole 1 was especially equipped for scientific work. Ten years after the expedition, however, the full results of its investigation had still not been made available although some of its materials had been published.[15] In 1948 Zubov wrote:

> On February 19, 1938, the station North Pole ended its research . . . [but] there still remains the tremendous task of final processing and publication of the collected materials. Another big task is to compare the observations of the North Pole station with those of the numerous earlier expeditions and of the coastal polar stations.[16]

After World War II new expeditions were sent out. A report of the Arctic Scientific Research Institute of Glavsevmorput' to the Presidium of the U.S.S.R. Academy of Sciences in April 1954 cited the discovery of the Lomonosov underwater mountain range by Soviet expeditions in 1948-1949 and announced other achievements in central Arctic exploration during postwar years.[17] In 1950 and 1951 a new drift ice station (the North Pole 2) was in operation, and in spring 1954 two more central Arctic research stations (North Pole 3 and North Pole 4) were set up on drift ice by joint action of Glavsevmorput' and the U.S.S.R. Academy of Sciences.[18]

V. Frolov, director of the Arctic Scientific Research Institute of Glavsevmorput' stated:

> In the postwar period much expeditionary work has been conducted. . . . The accumulated experience of reconnaissance work, which encompassed all of the central Arctic, has made it possible to proceed from episodic to systematic research.[19]

Frolov added that the knowledge gained had been used to ensure the practicability of navigation along the Northern Sea Route.[20]

Regular meteorologic, hydrographic and sea ice observations, as well as the maintenance of radio communications, are the job of the polar stations distributed along the Arctic coast and on adjacent islands. Long-term forecasting is based also on the data from air reconnaissance, to be discussed later. As a rule each polar station sends its data once a day, and during the navigation season three times a day, to Dickson Island, where the reports are assembled and forwarded to the Administration of Polar Stations of Glavsevmorput' in Moscow and then to the Arctic Institute in Leningrad. On the basis of these data, synoptic maps are prepared and weather forecasts issued not only for the Arctic but also for the greater part of the Eurasian continent. Information concerning the observation and forecasting work of polar stations and central agencies is not released for general consumption. Personnel working in this field before the war informed the author that in the eastern sector forecasts of sea ice conditions can be made during the spring and fall for not more than one day, but during summer and winter for four or five days if radio connections with other stations can be maintained. In the western sector sea ice forecasting is more difficult because of the frequent changes in weather. Here too, however, it is somewhat better during summer and winter. Forecasts for flying conditions can be made over longer periods because the factors affecting climate have been more fully studied than those affecting sea ice conditions.[21]

The basic network of 55 polar stations had been established by the end of the Second Five-Year Plan (1937).[22] When necessary the permanent network is supplemented by temporary stations. The need for expanding the network was reflected in plans for establishing 22 new permanent stations during the Third Five-Year Plan (1938-1942).[23]

Five of the stations (Tikhaya Bay, Matochkin Shar, Dickson, Chelyuskin, and Uelen) are more in the nature of geophysical observatories. Their program includes observations in actinometry, aerology, terrestrial magnetism, atmospheric electricity, and radio waves.[24]

c. Icebreakers, Freighters and Other Vessels

To make navigation possible for even three months in Arctic seas an icebreaker fleet is indispensable. In the early years icebreaker service was poor because of the small number and obsolescence of the vessels available to Glavsevmorput', which up to 1939 had only four icebreakers at its disposal. The most powerful was the "Krasin" with 10,000 horsepower, followed by the "Yermak" with 9,500, the "Lenin" with 7,980, and the "Litke" with 7,000. In addition, Glavsevmorput' had five ice-forcing ships: "A. Sibiryakov" of 2,000 h.p., "R. Rusanov" of 2,200, "G. Sedov" of 2,360, "Malygin" of 2,800, and "Sadko" of 3,500. The newest of these, the "Krasin" and "Lenin," were built in 1917. The venerable "Yermak," still in active service, was built in 1899.

The reconstruction of the icebreaker fleet became one of the main tasks of Glavsevmorput'. In 1935 and 1936, expenditures for the construction of icebreakers represented the chief item in the organization's budget of expenditures.[25] During the Second Five-Year Plan (1933-1937) the construction of four icebreakers and two ice-forcing ships was started. In 1935 systematic servicing of the Northern Sea Route with icebreakers began, and Glavsevmorput' declared that it had been transformed into a normally functioning seaway.[26] The "Lenin" was assigned to the Kara Sea as far east as Dickson. The "Yermak" escorted eleven ships through the eastern part of the Kara Sea and Vil'kitski Strait; the "Litke" worked the Laptev Sea up to Dmitri Laptev Strait; and the "Krasin" escorted ships as far as the Bering Strait. Three ice-forcing ships, the "Rusanov," "Sedov" and "Sibiryakov," were held in reserve.[27] That normal commercial navigation was not in fact established on the Northern Sea Route is clear from the 1946-1950 plan, which treated the solution of the problem as a goal still to be attained.[28]

Before World War II the Maritime Department of Glavsevmorput' called for a minimum of ten icebreakers. The available icebreakers were described as not fully suited to Arctic service and obsolescent. Their limited fuel capacity had frequently been discussed at Glavsevmorput' meetings and in the Arctic literature. It was pointed out that the "Krasin" and the "Yermak" carried only a little over 2,500 tons of coal, the "Lenin" only 1,200 tons, the "Litke" 750 tons, and the ice-forcing ships 300 tons or less. It was not rare for an icebreaker to leave its convoy for refueling, which sometimes required a long run. For vessels in Arctic service before World II, half of the idle time (the latter averaging 40 to 50 per cent of the total voyage time) was spent waiting for an ice-breaker.[29]

Shortly after World War II it was reported that there were nine icebreakers of 10,000 to 12,000 h.p. in service in the Arctic: the "Iosif Stalin,"[30] "L. Kaganovich," "A. Mikoyan," "V. Molotov," "Yermak," "Krasin," "Kapitan Belousov," "Admiral Makarov," and "Severnyi Polyus."[31] Three of the icebreakers were Lend-Lease vessels which were returned to the United States in 1949 and 1951.[32] Ships such as these "can make their way through [ice] with a firmness of nine points."[33] The "Lenin" is also sometimes used in heavy ice. Convoy work in lighter ice is done by special ice-forcing ships. Especially with the return of Lend-Lease vessels the ice-breaker fleet was inadequate to assure stable shipping the entire length of the Northern Sea Route—a fact tacitly acknowledged by the Party in 1952, when it ordered that new icebreakers be added to the merchant marine.[34] In accordance with a Finno-Soviet trade agreement, a Finnish firm was given an order to build three powerful Diesel-electric ice-breakers of the same class for the Arctic, to be named the "Kapitan Belousov," "Kapitan Voronin" and "Kapitan Mele-khov."[35] Their general specifications were: length 83.16 meters, beam 19.4 meters, displacement tonnage 5,360, and maximum speed 16.5 knots. They were designed to develop 10,500 h.p. and to carry about a two-month supply of fuel.[36] In December 1953 one of the icebreakers was launched (probably the new "Kapitan Belousov"), and on this occasion the Minister of Foreign Trade stated that the Soviet Union was ready to give Finland additional orders for icebreakers, freighters, tankers, lighters, and barges.[37] A press report a year later said that the icebreaker "Kapitan Voronin" had also been launched, that the keel had been laid for the ice-breaker "Kapitan Melekhov," and that a flag-raising ceremony had been held on the icebreaker "Kapitan Belousov" during a visit by Mikoyan to Finland in November-December 1954.[38] The fitting out of the "Kapitan Belousov" was completed in Leningrad, and in February 1955 the icebreaker was operating in Baltic waters with a crew of 106 persons.[39]

In addition to the icebreakers, the maritime fleet of Glavsevmorput' before World War II consisted of only fourteen steamers and motor sailboats, six hunting schooners and a few other vessels.[40] Every year Glavsevmorput' was forced to charter freighters suitable for Arctic navigation. Since for the export of Igarka lumber via the Kara Sea the government permitted the chartering of foreign vessels from England, Norway, Germany, Estonia, Belgium, Latvia, and Denmark, it was possible to select desirable types for these runs. The largest percentage of the tonnage used in the Kara Sea was British, and the number of Soviet ships negligible.

For other sectors of the Northern Sea Route the use of foreign ships was not authorized and Glavsevmorput' chartered bottoms from the People's Commissariat of Water Transport, which had difficulty in furnishing vessels suitable for Arctic navigation from the small and ill-equipped merchant marine.[41]

Up to World War II little or no progress had been made in reinforcing cargo vessels against ice for use on the Northern Sea Route, although the necessity had long been recognized. At the Eighteenth Party Congress in 1939, Papanin declared:

> For execution of the tasks placed before us by Comrades Stalin and Molotov, [Glavsevmorput'] must have not only a large icebreaker fleet but also a powerful northern freighter fleet especially adapted for use under the ice conditions [of the Northern Sea Route].[42]

He also requested that Stalin and Molotov instruct the People's Commissariat of the Shipbuilding Industry to begin construction of the needed ships that year. Even earlier the

Third Five-Year Plan (1938-42) had provided for such large-scale additions to the merchant fleet that it was informally referred to as "the five-year plan for shipbuilding." Glavsevmorput' was counting on its share of vessels for northern navigation. However, the plan was cut short by the war. In 1946 one authority cited by name only fifteen cargo vessels as suitable for navigation in Arctic waters, but implied that others in the same category were available.[43]

Efficient operation of traffic on the Northern Sea Route requires freighters of suitable deadweight tonnage. Even during the period of Komseverput' it was clear that vessels with greater cargo capacity could and should be used in the Arctic. Among their advantages is the fact that they require less ice-breaker and plane assistance. Heavier ships can make greater speed and longer voyages without refueling because they overcome water and air resistance more readily, have more powerful engines and can carry more fuel. These attributes are particularly valuable on the Northern Sea Route where the navigation period is short and voyages long. Larger vessels afford economics of scale, both in their construction and operation. An increase in the size of a vessel does not mean a proportionate increase in the cost of construction, nor does the increase of carrying capacity demand a proportionate increase in the horsepower. Tripling the capacity often requires only a doubling of the power. Fuel consumption per ton of cargo of larger freighters is relatively low. In addition, the increase in tonnage does not require a corresponding increase in personnel, port facilities, and so on. The unit costs of transportation are thus lowered. Finally, ships with greater deadweight tonnage are more efficient in coping with the cargo congestion which is caused in ports by the short navigation period. Igarka, for example, accumulates lumber for nine months of the year. At the same time shipments to the Arctic can be handled more expeditiously if the goods are assembled and waiting at the ports. For this reason the Murmansk Arctic Shipping Administration required that industrial goods and certain foods be at Murmansk by June 1, and other cargo by July 25.[44]

The use of large ships raises the problem of the depth of the Northern Sea Route and the harbors. Glavsevmorput' in its hydrographic work devotes much attention to straits, shallow waters, and so on. As a result of measures taken even before World War II vessels of deep draft can now freely navigate the greater part of the Route. The average deadweight tonnage of ships used in the Arctic run is between 3,500 and 4,000, while that of individual ships may vary from 3,000 to 8,350. Although in some years ships with a carrying capacity of 8,000 tons have successfully docked at Igarka, the average tonnage of vessels berthing there is only 3,500 to 4,500. The smallness of the ships in use has been quite justly criticized at Glavsevmorput' conferences and in the Arctic literature, and it has been urged that ships of deeper draft be constructed and selected on charter for the Northern Sea Route.[45] It has not been easy to follow this recommendation because of the poverty of the Soviet merchant marine.

One of the reasons for the failure of the 1937 navigation season of the Northern Sea Route was the unsatisfactory character of the ships chartered from the Commissariat of Water Transport. Many required immediate repairs; many others were totally unfit for polar navigation. The "Desna," for example, was sent to Nordvik with 400 passengers although she had been pronounced unfit to sail in Arctic waters. The "Unzha," "Sura" and "Sviyaga," which were under a similar prohibition, were routed to Tiksi, Cape Chelyuskin and Igarka respectively. The "Tobol," built with a thinly ribbed bow, was also sent to Tiksi. The "Chita" was dispatched on an Arctic run with her engines in need of repair. Ample time had been allowed for the replacement of these vessels with others, since the Registry had warned about their unfitness in May 1937.[46] The year 1937 brought the ruthless and far-reaching purge into all corners of Soviet life, and the failures of Arctic navigation were attributed to "wreckers" who took advantage of the "complacency and conceit" of the Glavsevmorput' authorities.[47] But Glavsevmorput' officials were only partly to blame for the failure, considering the poverty of the merchant marine from which they had to choose.

Along with vessels for long-distance northern sea transportation, ships were needed for local coastwise shipping which developed to serve the increasing number of settlements along the Arctic coast. Frequent discharging by the larger deep sea vessels plying the Northern Sea Route wastes the brief navigation period. It is economically sounder to have these ships discharge at key points, and then use coasting craft to distribute the freight to the scattered settlements. Bottoms were also needed to carry goods which had been brought up from the south to the mouths of the Lena, the Ob' and the Yenisei for onward shipment to various points along the Arctic coast. Part of the coastwise shipping was done by river craft solely because of the shortage of vessels suitable for cabotage. Glavsevmorput' had hoped to supply the ports of Tiksi, Dickson and Provideniya Bay with coasting craft during the Third Five-Year Plan (1938-42).[48] The first postwar Five-Year Plan (1946-50) provided for increased production of lighters,[49] which are very useful in coastwise shipping. They require only a small crew and modest operating costs, and can be dropped by a tug for unloading and then picked up on the return trip.

The increasing population of the North poses the problem of establishing normal passenger transportation via the Route. The vessels used for this purpose were not built for passengers. Although before the war some of the vessels chartered by Glavsevmorput' from the Commissariat of Water Transport were suitable—the "Suchan," "Stalingrad" and "Smolensk"—their charter prohibited their use in passenger service;[50] and passengers continued to be carried on vessels without proper accommodations.

d. Port Facilities

The short navigation period in Arctic seas requires well equipped ports for prompt and efficient loading and unloading. Before the war, however, the cargo discharge points of the Northern Sea Route could hardly be called ports. Instead of four or five days turnaround time, vessels were held up for ten and twelve days. The cost of cargo discharge and loading in the Arctic was from eight to ten times higher than in other Soviet waters.[51] Most offloading of cargo was carried out in harbors that were hardly more than anchorages, inadequately equipped with auxiliary craft such as lighters and barges. Along the whole Northern Sea Route it is essential to deepen the approaches to the harbors, build more quay frontage and augment port facilities—warehouses, cranes, transportation on piers, and so on.

Up to World War II the only port in the central Arctic supplied with the necessary cargo-handling facilities was Igarka, the lumber export town on the Yenisei, where there were seven permanent wharves totaling 715 meters in length and two floating wharves totaling 182 meters in length.[52] On Dickson Island a well equipped bunkering port was nearing completion in 1937. Plans were then being made for the construction of large ports at Provideniya Bay, Tiksi and Kozhevnikovo Gulf, and of coal stations at various points, as well as more adequate installations in Ambarchik Bay at the Kolyma estuary, Chaun Bay and other harbors.[53] A wartime article by personnel of the Arctic Institute indicates that these plans were far from realization except in the case of Provideniya Bay:

> The transshipment of cargo for the Khatanga River Basin takes place in Syndasko Bay (in the Gulf of Khatanga). In the Laptev Sea area vessels discharge and load in Nordvik Bay, Kozhevnikovo Gulf, Tiksi Bay, and in the estuary of the Yana River. Freight destined for the Anabar River basin is offloaded to river boats in the estuary at Cape Khorgo. Tiksi, a large port on the lane of the Northern Sea Route . . . is situated in the eastern part of the Lena delta near the Bykovo Channel. Freight for the Yana River basin is transshipped in the anchorage opposite the [Yana] estuary, and for the Indigirka River basin is offloaded to river ships in an anchorage. For transshipping goods to the Kolyma basin, tugboat stations and an anchorage have been set up in Ambarchik Bay.[54]

In Provideniya Bay a large mechanized port had been built by 1944, mainly as a transshipment point for Lend-Lease war material from the United States. During the war the population of Provideniya Bay increased greatly; assembly plants for Lend-Lease planes and three or four shore artillery batteries were set up in the area.[55]

Elsewhere the construction program has apparently not advanced beyond the paper stage, even after the war. Zubov in his 1948 work states that crew members of cargo ships and the accompanying icebreakers often work as stevedores to shorten the turnaround time in Arctic ports for freighters under convoy.[56] Tiksi, one of the most important ports on the Northern Sea Route, has been neglected, according to all indications.[57] Tiksi, of course, has the disadvantage of its remote location in the central Arctic. But even the ports of Murmansk and Archangel, which are important to other shipping lanes as well as the Northern Sea Route, are also inadequately equipped. It was not until 1951 that plans were made to construct a station building at the port of Murmansk.[58] In 1949 the station building of the Archangel port was in a state of neglect.[59] From such conditions it is obvious that the

Soviet government has been allocating meager resources of manpower and material to the development of Arctic ports in general.

2. *Aviation in the North*

a. Air Ice Reconnaisance

The development of aviation and radio after World War I greatly facilitated navigation in the Arctic Ocean. The ice in the water is not a solid mass. With a good understanding of ice movements it is possible to make voyages from the end of July through September. A plane reconnoiters and determines the most favorable route. It then transmits the information by radio to the icebreaker, which leads the convoy of ships through the clearest lanes. Island and shore-based polar stations, which carry out observations all year around in order to improve the forecasts of the movement of the ice fields during the navigation season also contribute important information. In 1939 Glavsevmorput' introduced the practice of air ice reconnaissance before the opening of the navigation season. That year N. N. Zubov made a special flight to clarify the position of ice floes in the Kara Sea before starting on an Arctic voyage. During the war years air ice reconnaissance in the fall, after the navigation season, was begun,[60] and even year-round air reconaissance proved feasible.[61] The approximate length of the period during which such work can be carried out is shown in the following table:[62]

Reconnaissance Season	Beginning	End	Average Duration (months)
Winter	February 20-28	May 5-15	2.5
Spring (prenavigation)	June 10-20	July 10-20	1
Summer	July 10-20	October 1-10	2.5-3
Fall	October 1-10	November 1-10	1

There are two interruptions in air reconnaissance: in the fall and winter for over three months, and in the spring for about a month. The first interruption is caused by the Arctic polar night, and the second by organizational and technical difficulties, which can be lessened by building land airfields and even by seaplane landings on the mouths of rivers at certain times.[63] After World War II an additional type of air reconaissance was introduced. During the navigation season a plane periodically makes a quick run along the whole sea route to get a general picture of ice conditions.[64]

The development of Soviet polar aviation has presented great difficulties, in particular the purely technical obstacles inherent in working in a sparsely populated territory far from civilization and in a harsh climate. Everything is complicated, from fueling planes to building landing fields. Even after the close of the navigation season, air ice reconnaissance is a hardship because of the inadequate network of airfields, brief periods of daylight and adverse meteorological conditions such as low-hanging clouds, limited visibility and heavy icing.[65] It has always been recognized that coastal air bases were essential. As Glavsevmorput' pointed out in 1933,

> reconnaissance by icebreaker-based planes does not always provide satisfactory results because of the difficulty of landing on and taking off from the uneven ice [in the vicinity of the icebreaker]. Shore air facilities are therefore necessary. The existing airfield on Dickson is not enough. There should be others on the Northern Sea Route.[66]

In the same year O. Yu. Shmidt, then head of Glavsevmorput', announced that the government had decided to construct air bases near Cape Chelyuskin and at Cape Shmidt, each of which was to be provided with two specially built planes that would winter there and conduct regular year-round ice observations.[67] Although a number of new airfields may have been constructed, particularly during the war—in the Provideniya Bay area, for instance—they apparently do not satisfy the requirements for ice reconnaissance for vessels in the Arctic passage. In 1946, when convoys on the Northern Sea Route were experiencing serious difficulties with ice, Glavsevmorput' was forced to dispatch a plane from Moscow to reconnoiter the entire length of the Route. In the course of its flight the plane advised three convoys of less difficult paths through the ice.[68] There may have been local land-based planes in the vicinity but the fact remains that none were assigned to aid the ships. Akkuratov, after his postwar high-altitude reconnaissance flight over the entire Northern Sea Route in 1945 indicated that Cape Chelyuskin had no air base of its own:

> Once a year a ship arrives bringing everything needed to those who spend the winter here. The rest of the time the only communication with the outside world is by radio. Now and then a plane visits the cape, bringing mail and newspapers.[69]

b. Transport and Communication

In attempts to develop northern communications, which began immediately after the Civil War, much attention was given to air routes for the simple reason that aircraft are free from the greatest obstacle to Arctic travel, moving ice. "For the Arctic, with its tremendous unconquered regions and unique natural conditions," the chairman of the government Arctic Commission, S. S. Kamenev, stated in 1933,

> air routes take on special . . . significance. In the face of these conditions all the usual types of transportation and communication are helpless. Even an icebreaker, the most powerful type of transportation in the Arctic, can visit many districts of our northern shore and its adjacent islands only once a year. Some lands of the Arctic Ocean and their shores are inaccessible.[70]

In general the Soviet government put tremendous effort into developing aviation, with the expectation that, once the U.S.S.R. was industrialized, it could soon surpass other countries in this newer field, if not in all transportation facilities. Furthermore, in the sub-Arctic at least, and possibly also in the Arctic, the cost of setting up air lines was less than that required for other types of transportation. Still another factor in the desire to master the polar air theater was the prevalence among Soviet specialists in the early period of extremely pessimistic views on the practicability of regular navigation the entire length of the Northern Sea Route.[71] Success in this endeavor was regarded as prerequisite to any further conquests of more northerly Arctic regions by ship.

Furthermore, aviation offered the possibility of maintaining winter communications in the North. The following table, which shows the number of flying hours per year in the extreme North by civil aviation, indicates the rapid progress made in winter flying:[72]

	1932	1933	1934	1935	1936	1937
Winter	—	152	635	2,800	6,111	7,526
Summer	570	1,261	2,131	6,154	8,945	9,685
Total hours flown in extreme North	570	1,413	2,766	8,954	15,056	17,211

After World War II frequent winter flights were made on a regular schedule.[73] During the winter of 1948-1949 almost all the civil air lines that were kept busy during the summer operated in the winter also, especially the eastern lines.[74]

The Leningrad-Archangel line is one of the oldest prewar civil air lines. Moscow-Leningrad-Archangel flights were scheduled for the winter of 1948-1949.[75] The Leningrad-Murmansk line was opened in 1948.[76] There are smaller civil air lines operating between Archangel and Onega, between Archangel and Nar'yan-Mar, between Igarka and Dudinka, and occasional flights in other districts.

The three main north-south civil air lines in Siberia, along the Ob', Yenisei and Lena, began to function during 1930-1931. They greatly reduce travel time between the interior of western Siberia and the Arctic, as the following table shows:[77]

The Northern Sea Route

I. *Transportation Time Between Krasnoyarsk and Igarka*

a. Summer, north by water via the Yenisei   9-11 days
    Summer, south by water via the Yenisei   15-18 days
b. Winter, by horse or reindeer-drawn sleigh   50-60 days
c. Plane, good weather   10-12 hours
    Plane, bad weather   2 days

II. *Transportation Time Between Irkutsk and Tiksi*

a. Summer, north by water via the Lena   10-12 days
    Summer, south by water via the Lena   16-19 days
b. Winter, by horse or reindeer-drawn sleigh   Travel almost impossible
c. Plane, good weather   12-14 hours
    Plane, bad weather   2-3 days

The Yana line began operations during World War II.[78] Regular flights between Vladivostok and Petropvalovsk (Kamchatka) were started in 1933.[79]

Southbound freight carried by these civil air lines includes furs, fresh-frozen fish, gold and other products from northern enterprises (such as Noril'sk platinum), mail and other reading matter; and northbound freight consists largely of equipment and supplies for industries and polar stations.[80]

Passenger transportation has also developed in the North, but with a few exceptions it is merely an adjunct of freight transportation. Passengers are usually carried in mail planes, which are not equipped for passenger service.

In addition to their ice reconnaissance and transportation functions, planes perform many valuable services in the North: (a) Air photography. Professor Vize describes the plane as the most effective means for geographic study of the central polar basin.[81] Studies by air photography have been made of the eastern part of the Taimyr Peninsula, the mouth of the Khatanga, the Olenyok river, certain parts of the Lena river, and many other areas. (b) Servicing expeditions by transporting personnel and supplies. (c) Observation of the movement of fish and sea animals as an aid to hunting and fishing. (d)

Medical and "cultural" services for the personnel of polar stations and other remote points.[82]

Civil aviation in the Soviet Union is considered an important military potential, and polar aviation preeminently so.

The Main Administration for the Civil Air Fleet (Aeroflot) and the Department of Polar Aviation of Glavsevmorput' had many features characteristic of paramilitary organizations, such as army-like discipline, uniforms, and close liaison and joint operations with regular military personnel. All of the experience gained by Aeroflot and Glavsevmorput' aviation in the extreme North is applicable to solving the problems of military polar aviation.

In addition to the aviation facilities and personnel of Glavsevmorput' and Aeroflot in Siberia, the military forces, of course, maintain their own sizable airbases. In or near many of the larger cities there are both civil and military air establishments.

3. River Transportation

a. The Main Siberian Rivers

In the economic development of the northern regions the three great rivers of Siberia, the Ob', Yenisei and Lena, may be utilized either as adjuncts to the Northern Sea Route or as competing transportation routes. If the rivers carry mainly freight brought in and shipped out by sea, they become economic subsidiaries of the Northern Sea Route, at least in their lower course. On the other hand, given the necessary navigation facilities, they can function as competitors of the Northern Sea Route by connecting the northern regions with markets and supply bases in southern Siberia—or in other regions of the U.S.S.R. through further shipment via the Trans-Siberian Railroad.

As transportation arteries in the extreme North, the main

Siberian rivers have certain natural advantages. Whereas on the average the Northern Sea Route is navigable for only ninety days a year, the Ob' at Salekhard is navigable for 130 to 170 days, the Yenisei for 190 to 200 days at Krasnoyarsk and for 120 days at Dudinka, and the Lena for 160 days in the upper reaches and 120 days in its lower course.[83] During the navigation season the rivers are not obstructed by ice fields, and therefore there is no need for special equipment such as is required on the Northern Sea Route.[84] The Ob' (3,680 kilometers long) and the Yenisei (3,350 kilometers long) are navigable almost their entire length. Their depth averages over five meters, and in most sections their breadth is three or more kilometers.[85] Although the Lena has many rapids and shallows, it is navigable from its mouth to Ust'-Kut, a distance of about 3,450 kilometers; from Ust'-Kut to Kachuga it can be used only by small vessels, and thereafter is nonnavigable. Thus goods consigned to the North, after arrival in Irkutsk via the Trans-Siberian Railroad, were formerly sent overland to Kachuga (254 kilometers), thence by raft to Ust'-Kut (501 kilometers), where they were transferred to river craft for shipment to Yakutsk and beyond.[86] Shipments in the reverse direction of course involved the same difficulties. Transportation in this area has now been greatly simplified by a direct rail connection from Taishet, on the Trans-Siberian, to Ust'-Kut. The line was reported still under construction, but in temporary operation, in November 1954.[87]

Hydrographic studies of the Siberian rivers are incomplete. Ships plying the Yenisei must frequently rely on luck in avoiding rocks—a hazard worse than the shallows found at places in the Ob'—and are frequently severely damaged by running aground. Stretches of the Lena may well be characterized as *terra incognita*. In 1948 it was reported that

> a new chart of the Lena from the estuary to the city of Yakutsk has been made. . . . Until now the captains of Lena ships have

been forced to use a chart prepared twelve years ago, which, with the changing hydrography of the Lena, made navigation difficult.[88]

A thorough charting of the Lena is a major task requiring a large allocation of equipment and personnel; the river stretches through uninhabited and largely unexplored territory over much of its navigable length (over 3,900 kilometers). In the light of the meager resources available elsewhere in Siberia for such purposes, it is doubtful that the new chart represents a definitive study even of the distance covered. For instance, the technical equipment supplied to the buoy attendants stationed along the banks of the Yenisei, who "measure the depth and study every inch of the river's bottom,"[89] is not complicated—a pole and a rowboat.[90] Furthermore, there are only 356 such posts along the whole Yenisei, most of them being concentrated upriver from Turukhansk.[91]

Siberian river transportation has been handicapped by primitive fueling facilities. In 1940, on a trip from Krasnoyarsk to Igarka on the ship "Maria Ul'yanova," the author was able to observe the fueling methods not often described in official materials. Along the Yenisei, both in the settlements and in the uninhabited taiga, small wood-supply stations were maintained by groups of woodcutters who lived in the forest and piled the wood on the riverbank. Vessels approached and helped themselves. The "Maria Ul'yanova," which had old, inefficient equipment, was forced to refuel two or three times in twenty-four hours and burned 100 to 120 square meters of wood on the trip. As the vessel approached the fuel point, three or four of the crew put out in a small boat for the riverbank, where they moored the ship to tree trunks with ropes. When they had rowed back halfway to the vessel, a wooden gangplank was extended to the shore, their boat acting as a floating support. Stevedores, working in pairs, then carted the wood aboard in handbarrows.

This method of landing is the usual one for Yenisei craft, even at settlements, and despite the skill and experience of the crew, often causes long delays. Along the entire Yenisei north from Krasnoyarsk, only Krasnoyarsk itself, Yeniseisk, Igarka, and Dudinka had regular warves. Although Turu-khansk had a few small piers which could be used for loading and unloading, ships stopping there were still moored to rocks. Even the city of Krasnoyarsk had no building for the river station; such construction, provided for in previous five-year plans, was started only in 1949.[92]

Transportation on the Ob' was similarly affected by faulty shore installations and operations. In 1949 the Minister of the River Fleet of the U.S.S.R. drew attention to the lack of mechanization in river ports of the Ob'-Irtysh Basin.[93]

Of port installations and cargo handling on the Lena in 1952, a high trade official of the Yakut A.S.S.R. declared:

> On the Osetrovo wharf much cargo has been left standing since the year before last. . . . On the Yakutsk wharf there is a freight bureau, but it does not work. Clients themselves load the barges. . . . There is not enough mechanization of loading and unloading, and when large cargo shipments arrive, whatever mechanical equipment there is is not utilized. There is no order on the wharves, not even in Yakutsk; everything is in a neglected state.[94]

The Nineteenth Party Congress directed that during the 1951-1955 Plan Osetrovo was to become a highly-mechanized port, and articles in the Soviet press indicated that by mid-1954 about 70 per cent of the projected work had been completed.[95] The improvement of facilities at Osetrovo is a logical complement of the construction of the rail line from Taishet to Ust'-Kut. Both measures contribute materially to the usefulness of the Lena as a transportation link between the extreme North and southern Siberia.

Quantitatively and qualitatively the Soviet northern river fleet has not been fully adequate to handle freight traffic on the main Siberian rivers. The deficiency is least noticeable in the Ob'-Irtysh basin, where the shipyards at Tyumen' have been building ships since the nineteenth century. The development of agriculture in western Siberia stimulated the early growth of the Ob' fleet.

When Glavsevmorput' was established in 1932 it was given the responsibility of developing navigation in the northern reaches of the Ob', Yenisei and Lena rivers. As nucleus of the fleet, it inherited from Komseverput' three Diesel ships, six steamers and forty-three lighters and barges. To provide service on the Lena, over which Komseverput' had not had jurisdiction, Glavsevmorput' transferred to it several ships from other rivers. In 1933 the Diesel ship "Pervaya Pyatiletka" and an iron lighter were moved from the Ob' to the Lena, and in 1934 the tug "Partizan Shchetinkin" was transferred from the Yenisei. The efforts of Glavsevmorput' to augment the river fleet began in 1933 with the construction of a small shipyard at the Lena-Peledui confluence; the following year the yard turned out several wooden barges. In 1934 Glavsevmorput' equipped a minor yard on the Ob' for the building of fishing and animal-hunting schooners, fishing sailboats and cutters. A reconstructed yard on the Yenisei at Predivinsk soon began to turn out large barges up to 5,500 tons, small steamers and boats. In addition, in 1941 Glavsevmorput' was operating a shipyard for metal ships at Kachuga on the Lena.[96] Glavsevmorput' also purchased vessels and equipment from other Soviet enterprises and from foreign concerns.[97]

In 1938 in conjunction with the changes in the jurisdiction of Glavsevmorput', the Commissariat of Water Transport assumed responsibility for all transportation on the Ob' and Yenisei. On the Lena only the section north of Yakutsk remained under the jurisdiction of Glavsevmorput'.

On the Yenisei at the end of the thirties the Commissariat of Water Transport was operating three passenger vessels[98] (actually a combination of freight and passenger), forty to forty-five steamers with an average of 275 to 300 horsepower, and fifty to fifty-five lighters and other such vessels, with an average cargo capacity of 430 tons.[99] On the Lena the Commissariat and Glavsevmorput' had a combined total of twenty-eight steamers with an aggregate of 4,469 horsepower, three small combination freight and passenger vessels, and 114 lighters with a total cargo capacity of 22,065 tons.[100]

The widening gap between the number of available river craft on the main Siberian rivers and the yearly increase in cargo was noted in most of the prewar annual reports of Glavsevmorput'. The Department of the North of R.S.F.S.R. Gosplan and other administrative bodies concerned with the northern economy were also aware of the inadequate size of the river fleets.

Furthermore, the vessels in use were on the whole antiquated. As an illustration, the "Shchetinkin," built in 1869 in Tyumen', was still plying the Ob' in 1949.[101] Craft employed in the extreme North were ill suited to the geographic and economic conditions there. Barges, of design similar to that used on the Volga, were in general serviceable, as were the steamers available, but little attempt had been made to adapt either to conditions in the North. Another disadvantage was the lack of standardization of barges and engines.

Transportation was slowed down by the inappropriate character of the tugboat fleet, which included a number of powerful tugs (1,400 to 1,500 horsepower) instead of a larger fleet of less powerful vessels. As a result, one tug towed many barges in a long train, sometimes a kilometer in length. The loss of time in separating the barges and the congestion caused at unloading points by the simultaneous arrival of many barges reduced the effectiveness of the tugboat fleet. Both Glavsevmorput' and the river shipping organizations sought to obtain more tugs of 400 to 800 horsepower.

A major effort to remedy the deficiencies of the Siberian river fleets began in the spring of 1949, when a convoy of "a few dozen steamers, diesel vessels, lighters and barges" was formed in Archangel under the command of the "Fleet of the Arctic Expedition."[102] The vessels, delivered from Gor'ki and other cities of the northern European U.S.S.R., were escorted via the Kara Sea and distributed among the river shipping administrations of the Ob', Irtysh and the Yenisei. By the fall of that year the ships were in operation. The Minister of the River Fleet stated that the convoy of vessels contained

> . . . not a few new ones, which were built during the past few years by the Krasnoye Sormovo plant. . . . The designers and builders of these ships were recently honored with Stalin Prizes.[103]

In the language of Soviet public announcements, the phrase "not a few new ones" carries the connotation that most of the vessels were of old construction. It may be assumed that the new vessels were built with northern river transportation conditions in mind. In 1951 the Minister of the River Fleet announced that the Ob', Irtysh and Yenisei fleets had been reinforced by new acquisitions, but that the fleets of the eastern rivers had still not been built up to the desired strength.[104] In 1952 a number of Volga diesel tugs, built by the Krasnoye Sormovo plant and hailed as "the pride of our national shipbuilding,"[105] were delivered to the Lena via the Northern Sea Route. In September 1954, the Soviet press reported that another transfer of vessels via the Northern Sea Route from the west to the river fleets of the Ob', Yenesei, and Lena had been made.[106]

Additions to the physical equipment cannot guarantee the proper functioning of Siberian river transportation without more efficient utilization of available facilities than has been achieved by river shipping agencies in the past. For many years in the upper reaches of the Lena, for example, no cargo had been assembled at the wharves for shipment downriver during the first six weeks of the navigation season; or, if cargo was on hand, the construction of expendable wooden rafts and barges on which it was to be floated northward had not yet been completed.[107] All this time tugs and other vessels, which had been concentrated since the preceding fall in Ust'-Kut and which were to take the rafts and barges in tow, remained idle.

The consequences of poor organization, compounded with inadequate facilities, are well illustrated in the utilization of shipping tonnage during the navigation seasons of 1934-1936 on the northern sections of the Ob' and the Yenisei (which were under the jurisdiction of Glavsevmorput' agencies at that time):[108]

Omsk Territorial Administration (Ob' River)

	Idle time	Sailing time
	(per cent of navigation season)	
1934	62.9	37.1
1935	56.7	43.3
1936	72.0	28.0

Krasnoyarsk Territorial Administration (Yenisei River)

1934	56.3	43.7
1935	48.9	51.1
1936	76.0	24.0

Utilization of ship tonnage on the Lena was even less efficient in the same years. Despite the shortage of bottoms during this period, vessels were customarily loaded to only 70-80 per cent of capacity.[109]

At the end of the 1940's such problems had still not been solved. In 1949 the Minister of the River Fleet said that "idle time, reduced somewhat in 1948, is still very great."[110] In the official summary of the results of the 1954 economic plan, in contrast to reports of fulfillment and overfulfillment of the plan for various branches of the economy, it is laconically stated that the "program for utilization of the fleet has not been carried out by river transportation."[111]

The Route and Other Transportation

Correction of the basic shortcomings in human organization, which are characteristic of the whole Soviet economy, is no simple matter. Despite its weaknesses, however, transportation on the main Siberian rivers can compete effectively with the Northern Sea Route or serve as a useful subsidiary of the latter in connecting the extreme North of Siberia with the rest of the U.S.S.R.

b.   The Lesser Siberian Rivers

The provision of transportation facilities on the smaller northern rivers would stimulate the economic growth of virgin territories in the extreme North, which in turn might make a major freight contribution to the Northern Sea Route. Unlike the Ob', Yenisei and Lena, the smaller northern rivers do not extend far to the south where they could tap alternate markets and sources of supply for the extreme North. Thus, unable to compete with the Northern Sea Route as traffic arteries, they might well function as true economic subsidiaries of the Route. There is still the possibility, however, that the Route would play only a secondary role in freight transport on the smaller northern rivers if goods were routed north and south via the main Siberian rivers and carried by coastal craft along the Arctic coast to and from the mouths of the smaller northern rivers. The Northern Sea Route would then benefit only by an increase in local cabotage rather than by an increase in the long hauls which are more valuable for a shipping lane.

The physical characteristics of the more important of the the smaller northern rivers, none of which extends below the boundaries of the extreme North, can be seen in Table I. In 1932 preliminary investigations were made of the Pyasina, and in 1933 commercial navigation on that river began. Freight turnover on the Pyasina just before World War II amounted to about 25,000 to 30,000 tons yearly. The devel-

Table I. Physical Characteristics of the Smaller Northern Rivers[112]

Rivers	Total Length (kilometers)	Navigable Length (kilometers)	Ice Breakup		Freeze-up		Navigable Period
			Estuary	Upper Reaches	Estuary	Upper Reaches	
Pur	256	256					
Taz	779	779					
Pyasina	820	Downstream of the Dudypta[115]	Early June[113]		Middle October[114]		
Khatanga[116]	546		June 26*		Nov. 28*		
Anabar	924	260					
Olenyok	2162	1120	July 3	May 29	Nov. 3	Oct. 14	
Yana	1126	872	June 4	May 29	Oct. 3	Oct. 8	
Indigirka	1800	1140	June 16		Oct. 6		
Kolyma	2700	1863	June 6	May 28	Oct. 5	Oct. 22	110-120 days[117]
Anadyr'	1117[119]	500[120]	June 6†		Oct. 15†		3½- 4½ months[118]

* Data valid for the section near the Nizhnyaya River.
† Data valid for the section near the settlement Markovc

opment of river routes in the eastern part of the extreme North was started in 1936, but, except for the activities on the Lena, intensive navigation developed only on the Kolyma. In 1936 the "Sasyl-Sasy," a 150-horsepower steamer, was transferred with 500 tons of cargo from the Lena to the Yana, where it sailed up to Verkhoyansk, 800 kilometers from the estuary, and another steamer, the 300-horsepower "O. Yu Shmidt," was transferred from the Lena to the Indigirka.[121] In 1937 commercial navigation began on the Olenyok and on the Anabar.[122] Postwar activity on the Taz and Pur rivers, which empty into the Kara Sea, remains very limited. During the navigation season of 1949 two tugboats, the "Vorkuta" and the "Irtysh" served to carry out what was described as "a tremendous task of delivering food and various materials to the population of the districts deep in the tundra."[123]

The interest of the Soviet government in the development of transportation on the smaller rivers is indicated by the existence in 1953 of a Main Administration for the Transport Development of Small Rivers under one of the transportation ministries of the R.S.F.S.R.[124] It is not known what progress this agency has made in developing the smaller northern rivers or, indeed, whether its jurisdiction extends to the northern regions. A report on its operations for 1953 made no mention of the smaller northern rivers and seemed to indicate a concentration of the Administration's activities in southwestern Siberia and the European U.S.S.R.[125]

NOTES

[1] See *Klimaticheskii ocherk Karskovo morya* [Climatic Outline of the Kara Sea], ed. by Ye. I. Tikhomirov, Moscow, Glavsevmorput', 1946, p. 6 (*Trudy Arkticheskovo Nauchno-Issledovatel'skovo Instituta Glavnovo upravleniya Severnovo morskovo puti pri Sovete Ministrov SSSR* [Works of the Arctic Scientific Research Institute of Glavsevmorput' of the U.S.S.R. Council of Ministers], Vol. 187).
[2] *Ibid.*, p. 7.

The Northern Sea Route

3 Suslov, S. P., *Fizicheskaya geografiya SSSR: Zapadnaya Sibir', Vostochnaya Sibir', Dal'nii Vostok, Srednyaya Aziya* [Physical Geography of the U.S.S.R.: Western Siberia, Eastern Siberia, the Far East, Central Asia], Moscow-Leningrad, Uchpedgiz, 1947, p. 177.

4 *Ibid.*, p. 178.

5 These attempts were known even to the captain of the German warship "Komet," which traversed the Northern Sea Route in 1940 (see p. 167). Thorwald, Juergen, "Das Gespensterschiff im Pazifik," *Revuedie Weltillustrierte*, Munich, No. 33, August 19, 1950, p. 20. See also Armstrong, Terence, *The Northern Sea Route: Soviet Exploitation of the North East Passage,* Cambridge, Cambridge University Press, 1952, pp. 32, 38 (Scott Polar Research Institute, Special Publication No. 1).

6 Akkuratov, V., *Pokoryonnaya Arktika* [The Conquered Arctic], Moscow, Molodaya Gvardiya, 1948, pp. 113-14.

7 "V nevedomuyu gornuyu stranu" [Into Unknown Mountain Country], *Izvestiya,* July 9, August 13, 20 and 27, 1947. It appears from the accounts that the expedition studied the broad plains between the mountains, where there are many lakes and small rivers flowing in a latitudinal direction. Lakes were also discovered in the Byrranga Mountains.

8 Akkuratov, *op. cit.,* pp. 113-14.

9 Polovinkin, A. A., *Obshchaya fizicheskaya geografiya: Uchebnik dlya uchitel'skikh institutov* [General Physical Geography: A Textbook for Teachers' Institutes], Moscow, Gosuchebizdat RSFSR, 1948, p. 185; "Arktika" [The Arctic], *Bol'shaya Sovetskaya entsiklopediya* [Large Soviet Encyclopedia], 2d ed., Moscow, Vol. III, 1950, p. 29.

10 Suslov, *op. cit.,* p. 177.

11 Zubov, N. N., *V tsentre Arktiki: Ocherki po istorii issledovaniya i fizicheskoi geografii tsentral'noi Arktiki* [In the Center of the Arctic: Notes on the History of Exploration and Physical Geography of the Central Arctic], Moscow-Leningrad, Glavsevmorput', 1948, pp. 103-4.

12 See Buinitski, V. Kh., *812 dnei v dreifuyushchikh l'dakh* [812 Days on Drifting Ice], Moscow, Glavsevmorput', 1945; Spirin, I., *Pokoreniye Severnovo polyusa* [The Conquest of the North Pole], Moscow, Gosudarstvennoye izdatel'stvo geograficheskoi literatury, 1950; Badigin, K. S., *Tri zimovki vo l'dakh Arktiki* [Three Winters in the Arctic Ice], Moscow, Molodaya Gvardiya, 1950.

13 The "Fram," which was used by the Nansen party during 1893-96, drifted a total of 1,055 days between 83° N. lat. and 86° N. lat. Zubov, *op. cit.,* p. 126.

14 *Ibid.*

15 *Trudy dreifuyushchei stantsii "Severnyi Polyus": Nauchnye otchoty i rezul'taty nablyudenii dreifuyushchei ekspeditsii Glavsevmorputi 1937-1938 g.g.* [Works of the Drifting Station "North Pole": Scientific Reports and Results of Observations of the Drifting Expedition of Glavsevmorput' in 1937-1938], Leningrad-Moscow, Izd-vo Glavsevmorputi, 2 vols., 1940-1945.

16 Zubov, *op. cit.,* p. 112.

The Route and Other Transportation

[17] "V Prezidiume Akademii Nauk SSSR" [In the Presidium of the Academy of Sciences of the U.S.S.R.], *Izvestiya*, April 29, 1954.

[18] Shcherbakov, D. I., "V serdtse Arktiki" [In the Heart of the Arctic], *Nauka i zhizn'* [Science and Life], Moscow, No. 9, 1954, p. 30; and Treshnikov, A., "Sevodnya na dreifuyushchikh nauchnykh stantsiyakh" [Today at the Drifting Research Stations], *Pravda*, July 19, 1954. See also Ryumkin, Ya., and S. Morozov, "Na l'dakh tsentral'noi Arktiki" [On the Central Arctic Ice], *Ogonyok* [The Light], Moscow, No. 30, July 1954, p. 7. The personnel for another drift ice station (North Pole 5) set out for the Arctic in April 1955. "V tsentral'nuyu Arktiku" [To the Central Arctic], *Pravda*, April 4, 1955.

[19] Frolov, V., "Novye issledovaniya v Arktike" [New Studies in the Arctic], *Izvestiya*, June 25, 1954.

[20] *Ibid.* For other articles on postwar Soviet Arctic research see Morozov, S., "K poslednim parallelyam" [At the Last Parallels], *Ogonyok*, Nos. 31-33, August 1954; Burkhanov, V., "Novye issledovaniya sovetskikh uchonykh v Arktike [New Research of Soviet Scientists in the Arctic], *Pravda*, May 16, 1954; and "Dreifuyushchiye nauchnye stantsii na l'dakh tsentral'noi Arktiki" [Drifting Research Stations on Central Arctic Ice], *Pravda*, July 17, 1954.

[21] The level of knowledge concerning sea ice movements and the difficulties in forecasting were characterized as follows: "There is much that is not understood in the movement of [sea] ice. Where a steamer makes a passage freely one day, the next day heavy ice appears, and the most powerful icebreaker is stopped by the impassable obstacle." Akkuratov, *op. cit.,* pp. 113-14.

[22] Zubov wrote in 1948 as follows: "By May 21, 1937, the number of polar stations located on the Arctic littoral and adjacent islands had reached 55. As a result there were almost no points left in the Soviet Arctic where it would be necessary to build a scientific station farther north than those already in existence." Zubov, *op. cit.,* p. 99. The statement may have been intended to convey the impression that the number of permanent stations was adequate in 1937. It is noteworthy, however, that Zubov leaves open the question whether additional stations were required to the south of or at the same latitude as the most northerly stations, and he even implies that a few permanent stations north of those in existence were needed. It is possible that inadequate resources were available for the construction of new stations and that Zubov's curiously ambiguous statement was intended to cover up that fact.

[23] Some of the additional stations were needed to study weather and ice conditions for the proposed variant of the Route passing north of Severnaya Zemlya, the New Siberian Islands and Wrangel Island. See Mikhailov, A. P., "Set' polyarnykh stantsii v tret'yei pyatiletke" [The Network of Polar Stations in the Third Five-Year Plan] *Sovetskaya Arktika* [The Soviet Arctic], Moscow, No. 10, 1937, p. 25.

[24] "Severnyi morskoi put'" [The Northern Sea Route], *Bol'shaya Sovetskaya entsiklopediya,* Vol. L, 1944, col. 582.

[25] Shmidt, O. Yu., "Nashi zadachi v 1936 godu" [Our Tasks in 1936], *Sovetskaya Arktika,* No. 3, 1936, p. 34.

[26] *Raport Nachal'nika Glavsevmorputi O. Yu. Shmidta I. V. Stalinu* [Report of the Head of Glavsevmorput' O. Yu. Shmidt to J. V. Stalin], *Sovetskaya Arktika,* No. 1, 1935 (Supplement).

[27] Annual Report of Glavsevmorput' for 1935.

[28] *Zakon o pyatiletnem plane vosstanovleniya i razvitiya narodnovo khozyaistva SSSR na 1946-50 g.g.* [Law on the Five-Year Plan for the Reconstruction and Development of the National Economy of the U.S.S.R. for 1946-1950], Moscow, OGIZ, 1946, p. 48.

[29] Data from Glavsevmorput', 1939.

[30] The "Stalin" has been described in the Soviet press as the "flagship" of the northern icebreaker fleet. Its captain, the well known polar specialist V. I. Voronin, is a deputy in the U.S.S.R. Supreme Soviet. See photograph and caption in *Pravda,* March 13, 1949.

[31] Karelin, D. B., *Ledovaya aviatsionnaya razvedka* [Air Ice Reconnaissance], Moscow, Glavsevmorput', 1946, pp. 141-43.

[32] One of the vessels was returned in December 1949 (*The New York Times,* New York, December 29, 1949) and the other two in December 1951 (*ibid.,* December 16, 17 and 19, 1951, and February 26, 1952).

[33] Karelin, *op. cit.,* pp. 141-43. Soviet seamen and hydrographers evaluate the density of ice, or the degree to which the sea is covered by ice, in points (*bally*). Ten points means that the visible area of the sea is completely covered with ice, and zero points means that the sea is completely free of ice. Vize, V. Yu., *Na "Sibiryakove" i "Litke" cherez Ledovitye morya* [Through Arctic Seas in the "Sibiryakov" and "Litke"], Moscow-Leningrad, Glavsevmorput', 1946, p. 70, n. 3.

[34] "Direktivy XIX s"yezda partii po pyatomu pyatiletnemu planu razvitiya SSSR na 1951-1955 gody" [Directives of the Nineteenth Party Congress on the Fifth Five-Year Plan for the Development of the U.S.S.R. for 1951-1955], *Izvestiya,* August 20, 1952. The fact that more icebreakers were needed for stable sea communications does not necessarily imply that the commercial traffic on the Northern Sea Route was large enough to justify the expense of additional icebreakers or even the operation of the six icebreakers remaining after the return of the three Lend Lease vessels.

[35] Interview with the Minister of the Maritime and River Fleet. See Khodulin, G., "Novye ledokoly" [New Icebreakers], *Ogonyok,* No. 2, January 1954, p. 18. This second "Kapitan Belousov" is not to be confused with the icebreaker of the same name mentioned before.

[36] *Ibid.*

[37] "Tseremoniya spuska na vodu ledokola, stroyashchevosya v Finlyandii dlya Sovetskoyo Soyuza" [Launching Ceremony for the Icebreaker Built in Finland for the Soviet Union], *Pravda,* December 16, 1953.

[38] "Kommyunike o prebyvanii v Finlyandii zamestitelya Predsedatelya Soveta Ministrov SSSR A. I. Mikoyan" [Communique on the Stay in

The Route and Other Transportation

Finland of the Vice-Chairman of the Council of Ministers of the U.S.S.R., A. I. Mikoyan], *Pravda,* December 2, 1954.

[39] Nikitin, M., "Reis vo l'dakh" [Voyage in the Ice], *Pravda,* March 2, 1955.

[40] Data from Glavsevmorput', 1940.

[41] *XVIII S"yezd Vsesoyuznoi Kommunisticheskoi partii (b) 10-21 marta 1939 g.: Stenograficheskii otchot* [Eighteenth Congress of the All-Union Communist Party (Bolsheviks), March 10-21, 1939: Stenographic Report], Moscow-Leningrad, OGIZ, 1939, p. 333.

[42] *Ibid.*

[43] Among the fifteen vessels named were the "Nenets" and the "Yuka-gir," which were to be used for the transport of oil products. Karelin, *op. cit.,* p. 142. According to the 1941 State Plan, 21 vessels were to be chartered from the People's Commissariat of the Maritime Fleet by Glavsevmorput' for Arctic navigation in 1941, 13 of them for navigation in the western sector and 8 for the eastern sector. *Gosudarstvennyi plan razvitiya narodnovo khozyaistva SSSR na 1941 god* [State Plan for the Development of the National Economy of the U.S.S.R. for 1941], Photo-Lithoprint by Universal Lithographers, Baltimore, Md., Supplement No. 117, p. 466 (American Council of Learned Societies Reprints: Russian Series No. 30).

[44] Data from Glavsevmorput'.

[45] See Molodetski, K. G., "Voprosy ekonomiki eksploatatsii Severnovo morskovo puti" [Problems of the Economics of the Exploitation of the Northern Sea Route], *Sovetskii Sever* [Soviet North], Leningrad, No. 3, 1939, pp. 3-17.

[46] Annual Report of Glavsevmorput' for 1937.

[47] "O rabote Glavsevmorputi za 1937 god" [Concerning the Work of Glavsevmorput' in 1937], *Sovetskaya Arktika,* No. 5, 1938, p. 21.

[48] Data from Glavsevmorput', 1937.

[49] "Bol'shoi reserv morskovo transporta" [The Great Reserve for Sea Transport], *Izvestiya,* October 4, 1951.

[50] Data from Glavsevmorput'.

[51] Data from Glavsevmorput', 1937.

[52] Data from the Igarka Port Administration, 1940.

[53] Data from the Third Five-Year Plan of Glavsevmorput', 1937.

[54] "Severnyi morskoi put'," *op. cit.,* col. 581.

[55] Information from reliable persons who left Provideniya Bay in 1943. Construction of a large mechanized port in Provideniya Bay is reported in "Severnyi morskoi put'," *op. cit.,* col. 581.

[56] Zubov, *op. cit.,* p. 132.

[57] A 1946 article on Tiksi in the Soviet encyclopedia makes no comment on the port. "Tiksi," *Bol'shaya Sovetskaya entsiklopediya,* Vol. LIV, 1946, cols. 243-44. Although at the end of the first postwar Five-Year Plan (1946-50) and afterwards the Soviet press paid a good deal of attention to Tiksi, it failed to mention the port or port personnel. See "Za polyarnym krugom" [Above the Arctic Circle], *Pravda,* March 13, 1950; "Znatnye lyudi Arktiki" [Eminent Men of the

Arctic], *Izvestiya*, November 23, 1950; "V Sovetskoi Yakutii" [In Soviet Yakutiya], *Ogonyok*, No. 13, March 1951, pp. 25-26.

58 "Gorod v Zapolyar'ye" [City Above the Arctic Circle], *Sovetskii Soyuz* [The Soviet Union], Moscow, No. 2, February 1951, p. 18.

59 "Neporyadki na morskom vokzale" [Disorder in the Maritime Station], *Morskoi Flot* [Merchant Marine], Moscow, August 9, 1949.

60 Karelin, *op. cit.*, p. 12.

61 *Ibid.*, p. 22.

62 *Ibid.*, p. 102.

63 *Ibid.*

64 Zubov, *op. cit.*, pp. 5-6.

65 Karelin, *op. cit.*, p. 12.

66 Data from Glavsevmorput', appendix to the plan for 1933 of the Maritime Department. The planes take off from the ice after having been lowered from the icebreaker.

67 "Plan osvoyeniya Arktiki" [Plan for the Conquest of the Arctic], *Izvestiya*, March 16, 1933.

68 Zubov, *op. cit.*, p. 135. One of the many obstacles is the shortage of fuel in the Arctic. During World War II no fuel was dispensed at the polar station on Wrangel Island, and for two years the station relied on the wind generator alone. Mineyev, A. I., *Ostrov Vrangelya* [Wrangel Island], Moscow, Glavsevmorput', 1946, p. 268.

69 Akkuratov, *op. cit.*, p. 116.

70 Anvel't, Ya. Ya., *et al.*, eds., *Vozdushnye puti Severa* [Air Routes of the North], Moscow, Sovetskaya Aziya, 1933, p. xiii.

71 Vize, *op. cit.*, pp. 15-16.

72 Data from Glavsevmorput'.

73 "Despite the −40° C. temperature the air lines of the North are busy. Planes take off daily from the Archangel airports, carrying passengers, freight and mail." "Apel'siny zhitelyam Zapolyar'ya" [Oranges for Polar Residents], *Pravda*, January 10, 1950.

74 "Na vozdushnykh magistralyakh strany" [On the Main Air Routes of the Country], *Pravda*, October 6, 1948.

75 *Ibid.*

76 "Na vozdushnykh liniyakh" [On the Air Lines], *Izvestiya*, June 16, 1948.

77 Based on prewar data from Glavsevmorput', Aeroflot and personal observations of the author.

78 "Discovery of large tin deposits in the basin of the Yana and the development of industry helped to create an industrial population, an air line, navigation on the Yana. . . ." Lutski, S. L., *Geograficheskiye ocherki russkoi taigi* [Geographic Sketches of the Russian Taiga], Moscow, Geografgiz, 1947, pp. 142-43.

79 "Kamchatskaya oblast'," *Malaya Sovetskaya entsiklopediya* [Small Soviet Encyclopedia], 2d ed., Moscow, OGIZ RSFSR, Vol. V, 1936, col. 214.

80 Based on data from Glavsevmorput' and Aeroflot and the author's personal observations. See also "Aviatsiya" [Aviation], *Bol'shaya Sovetskaya entsiklopediya*, 2d ed., Vol. I, 1949, p. 110; Zakharov, F. A.,

The Route and Other Transportation

Grazhdanskaya aviatsiya na sluzhbe narodnomu khozyaistvu SSSR [Civil Aviation in the Service of the National Economy of the U.S.S.R.], Moscow, 1948; and "Na vozdushnykh magistralyakh" [On the Main Air Routes], *Izvestiya,* July 19, 1952. The shipment of fruit to the North is a post-World War II development possibly brought about by a concentration of military personnel in the Arctic. Before the war plane transportation of fruit to the North was prohibited except occasionally for polar stations. For reports of postwar shipments of fruit to the North, see "Soobshcheniye iz Yakutska" [Report from Yakutsk], *Izvestiya,* August 11, 1948; "Samolyoty dostavlyayut gruz kolkhozam" [Planes Deliver Freight to the Kolkhozes], *Izvestiya,* August 9, 1949; "Apel'siny zhitelyam Zapolyar'ya," *op. cit.*

[81] See Vize, V. Yu., *Morya Sovetskoi Arktiki* [Seas of the Soviet Arctic], Moscow-Leningrad, Glavsevmorput', 1948.

[82] Aeroflot planes transport large quantities of political literature and election materials to Anadyr', Salekhard, Nar'yan-Mar and other points. "Arkticheskii reis M. Kozlova" [The Arctic Flight of M. Kozlov], *Sovetskaya Sibir'* [Soviet Siberia], Novosibirsk, October 24, 1945. See also "Agitsamolyoty v Zapolyar'ye" [Propaganda Airplanes in the Polar Regions], *Izvestiya,* January 29, 1950.

[83] For information on the Ob' see Suslov, *op. cit.,* p. 22; on the Yenisei, see "Yenisei," *Bol'shaya Sovetskaya entsiklopediya,* 2d ed., Vol. XV, 1952, p. 514; and on the Lena, see "Lena," *ibid.,* Vol. XXIV, 1954, p. 487.

[84] On the Aldan river system it has proved possible to drive motorized and animal-drawn vehicles over the river ice after the freeze-up: "In the winter the rivers in the Aldan system are covered with thick layers of ice, which in most cases become excellent roads for motor transport and do not need any construction or repair. From fall to spring strings of trucks and buses and trains of sledges drawn by horses and reindeer move along the river ice." Lutski, *op. cit.,* pp. 150-51. Such transport is physically possible on the other Siberian rivers as well.

[85] According to Suslov the depth of the Yenisei below Turukhansk is fourteen to twenty-three meters, and of the Lena, below the Vilyui confluence, sixteen to twenty meters. Suslov, *op. cit.,* p. 173. At present ocean-going vessels sail freely up the Yenisei to Igarka.

[86] Margolin, A., "Puti zavoza gruzov na krainyi Sever" [Freight Routes to the Extreme North], *Sovetskaya Arktika,* No. 6, 1939, p. 35.

[87] "Zheleznaya doroga Taishet—Ust'-Kut" [The Taishet—Ust'-Kut Railroad], *Pravda,* November 4, 1954; see also "Na magistrali Taishet-Lena" [On the Taishet-Lena Main Line], *Izvestiya,* December 2, 1954.

[88] "Otovsyudu" [From Everywhere], *Izvestiya,* May 20, 1948.

[89] "U yeniseiskikh bakenshchikov" [With the Yenisei Buoy Attendants], *Izvestiya,* July 12, 1949.

[90] Even in southern Siberia, on the upper Irtysh, supplying the buoy attendants with motor boats was considered "an accomplishment." See "Sibirskiye bakenshchiki" [The Siberian Buoy Attendants], *Izvestiya,* May 28, 1953.

⁹¹ "U yeniseiskikh bakenshchikov," *op. cit.;* and "Ogni na Yeniseye" [Lights on the Yenisei], *Izvestiya,* August 7, 1952.

⁹² "Otovsyudu" [From Everywhere], *Pravda,* September 19, 1949. In 1951 it was reported that the building was being completed. "Rechnoi vokzal na Yeniseye" [River Station on the Yenisei], *Izvestiya,* February 24, 1951.

⁹³ Shashkov, Z., "Vazhneishiye zadachi rechnikov" [Most Important Tasks of River Workers], *Pravda,* September 10, 1949. Even in such a large commercial center as Novosibirsk loading and unloading operations are only 73 per cent mechanized. "Novosibirskii port pered navigatsiyei" [The Novosibirsk Port Before the Navigation Season], *Pravda,* April 15, 1953.

⁹⁴ Vernikovski, N., "Neporyadki v lenskom rechnom parokhodstve" [Disorders in the Lena River Shipping Administration], *Izvestiya,* September 13, 1952.

⁹⁵ Volkov, N., "Port v Osetrove" [A Port in Osetrovo], *Pravda,* March 4, 1954. See also "Port na Lene" [A Port on the Lena], *Izvestiya,* July 13, 1954.

⁹⁶ See Appendix to the Decree of the Council of People's Commissars of the U.S.S.R. of January 25, 1941 in Armstrong, *op. cit.,* Appendix VI, p. 126.

⁹⁷ Procurements from foreign concerns included motors from Japan. Data from Glavsevmorput'.

⁹⁸ The three vessels were the "Maria Ul'yanova," a large ship of the type used on the Volga, the "Spartak," a smaller version of the "Maria Ul'yanova," and the "Iosif Stalin," a diesel ship. The first two were built before the Revolution. The "Iosif Stalin" is faster and more comfortable than the other two.

⁹⁹ A separate river fleet was used for transport exclusively between Krasnoyarsk and Minusinsk. Data from the administrative office of the Yenisei River Shipping Administration, 1939.

¹⁰⁰ "Lena," *Bol'shaya Sovetskaya entsiklopediya,* Vol. XXXVI, 1938, col. 311.

¹⁰¹ "Sibirskiye sudostroiteli" [Siberian Shipbuilders], *Izvestiya,* August 5, 1949.

¹⁰² "Rechnaya flotiliya v vodakh Arktiki: Beseda s ministrom rechnovo flota SSSR tov. Z. A. Shashkovym" [The River Fleet in the Waters of the Arctic: An Interview with the Minister of the River Fleet of the U.S.S.R., Z. A. Shashkov], *Ogonyok,* No. 38, September 1949, pp. 10-11. See also "Raport nachal'nika Arkticheskoi Ekspeditsii, Pompolita i Nachal'nika morskoi provodki—Predsedatelyu Soveta Ministrov SSSR, I. V. Stalinu" [Report of the Head of the Arctic Expedition, the Assistant for Political Affairs, and the Head of the Sea Escort to the Chairman of the Council of Ministers of the U.S.S.R., J. V. Stalin], *Pravda,* September 9, 1949; "Zamechatel'nyi uspekh sovetskikh rechnikov" [The Remarkable Success of Soviet River Workers], *Pravda,* September 10, 1949.

¹⁰³ "Rechnaya flotiliya v vodakh Arktiki," *op. cit.*

¹⁰⁴ "Zasedaniye Verkhovnovo Soveta SSSR: V Sovete Natsional'nostei:

Rech' ministra rechnovo flota SSSR Z. A. Shashkova" [Session of the Supreme Soviet of the U.S.S.R.: In the Soviet of Nationalities: Address of the Minister of the River Fleet Z. A. Shashkov], *Pravda*, March 12, 1951.

[105] "Vydayushchiisya uspekh sovetskikh rechnikov" [An Outstanding Success of Soviet River Workers], *Izvestiya*, September 28, 1952.

[106] "Po Severnomu morskomu puti" [Along the Northern Sea Route], *Izvestiya*, September 1, 1954.

[107] See Margolin, A., "Nuzhen li karbasosplav po reke Lene" [Are High-Walled Barges Needed on the Lena River?], *Sovetskaya Arktika*, No. 10, 1940, pp. 21-29.

[108] Data from Glavsevmorput'.

[109] Data from Glavsevmorput'.

[110] "Rechnoi transport v 1949 godu" [River Transport in 1949], *Izvestiya*, February 8, 1949.

[111] "Ob itogakh vypolneniya gosudarstvennovo plana razvitiya narodnovo khozyaistva SSSR v 1954 godu: Soobshcheniye Tsentral'novo statisticheskovo upravleniya pri Sovete Ministrov SSSR" [On the Results of the Fulfillment of the State Plan for the Development of the National Economy of the U.S.S.R. in 1954: Statement of the Central Statistical Administration Under the Council of Ministers of the U.S.S.R.], *Pravda*, January 21, 1955.

[112] Unless otherwise indicated, data from *Kursy politupravleniya dlya komandnovo sostava Glavsevmorputi: Ekonomgeografiya Krainevo Severa* [Courses in Political Administration for Executive Personnel of Glavsevmorput': Economic Geography of the Extreme North], Leningrad-Moscow, Glavsevmorput', 1940, p. 11.

[113] "Taz," *Bol'shaya Sovetskaya entsiklopediya*, Vol. LIII, 1946, col. 456.

[114] *Ibid.*

[115] "Pyasina," *ibid.*, Vol. VII, 1940, col. 717.

[116] In the data on the Khatanga no account is taken of later changes whereby the Khatanga is considered to end at the confluence of the Kheta; what was formerly the lower course of the Khatanga is now considered to be part of the Kotui. "Kotui," *Bol'shaya Sovetskaya entsiklopediya*, 2nd ed., Vol. XXIII, 1953, p. 162.

[117] "Indigirka," *ibid.*, Vol. XVIII, 1953, p. 12.

[118] "Kolyma," *ibid.*, Vol. XXII, 1953, p. 90.

[119] "Anadyr'," *ibid.*, Vol. II, 1950, p. 323.

[120] *Ibid.*

[121] Margolin, "Puti zavoza gruzov na Krainyi Sever," *op. cit.*, p. 34.

[122] Data from Glavsevmorput'. See also Margolin, "Puti zavoza gruzov na Krainyi Sever," *op. cit.*, p. 35.

[123] "Iz Tyumeni" [From Tyumen'], *Izvestiya*, October 22, 1949.

[124] In Russian the Administration is called *Glavnoye upravleniye po transportnomu osvoyeniyu malykh rek pri Ministerstva dorozhnotransportnovo khozyaistva RSFSR* [Main Administration for the Transport Development of Small Rivers Under the R.S.F.S.R. Min-

istry of Transportation]. See "Osvoyeniye malykh rek" [The Development of Small Rivers], *Izvestiya*, June 4, 1953.

[125] The report stated: "In 1953 it is intended to make an additional thousand kilometers of river routes navigable in the Tomsk, Tyumen', Omsk, Kemerovo, and Leningrad Oblasts and in the Altai Krai. . . . Along with the development of new routes the Main Administration is constructing water-power systems on the Moksha and the Tsna. This year the Rassypukhinskii, Morshanskii, Gorel'skii and other water-power systems will be constructed. It will thus be possible to travel from Tambov to the Oka entirely by water." *Ibid.* Of the areas mentioned only the Tyumen' Oblast contains any of the smaller northern rivers (the Pur and the Taz), and the term Tyumen' Oblast as used here may very well refer exclusively to Tyumen' Oblast proper, located south of the Yamal-Nenets and the Khanty-Mansi National Okrugs.

V. THE ROLE OF THE NORTHERN SEA ROUTE

1. Shipments to the North

When Soviet planners at the beginning of the thirties were working on the development of the North they realistically assumed that much of the equipment, building materials, consumer goods and so forth would be shipped from Leningrad, Moscow, and the upper Volga via the Northern Sea Route.[1] This assumption had some validity at the end of the NEP and the beginning of the First Five-Year Plan, when industry in southern Siberia had just started to expand and transportation facilities on the northern reaches of the Siberian rivers were still rudimentary. Since that time, however, changes in the economic geography of Siberia have presented more rational alternatives for supplying the North. Southern Siberia, particularly the area west of the upper Angara, as a result of its rapid economic development, is now able to supply the North with most of the goods which it needs or, rather, may expect to receive. Present plans for Siberia forecast a further decrease in the usefulness of the Route in supplying the North. Consumer goods still come in some measure from the European U.S.S.R., but government provisions for building up local industry and producers' cooperatives east of the Urals may decrease the need for non-Siberian sources of supply. The present dependence on the old industrial areas for certain types of equipment and machinery will also lessen as southern Siberia continues to expand and diversify its economy.

Transportation on the Siberian rivers, although inefficient and not fully developed, can nevertheless deliver southern Siberian supplies in quantity to the North. The usefulness of these rivers for such a purpose is enhanced by the existence of two north-south motor roads, the AYaM road running from the Bol'shoi Never station on the Trans-Siberian Railroad through Aldan to Yakutsk on the Lena,[2] and the road from Magadan on the Okhotsk coast which crosses the navigable part of the Kolyma River (downstream of the point where the Bokhapcha River joins the Kolyma). Both roads are supply lanes in their own right in addition to their functions as adjuncts of the Siberian rivers. The significance of the port at Osetrovo and the rail line running from Taishet on the Trans-Siberian Railroad to Ust'-Kut on the Lena has already been discussed.

The completion of a second Trans-Siberian railroad is one of the possible methods of easing the rail transport problem in supplying the North. Rail shipments from the European U.S.S.R. increase the burden on the European railway network and the Trans-Siberian, and even goods originating in southwestern Siberia must ordinarily travel some distance by rail before reaching the approach routes to the North. The official Glavsevmorput' view in 1940 was that the Northern Sea Route "relieves the Siberian railroad from carrying freight for the extreme North."[3] Although exclusive use of the Route could potentially relieve the Trans-Siberian, goods from the European U.S.S.R. must travel over considerable distances by rail in order to reach Murmansk or Archangel for further shipment via the Route, and this extra load on the railroads in the European U.S.S.R. is one they are not prepared to assume. If the rail line from Taishet to Ust'-Kut is extended to the Pacific coast running parallel to the Trans-Siberian and if eventually a rail link is forged between Taishet and the South Siberian rail line (which is scheduled to reach Abakan by 1955), it will become still more advantageous to supply the

North from southwestern Siberia rather than via the Northern Sea Route.

The arguments in favor of using the Northern Sea Route for supplying the North continued to be based on the assumption that shipments would originate in the European U.S.S.R. In 1939 Glavsevmorput' calculated that the distance for shipments from Moscow to Tiksi via the Route was thousands of kilometers shorter than via the railroad and the Lena; shipments would also go twice as fast and cost 60 per cent less when sent by sea. The findings were that, of seventy-one commodities—including foodstuffs, manufactured goods and technical equipment—thirty-two could be shipped more advantageously via the Route from Archangel to Igarka, Dudinka and other ports and thence by river and coastal craft to their final destinations.[4] Given the underlying assumption, the calculations may have been correct. However, in seeking the most rational supply route for the North the central question is no longer the comparative cost, distance and speed of delivery from the western U.S.S.R. industrial centers via the Northern Sea Route or other transport. Instead, calculations must now first take into account the probability that most items can be supplied from a base closer at hand, that is, from southern Siberia.

The administrative structure of Siberia also favors this solution. The northern districts are part of large administrative units which extend far to the south.[5] Under Soviet conditions, officials of the large administrative units prefer to obtain supplies for their northern districts from areas under their own jurisdiction.

In spite of the changing situation it remains official Soviet dogma that the Northern Sea Route is the key to the economic development of the North. This fiction has been maintained for several reasons. First, it is a general Soviet policy to stress the peacetime aspects of projects which are of vital strategic importance. Second, for a Soviet citizen, public reevaluation of the role of the Northern Sea Route would have been a hazardous undertaking, in the teeth of the rumor that to prove the Route's economic usefulness was an *idée fixe* of Stalin.

The consequences of an open statement to the contrary were demonstrated by the experience of Molodykh, one of the most prominent authorities on northern transportation. At the beginning of the thirties he strongly urged that the Kolyma and Chukotsk regions be supplied from the south rather than from the north and adduced comparative cost analyses to support his contention.[6] His report was rejected and branded as "harmful" by Soviet authorities. Subsequent expressions of doubt, whether based on lack of cargo to or from the North or on inherent problems in transportation via the Route, were unfailingly subjected to sharp criticism.

The long-established practice for Soviet economic geographers in this and other matters is to conform to the officially sanctioned position, and they take to heart the warnings against "overemphasizing" physical factors in their studies on interregional economic relations whenever these factors seem to run counter to the regime's announced desires.[7] Thus treatises touching upon the northern economy or transportation usually refer to the value of the Route. Baranski, in postwar editions of his standard text on Soviet economic geography still wrote:

> The significance [of the Route] . . . lies in the fact that it opened the possibility for transporting timber and minerals from northern Siberia and at the same time made it easier to ship into Siberia machines and various kinds of agricultural and mining equipment. . . .[8]

In another text on the same subject published in the Soviet Union in 1940, it was stated that the Route, "exceptionally important to the U.S.S.R.," had "begun to be utilized" for direct shipments from the West to the mouths of the Lena, Kolyma and other northern rivers.[9]

The propagation of the official line on the Northern Sea Route did not prevent the supply of the North from developing in accordance with the economic realities. When the NKVD, an "experienced economic institution," set out in the thirties to develop the Kolyma gold mining area, it soon abandoned the attempt to depend exclusively on supplies shipped via the Route. Instead, the motor road was built northward from the Okhotsk coast to carry supplies which had been brought via the Trans-Siberian Railroad to Vladivostok and thence by sea to the Port of Nagayevo and the city of Magadan.[10] Of the materials used in the construction of the Noril'sk Polymetal Combine in the thirties, 60 per cent came from the south (mainly from the Kuznetsk Basin) and 40 per cent via the Route.[11]

A corollary of the official line was the idea that the main Siberian rivers, at least in their northern course, were extensions of the Route, carrying supplies southward to inland areas after delivery via the Route at Arctic ports. Available evidence from unpublished sources, although limited, indicated that this was not the case, that is, that the main Siberian rivers carried mostly southern-supplied goods to the North, and the inland flow of goods from the Arctic coast was very limited.[12] In current descriptions of freight movements on the Yenisei and the Lena, the Route and the Siberian rivers are frequently mentioned as of equal importance in supplying the North, and sometimes the independent role of the rivers is clearly expressed; but never is it indicated that the rivers are mainly subsidiaries of the Route.

Published Soviet sources give the following picture of the cargo turnover of the Yenisei River Shipping Administration, which is charged with shipping on the entire navigable portion of the Yenisei:

> Predominating in the cargo turnover of the Yenisei River Shipping Administration is rafted timber which is towed to the lower reaches of the Yenisei for local use and for loading on maritime vessels for export [*eksport*] after processing in sawmills. . . . An important role in the cargo turnover of the Yenisei River Shipping Administration is taken by the shipment of freight into the northern regions of the area, that is, to the lower reaches of the Yenisei as well as on its tributaries, and also the shipment from these places of the production of industrial enterprises.[13]

The southbound shipment of the "production of industrial enterprises" probably refers to the shipment of the output of the Noril'sk Polymetal Combine.

The activity of the Lena River Shipping enterprise, the vessels of which ply the Lena all along the stretch from Kachuga to the river's mouth, illustrates more clearly the importance of supply from the South:

> Shipments of equipment, fuel, industrial and food cargoes which come into the Yakut A.S.S.R. from the landing stages in the upper reaches of the Lena River account for most of the freight turnover of the Lena River Shipping Administration.[14]

Even when Soviet publications take pains to render the Northern Sea Route its conventional due as a supply channel for the North, no attempt is made to minimize shipments from the south:

> The river fleet of the Lena River Shipping Administration has been enlarged by the addition of new vessels which will carry passengers and freight from Yakutsk to the polar port of Tiksi. Freight which arrives via the Northern Sea Route for Yakutiya will now reach the population deep within the republic considerably faster.[15]
>
> One of the main routes for shipping goods into Yakutiya is the route downriver from the landing stages Ust'-Kut and Osetrovo. Beginning with the first prewar Five-Year Plans, in connection with the development of the Northern Sea Route, another route for the shipment of goods (chiefly industrial manufactures) took on great significance, [namely] from Archangel to the Bay of Tiksi and up the Lena to Yakutsk and beyond.[16]

Role of the Northern Sea Route

In spite of the recurrent attempts to keep alive the myth of the Northern Sea Route, on balance it is clear even from published Soviet sources that the volume of freight from the south is sizable.

Coastal shipping along the Arctic littoral at first handled mainly cargo brought in via the Northern Sea Route and discharged at key points such as Tiksi, Dickson Island and Provideniya Bay. From these points the cargo was trans-shipped and carried to the mouths of the smaller northern rivers or other points along the coast. For example, cargo offloaded at Tiksi was shipped west to the Olenyok, Anabar and Khatanga rivers and east to the Yana and the Indigirka. With the economic development of southern Siberia and the growth of transportation on the main Siberian rivers, the Northern Sea Route began to take a secondary role in the pattern of coastal shipping. An increasingly large percentage of the cargo delivered to key coastal points now comes from the south via the main Siberian rivers. To a considerable extent cargoes distributed out of Tiksi come from the south via the Lena River.[17] Onward shipping of southern-supplied cargo in cabotage contributes to the total cargo turnover on the Northern Sea Route, but the loss of anticipated long hauls originating at Murmansk and Archangel is a serious blow to its economic usefulness.

Shipments via the Northern Sea Route from Murmansk and Archangel or Soviet Far Eastern ports still supply the polar stations and islands in the Arctic, and in the main shipments to the Chutotsk Peninsula continue to go by sea from Soviet Far Eastern ports. Otherwise the Northern Sea Route has yielded its position as the main supply route of the North to the southern approaches. The subsequent analysis of the data available on Arctic cargo turnover will show the effects on the economic prospects of the Northern Sea Route.

2. Shipments from the North

The export of lumber took on particular importance for the Northern Sea Route toward the end of the First Five-Year Plan. From 1925 up to 1929 the mainstay of the Kara Sea runs, and in effect, of the whole Northern Sea Route, had been the import of European goods into Siberia and the export of Siberian lumber and agricultural products. When agricultural exports were almost entirely cut off during the First Five-Year Plan, Siberia began to place great reliance on the increased export of lumber:

> The Kara runs were responsible for the creation of the Siberian lumber export industry, which is developing at a rapid pace. In the near future lumber export will undoubtedly be of prime importance in the foreign trade balance of Siberia and thereafter will rapidly become a factor of national significance.[18]

As pointed out in the earlier discussion of the lumber industry, no solid foundation for an expanded Siberian lumber export trade was developed before World War II, and no significant expansion in the postwar period seems to have taken place. Primarily because of the lack of manpower and matériel the three sawmills of the Igarka Lumber Combine have remained the only producers of lumber for export in the extreme North. The Salekhard mills apparently ship their output to the southwest. The more southerly enterprises on the Ob' and Yenisei (at Mogochin and Kolpashevo for example) had begun before 1933 to export via the Northern Sea Route, but their production was later preempted for the Siberian market, particularly for the growing needs of the Kuznetsk Basin.[19]

Although the volume of lumber exports from Igarka after 1935 never reached proportions of such "national significance" that it could by itself justify the economic and human resources devoted to the Northern Sea Route, these shipments were of cardinal importance to the Route in that they usually contributed well over half its annual cargo turnover.[20]

The United Kingdom was the main customer for lumber exports through the Kara Sea, taking over 80 per cent of the total in the period from 1935 to 1938.[21] The outbreak of the war in Europe and the discontinuance of lumber shipments to the United Kingdom in 1940[22] threatened a severe reduction in cargo turnover on the Route. In early September 1940, with only a few weeks remaining of the navigation season, the author observed the Igarka wharves congested with lumber waiting for shipment. At that time the local expectation was that Germany was to replace the United Kingdom as a taker of Igarka lumber.[23] The German invasion of the Soviet Union in June 1941 put an end to such plans.

In 1949-1952 the volume of Igarka lumber shipments to the United Kingdom via the Kara sea was less than half of the volume in 1935-1938.[24] It is not known whether other countries have replaced the United Kingdom as a market for Igarka lumber, although there is frequent mention of wood products to be supplied by the U.S.S.R. under existing foreign trade agreements.[25] In the absence of reports indicating an expansion of the northern timber industry, we may assume that postwar outbound lumber shipments via the Northern Sea Route are comparable in scale to those of the late thirties.

The other industries in the North provide less freight for the Northern Sea Route than the lumber industry. Shortly before the beginning of World War II Glavsevmorput' had hoped for a substantial increase in the shipment of Noril'sk coal via the Route. The great resources of the Noril'sk deposits and the high quality of the coal made it appear expedient at that time to supply this fuel to industrial enterprises of the northern European U.S.S.R. and to the naval fleet based in Murmansk.[26] Even for the initial years of the project Glavsevmorput' had planned such shipments to an annual volume of 250,000 to 300,00 tons,[27] but the war and the development of the Pechora coal fields frustrated these plans. As the situation now stands, coal mining in areas along the Northern Sea Route serves local needs and provides bunkers for vessels plying the seaway.

Other mining enterprises contribute little cargo to the Route. The output of the Noril'sk Polymetal Combine goes to the industries of the Kuzbass and the Urals mainly via southern routes; any part that may be shipped to the north-west via the Kara Sea is very small. Presumably any other extractive industries that may spring up in the North in the future will also be oriented chiefly to the Siberian market. As two exceptions to this trend, the limited output of Nordvik salt workings is probably being shipped to northern fisheries via the Route, and although oil is being shipped into the Arctic districts, future production may grow enough to reverse the situation and provide outbound freight.

As for the northern fishing and reindeer-raising industries, their insignificant surpluses serve the domestic market via the river systems.

Marketable furs from the North are shipped out by air transport rather than via the Northern Sea Route. Before the development of northern air lines, furs of the autumn catch (and some of the spring catch) reached the Arctic ports after the departure of the last ship in the navigation season and were forced to wait until the next spring for shipment to fur-processing centers and markets in the European U.S.S.R. The dead capital and other costs resulting from such delay were high enough to make air transport advantageous for shipping out of furs,[28] as it has apparently been found to be in other regions as well. In the postwar period furs (and gold) were shipped from the Aldan region by air rather than via the AYaM highway, which is used to bring in supplies.[29]

3. Other Shipments

Efforts to prove the economic advantage of through voy-ages on the Northern Sea Route between Murmansk and Vlad-ivostok boomeranged from the start. Shipments of grain from Leningrad to Vladivostok on the vessels "Iskra" and "Van-zetti" in 1935 had discouraging results:

> Direct expenditures (without counting icebreaker service) amounted to over 275 rubles per ton. Delivery of this cargo by railroad is almost 50 per cent cheaper.[30]

In the same year Glavsevmorput' attempted to combine through voyages with calls en route to deliver and take on cargo. On a westbound passage from Vladivostok the "Ana-dyr'" and the "Stalingrad" delivered 4,100 tons of cargo to the Kolyma,[31] and 408 passengers, 55 horses and 15 cows with a year's supply of fodder to the estuaries of Siberian rivers far-ther west.[32] At Igarka each ship picked up 1,500 standards of timber, which the "Anadyr'" delivered to Murmansk and the "Stalingrad" to London.[33] The "Stalingrad" voyage was hailed as the first through voyage from Vladivostok to London via the Northern Sea Route.[34]

These two runs by no means prove the economic expediency of through voyages along the Northern Sea Route. After de-livering the 4,100 tons of freight at the Kolyma, the vessels made a large part of the costly voyage, from the Kolyma to Igarka, with a load of negligible proportions. The passengers and livestock could have been transported from the south over the cheaper, more highly developed river routes to the estu-aries of the larger Siberian rivers and further, if necessary, by local transportation.

Like the "Anadyr'" and the "Stalingrad" on this early pas-sage, vessels making the through voyage on the Northern Sea Route are seldom fully loaded with commercial cargo for the entire run. The real value of the seaway to the Soviet govern-ment lies in the transportation of military cargo in time of war.

One means of providing economically profitable freight for the Northern Sea Route would be a return to the export of Siberian agricultural products via the Kara Sea. When plans for traffic on the Route were first being drawn up, Professor V. I. Orlov pointed up the possibility of exporting 2 to 3 million tons of agricultural products annually over the Kara Sea if a suitable merchant fleet were provided.[35] Instead, after a time the export of Siberian agricultural products was stopped completely. In 1954, however, the Party resolution of March 2, on the development of new grain lands in southwestern Siberia and other areas, referred to the need for surpluses of grain in order to expand exports.[36] At the same time statements were being made in other quarters regarding the "need for increasing the role of the Soviet maritime fleet in the development of foreign trade relations with the People's Democracies in Europe and with the Chinese People's Republic."[37] It is possible that the Soviet government was contemplating a resumption of the grain export carried on via the Kara Sea before the Second Five-Year Plan. The outlook for such grain exports would be improved if the new grain lands program brings the results expected by the Soviet authorities.

Furthermore, the growth of population in the northern European U.S.S.R. may dictate the shipment of Siberian agricultural products via the Route to this area. From 1926 to 1939, the population of Archangel increased from 76,774 to 281,091 and Murmansk from 8,777 to 117,054.[38] There is evidence that since 1939, the population of these cities has continued to increase, as has that of the northern European U.S.S.R. as a whole. New industrial centers are growing up in Kirovsk (Khibinogorsk), Monchegorsk, Molotovsk, Vorkuta, Ukhta, Nar'yan-Mar, and elsewhere. In addition, the hundreds of thousands of prisoners in concentration camps located in the area must be fed, even if on a limited scale. Grain and other foodstuffs for the northern European U.S.S.R. come partly from the central chernozem regions of the U.S.S.R. and partly from Siberia. In either case a long railroad haul is involved (1,800 kilometers from the central chernozem region and 4,000 kilometers from western Siberia over the Kirov-Kotlas rail line). Pressure on the railroads would be relieved and the cost of transporting foodstuffs to the northern European U.S.S.R. considerably reduced if southwestern Siberian foodstuffs were shipped by the water route down the Yenisei or the Ob' and via the Kara Sea route to Archangel, Murmansk and Nar'yan-Mar.

Additional freight, although of lesser volume, would be provided for the Northern Sea Route if eastern Arctic areas such as the Chukotsk Peninsula were supplied to a greater extent through shipments from the estuaries of the main Siberian rivers instead of shipments originating in Soviet Far Eastern ports. The adoption of this pattern of supply would probably result in overall economies, especially in the use of goods which must now travel over long distances by rail before they reach the Soviet Far Eastern ports for further shipment northward. If the Yenisei and also the Ob' were used in such shipments in preference to the Lena, additional savings in rail transport would result, and the Route would benefit from the longer haul by sea.

It is always possible that northern production may increase significantly in the future and that the Soviet government may market these products in areas served by the Route. On the basis of the existing situation, however, a revival of agricultural exports from Siberia and a new pattern of supply for the northern European U.S.S.R. as well as for the extreme eastern Arctic are the prospects which hold the greatest promise for a substantial increase in the yearly cargo turnover on the Route.

4. *The Economic Impasse of the Northern Sea Route*

The discontinuance of exports from southwestern Siberia, the competition from Siberian rivers in supplying the North and the limited prospects for cargoes from the North frustrated the efforts of Glavsevmorput' to increase the cargo turnover on the Northern Sea Route. During 1934-1935 B. V. Lavrov, director of the Glavsevmorput' Institute of Economics of the North and former Chairman of Komseverput', and N. Ye. Shadrin wrote a monograph exploring this question.[39] Their position was a difficult one. They could not fail to see that the only solution to the problem was a return to the export of agricultural products from southern Siberia and an increase in the export of lumber;[40] at the same time official policy inflexibly banned the export of Siberian agricultural products, and the projected expansion of the lumber industry had not occurred. The government nevertheless demanded in the Second Five-Year Plan (1933-1937) that Glavsevmorput' increase the shipment of cargo from the North. Bowing to the inevitable, in the fragment of their monograph published in 1936 Lavrov and Shadrin proposed the following arbitrary plan for tonnage to be shipped via the Northern Sea Route in 1937:[41]

Through shipping	61,900 tons
Shipping in the western sector	462,500 tons
Shipping in the eastern sector	118,000 tons
Total	642,400 tons

The proposal displeased even Glavsevmorput'. The new director of the Planning Department, S. P. Natsarenus, sharply criticized Lavrov and Shadrin for their distortion of economic reality.[42] He was right. In 1937, and in the following years as well, cargo shipments amounted to about one third of their estimates. Demands from above, however, were unremitting. In 1938 the Council of People's Commissars called for the expansion of commercial runs and ordered that all ships should be put on the cost accounting budgeting system beginning with the 1939 navigation season.[43]

The results of efforts to gain an economic return for the resources devoted to the Northern Sea Route and the relative importance of the Route in the economic development of the North are indicated by the available figures on the cargo turnover of the Route and by comparison of its turnover with that of competing lines of transportation.

According to an official Soviet statement published in 1944, the cargo turnover on the Northern Sea Route from its inception through 1942 totaled 2,646,000 tons, and the average yearly cargo turnover during the Third Five-Year Plan period (1938-1942) was 230,000 tons (see Table I). Data obtained

Table I. Cargo Turnover on the Northern Sea Route (according to the *Bol'shaya Sovetskaya entsiklopediya*)[44]

A. Total Cargo Turnover

Period	Tons
Beginning through 1942	2,646,000
1876-1919	55,182

B. Average Yearly Cargo Turnover*

Period	Tons
1920-1928	12,300
First Five-Year Plan [1929-1932]	110,000
Second Five-Year Plan [1933-1937]	179,400
Third Five-Year Plan [1938-1942]	230,000

* The figures are evidently rounded off to the nearest hundred tons.

from Glavsevmorput' are in substantial agreement (see Table II). From these data it can be established that in no single year before 1942 did the cargo turnover on the Northern Sea Route reach 300,000 tons, a generalization which possibly can be extended to the year 1942 as well.[45]

Table II. Cargo Turnover on the Northern Sea Route
(according to Glavsevmorput' data unless otherwise indicated)

Period	Tons	Remarks
1920-1932	538,000	Includes only Kara Sea runs.
1933-1938	1,188,000	In 1934, Kara Sea runs totaled 112,337 tons, of which 7,775 tons went to the Arctic and 104,562 tons from the Arctic.
1939	222,100	Outbound shipments of lumber over the Kara Sea totaled 94,-400 tons.[46]
1940	197,600	To the Arctic, 70,600 tons; from the Arctic, 80,600 tons; local coastal shipping, 46,400 tons.
1941 (planned)[47]	240,400	To the Arctic, 88,700 tons; from the Arctic, 77,300 tons; between ports, 3,400 tons; local coastal shipping, 71,000 tons.[48]
Total 1920-1941	2,386,100	

Because of the meager available data, comparison between cargo turnover on the Route and on the main Siberian rivers must rest on the record of a single year, 1940, for which the figures on freight shipments both via the Route and via the northern half of the Lena River are known:[49]

	Total Cargo Turnover	Cargo to the Arctic
Northern Sea Route	197,600 tons	70,600 tons
Lena River (excluding section south of Yakutsk)	173,400 tons	161,200 tons

These figures express eloquently the relative importance of supply from the south via the Siberian rivers and supply via the Northern Sea Route. The exceedingly small tonnage (12,-200 tons) going south on this portion of the Lena is noteworthy.[50] It is only within this limited framework that we can speak of the use of the main Siberian rivers as extensions of the Route for supplying inland areas of the extreme North.

This fact effectively dispels any notion that the main Siberian rivers are "economic subsidiaries" of the Northern Sea Route.

It should be noted that the comparison is between shipments via the Route to all points in the Arctic and shipments to the Arctic via one river, the Lena. The relevant figures for the Ob' and the Yenisei are not available,[51] but they could only contribute further to the conviction that Arctic shipments by river far outweigh shipments via the Northern Sea Route.

Another index of the economic usefulness of the Route is the unit cost of transportation. One of the factors causing high unit costs is that cargo ships are not always provided with full loads. In both the western and eastern sectors of the Route before World War II there was a marked imbalance between incoming and outgoing freight. In shipping over the Kara Sea the outgoing freight exceeded incoming with a ratio of 5 to 1 or more, while in other areas a reverse ratio prevailed, ranging between 2.4 to 1 and 5 to 1.[52]

The reduction of unit costs by limiting total cost is inherently difficult in the case of the Route. It is true that water transport is cheaper than rail transport because, for one thing, there is no major outlay for the construction or upkeep of a roadbed. Unlike the ordinary water transport line, however, the Northern Sea Route requires the use of special equipment such as icebreakers and aviation, and the ratio of these expenditures to total costs is quite high. The operating costs of icebreakers, for example, amount to 50 per cent or more of total operating costs.[53]

In the Kara Sea after the Revolution the expense of icebreaker services in relation to the small cargo turnover made the cost of exporting Siberian products prohibitive. Komseverput' therefore discontinued the use of the icebreaker "Lenin," which had been convoying commercial vessels in the Kara run. Only in 1929, when it "became economically permissible with the cargo turnover achieved," did Komseverput' return to the use of the icebreaker.[54] The turnover referred to amounted to 73,202 tons.[55]

An investigation of the problem by Glavsevmorput' soon after its establishment led to the conclusion that a yearly cargo turnover of 95,000 to 100,000 tons was necessary to justify the use of the icebreaker "Krasin" or "Yermak." Up to World War II the conviction prevailed in Glavsevmorput' that a cargo turnover of this volume was required for each icebreaker of this class in use.[56] On this basis, for the nine large icebreakers which Glavsevmorput' will have with the addition of the three built in Finland, a minimum cargo turnover of 855,000 tons on the Northern Sea Route is needed. This calculation does not take into account the sporadic use of smaller icebreakers and a number of ice-forcing ships operated by Glavsevmorput' as well as other miscellaneous facilities. If we add the operating costs of these items, the total cargo turnover required is well over a million tons. The annual average of 230,000 tons from 1938 to 1942 does not even begin to solve the problem. Papanin, former chief of Glavsevmorput', stated in December 1945:

> Shortly before the war Comrade Stalin familiarized himself in detail with the work done by polar workers and the plans for the near future. Comrade Stalin informed us that the volume of Arctic cargo shipments was still paltry [*mizernyi*] and that it was necessary in the next years to increase the turnover on the Northern Sea Route about five or six times.[57]

In the postwar Soviet press reports on the bustling shipping activity in the Arctic continued, but the customary statements that the cargo turnover on the Route had increased during the year were usually missing.[58] Even in a sixteen-page article devoted entirely to the Route, the discussion of cargo turnover was limited to the following obscurantist statement:

> For the first twenty years of the [Soviet] utilization of the Route [1920-1940] almost forty times as much cargo was transported via the Route as in the half-century period under capitalism.[59]

It is interesting to note that in this article only one page was devoted to the work of Glavsevmorput'. In a brief reference to the postwar period the author expressed confidence that the economic problems of the Route would be solved—that is, in the future.

In one of the few concrete statements on the subject, Papanin announced in December 1945 that cargo turnover on the Northern Sea Route in 1945 was 180 per cent of the 1940 turnover.[60] His statement, taken at face value, would put the 1945 turnover at 355,680 tons,[61] an increase of about 55 per cent over the yearly average of 230,000 tons in 1938-1942. The requirements of the situation were, as Stalin himself had observed, that an increase of 500 per cent should be made in cargo turnover on the Route.

A statement by Zosim A. Shashkov, head of the former Ministry of the Maritime and River Fleet (which had jurisdiction over Glvasevmorput') might well create the impression that there had been a considerable postwar increase in cargo turnover on the Northern Sea Route. In June 1954 he stated that shipments within the Far Eastern Basin and along the Northern Sea Route had more than quadrupled in 1953 as compared with 1940.[62] To combine the figures for the Northern Sea Route and the Far Eastern Basin in this manner is misleading. There is no doubt that the turnover in the Far Eastern Basin was higher in 1953 than in 1940, not only because of the economic development in the area (coal and oil in Sakhalin, fishing and fish-processing, and so forth), but also because of the postwar Soviet annexations of former Japanese territories (Southern Sakhalin and the Kurile Islands). Furthermore, annual cargo turnover in the Far Eastern Basin was usually eight times larger than that of the Northern Sea Route.[63] Thus if the turnover in the Far Eastern Basin increased 4.5 times from 1940 to 1953, this increase alone would "more than quadruple" the cargo turnover on both sea lanes

165

taken together in 1953 as compared with the total in 1940, leaving the Northern Sea Route cargo turnover unchanged. Therefore Shashkov's statement cannot be taken as evidence that cargo turnover on the Route had increased significantly in 1953. Seen in the light of the background information which we have presented, the statement leaves the opposite impression, namely that Shashkov felt constrained to obscure unsatisfactory results on the Northern Sea Route by lumping them together with a description of more positive results achieved in the Far Eastern Basin.

The inescapable conclusion is that the Northern Sea Route has taken a secondary role in the economic development of the North and has not become a self-supporting project. Only its other uses explain Soviet efforts to develop the Route.

5. Strategic Significance of Arctic Facilities

a. The Northern Sea Route

Even in tsarist times the feasibility of navigation in Arctic waters was regarded as undermining the natural defense of the northern borders. In the light of later developments, however, the "ice sphinx" thus far seems less suitable as an avenue for an enemy approach than as an aid to Soviet maneuvers. This advantage was first demonstrated when the new rulers of Russia, in establishing their power, made use of the Northern Sea Route during the Civil War and the intervention by the Allied powers.[64]

In 1920 Soviet administrative agencies found an extremely difficult food situation when they arrived in Archangel; it was impossible to obtain relief from the south, since railroad transportation had been thoroughly crippled and the food supply in European Russia was exhausted. For the relief of the Archangel area the Siberian Revolutionary Committee was instructed to see to the delivery of supplies from southern Siberia via the Kara Sea. In 1920 the Committee created a Commission on the Northern Sea Route for this express purpose, and the latter sent twelve ships to Archangel carrying flour and other cargo. Such runs continued for the next few years.[65]

The strategic value of the Northern Sea Route in the transfer of warships from west to east was demonstrated during the 1940 navigation season, when the German auxiliary cruiser "Komet" (code name "Schiff 45") made the eastward passage along the entire length of the Soviet Arctic coast. Cut off from the Atlantic by the British blockade of the northern European waters, the captain of the "Komet" arranged to have the German naval attaché in Moscow approach the Soviet government on the matter of eastbound passage of the Northern Sea Route. At first permission was refused, out of unwillingness— according to the German interpretation—to disclose the Route to a foreign vessel. The Soviet government finally agreed, however, and promised its cooperation, even including ice-breaker service. Despite the fact that the "Komet" was divested of its icebreaker escort in the eastern sector of the Route, the ship completed the voyage successfully, aided by favorable ice conditions, and entered into active service.[66] Actual running time was only fourteen days although twenty-one were required for the passage.[67]

By the autumn of 1941, several months after the German invasion, enemy action had cut off the Kola Peninsula from the supplies normally received via the Kirov Railroad from Leningrad and other areas at the southern end of the railroad. The coal needs of the Kola Peninsula and of convoys bringing in Lend-Lease supplies were met by shipments from the Noril'sk coal fields in addition to the supply from the Pechora Basin, then still under development.[68] Describing the delivery of Lend-Lease materials without so specifying, Zubov comments that the experience of polar workers was put to good use during World War II in convoying ships from the Atlantic to ports on the Barents and White seas and via the Pacific to Vladivostok through the Seas of Okhotsk and Japan. He states that "navigation in these areas, which continued the whole year around [*sic*], required ice reconnaissance and icebreaker service."[69] Some foodstuffs and military supplies supplementing Lend-Lease deliveries were sent to the Kola Peninsula from Siberia over the Kara Sea in an operation reminiscent of the supply of Archangel during the Civil War. Ships carrying Lend-Lease goods from the United States sometimes proceeded to ports on the Northern Sea Route, such as Pevek, Ambarchik, the mouths of the Yana, Indigirka, Olenyok, Anabar and Khatanga rivers, Tiksi, and ports on the Yenisei.[70] Realizing the value of the Arctic supply line to the Soviet war effort, the German command dispatched aircraft, submarines and surface ships to the White, Barents and Kara Seas.[71]

For Soviet naval operations the communications between east and west afforded by the Northern Sea Route are of obvious importance. The Route lies entirely within waters under Soviet control and does not involve the use of foreign ports. At the Eighteenth Party Congress in 1939 Papanin, speaking of the military significance of the Route, declared quite frankly:

> In an emergency, if the enemy dares to attack us from the west or from the east, we shall be able, undisturbed and in a short time, to transfer warships from one sea border of our great Soviet Union to the other.[72]

Directly connected with the naval significance of the sea lane from Murmansk to Vladivostok is the development of the inland water route from the Baltic to the White Sea and of the naval base on the Kola Peninsula. The basic link of the inland route to the White Sea is the White Sea—Baltic Canal, running for over 225 kilometers from Povenets on Lake Onega to Belomorsk on the White Sea.[73] Completed in 1933 after an extraordinary expenditure of effort, matériel and human lives, the canal permits the passage of small merchant and naval vessels. Thus, certain ships of the Kronstadt naval forces, such as submarines, after passing through the Neva and Svir rivers, can proceed to the Arctic Ocean and the lanes of the Northern Sea Route. The fleet's mobility was further increased by the establishment in 1933 of a naval base on the Kola Peninsula with its main center at Polyarnoye.[74] The importance attached to the maintenance of the inland water connection between Kronstadt and the northern seas was exemplified during World War II when the White Sea Canal was destroyed by the Finns. As soon as they were driven out, despite the scope of the task and the general destruction and poverty of the country, unconcealed in those years, the Soviet government immediately rebuilt the canal.[75] This haste is all the more significant since commercial traffic on the canal, which passes through wild and undeveloped regions, was negligible before the war[76] and presumably remains so.

The strategic value of the Northern Sea Route is further enhanced by the growing availability of western Siberian food and military supplies, which can be shipped via the Route to the northern European U.S.S.R., the central Arctic littoral and the northeast.

Speaking of western Siberia, Voznesenski, the former chairman of the U.S.S.R. Gosplan, described industries which were already engaged in or could easily be converted to war production:

> During the war a number of new branches of the machine-building industry were set up in western Siberia: the production of planes, tanks, machine tools, tractors, motorcycles, ball-bearings, instruments, and electrical equipment. In western Siberia during the Patriotic War the production of high-grade metals and ferrous alloys was organized. Nonferrous metallurgy has grown considerably. The capacity of zinc production was increased, and the production of aluminum and tin was started.[77]

A government document recounted the importance of the wartime military production of the areas east of the Urals:

> The eastern districts of the Soviet Union, which grew and were

strengthened during the years of the Patriotic War, functioned as a powerful base for supplying the Red Army ammunition, arms, tanks, and planes.[78]

Thus in more than one respect the Route has a demonstrable strategic value. Investments in the icebreaker fleet, the network of polar stations, the coaling stations along the littoral, and other facilities of the Route as well as the reservoir of trained personnel and knowledge may have fallen short of Soviet desires and may have failed to secure an adequate economic return, but they have contributed to the potential strategic value of the Route and provided facilities which, in an emergency, could be transferred to other waters where ice reconnaissance and icebreaker service might be required.

b.   Polar Aviation

Mastery of the Arctic air spaces confers obvious strategic advantages. Air ice reconnaissance greatly facilitates the transfer of warships and military cargoes over the Northern Sea Route. Civil and military air transport in the North assures the continuity of communication and supply when other facilities break down. The most important strategic consideration, however, is that polar aviation opens a shorter path to the vital centers of the United States. The east-west air routes intended to connect the western part of the U.S.S.R. with the Chukotsk Peninsula and the Far East have frequently been referred to in Soviet literature. The potential north-south routes between the U.S.S.R. and America have received less publicity Soviet interest in meridional routes nevertheless goes back as far as 1934, when the Arctic Institute announced the possibility of using the northern coast of the U.S.S.R. as an "air transportation route between Europe and America."[79]

The first transpolar flights were made before World War II:

The world record for a nonstop flight was made by the Soviet flyer Chkalov [1937] . . . and later by Gromov (10,148 kilometers, in 1937), in flights from Moscow to North America over the North Pole in a Tupolev ANT-25.[80]

The early experimental flights—with the exception of the transpolar attempt by Levanevski, who was lost and never heard from again—have long been acclaimed in the Soviet Union as outstanding performances. The fliers did in fact display considerable skill, in view of the limited exploratory work that had previously been done in the central Arctic Basin, the inadequate meteorologic and other data on the Arctic, and the low technical level of Soviet aviation. The Soviet pilot Akkuratov, describing his 1936 flight to Franz Josef Land without precision instruments, wrote: "It was the first flight there, with no exact maps of the route."[81]

After World War II the level of Soviet aviation was much higher than before the war. In addition to its own progress, Soviet technology was advanced by American Lend-Lease equipment. Furthermore, after the war the Soviet Union had at its disposal German experience and technique.

The pilot of a 1945 Arctic flight declared:

> Two years ago this time of the year was not considered a season for flying. Now our technique has advanced so much, and people have acquired such experience that flights to the Arctic are possible in any weather.[82]

Akkuratov, comparing his postwar Arctic flight with his earlier ones and commenting particularly on the reliable radio communication with Moscow, boasted: "I am provided with many marvelous instruments which make it possible to pilot a plane under any conditions."[83] A postwar textbook for transport institutes declares:

> The Soviet Union has achieved extraordinary success in the field of air transportation and possesses the best aviation technique in the world, first-rate planes and highly qualified personnel, who have enriched their experience during the Great Patriotic War.[84]

Reports on postwar polar flights indicated Soviet interest in obtaining data that would be indispensable for purposes of transpolar bombing. Upon returning from a Moscow-

Chukotsk flight, the pilot Akkuratov, formerly member of a "squadron of long-range heavy bombers that had flown behind the fascist lines," was called to the polar aviation division of Glavsevmorput' to discuss a "more responsible task." The director of polar aviation, Major General Mazuruk, informed him:

> It is necessary to make deeper reconnaissance for our scientists, to visit the North Pole and observe the white spot [section of a map left blank for lack of data]. A complicated flight. Start from Moscow in twelve days.[85]

For a time, the study of the Arctic Ocean and the central polar regions did not seem to be keeping pace with the development of Soviet polar aviation. As was mentioned before, the data collected in the thirties by the drift-ice station North Pole 1 had not yet been fully processed after the war. With the sending out of three new drift-ice stations by mid-1954 and another in 1955, however, it became apparent that Soviet research on the central polar regions was being intensified. In spelling out the significance of these studies, Soviet commentators dwell on their value to the Northern Sea Route, to weather forecasting and other conceivably peaceful objectives.[86] The strategic value of research on the central polar regions, through which air routes to the United States can be laid out, is the unvoiced implication.

6. Summary

Officially enunciated Soviet policy in regard to the Arctic rests upon economic, scientific and cultural considerations. It is true that the region has relatively untapped natural resources, is a vantage ground for meteorologic research and is inhabited by a native population slow to accept sovietization.[87] The main incentives to Soviet activity in the Arctic, however, have been strategic. When, with the scientific and technological achievements of the twentieth century, especially in aviation, the frozen North became easily accessible even to other powers, the Soviet government took measures to assure itself of effective control over the expanses of its northern coast and the waters, islands and air spaces of the Arctic Ocean. The key to the attainment of this goal was at first considered to be the transformation of the Northern Sea Route into a normally functioning seaway between service areas able to provide sufficient freight to make the equipment and operation of the Route economically feasible.

Export-import traffic between Siberia and Western Europe would have provided ample freight, but Soviet policy halted imports into Siberia as well as the export of Siberian agricultural products and failed to expand the northern lumber trade to the point where it alone could serve as a sound economic basis for the Route. Thus the Route was deprived of its original service areas—southwestern Siberia and the central European countries and England—and not compensated by the opportunity to develop other commercial uses such as transporting agricultural products from southwestern Siberia to the northern European U.S.S.R.

Instead, the Northern Sea Route was assigned the role of establishing economic connections between the Arctic coast and islands and the European U.S.S.R. as well as the Soviet Far East. Traffic on the Route was thereby limited to shipments of food and manufactures to the Arctic and of raw materials and semi-finished goods from the Arctic, and to miscellaneous coasting trade.

The Northern Sea Route has failed to hold even the less advantageous service areas left to it. Its functions as a supply lane for the extreme North have been pre-empted by the great Siberian rivers carrying supplies from the south. As for the projected shipments from the extreme North, not only has exploitation of the natural resources of the region lagged behind expectations and potentialities, but in the main its products move south via the rivers, or, in some cases, are transported by plane.

In view of the limited economic usefulness of the Northern Sea Route, the advisability of further capital investments became questionable. The whole problem of what criteria should be used in making investment decisions is under dispute in the Soviet Union: the main goal is to "assure the independence of the U.S.S.R. and the absolute predominance of the socialist economic system," but there is a parallel desire to base decisions on what is in effect the rate of return on capital investments.[88] In branches of the economy such as transportation, more weight is given to the non-economic criteria,[89] and what really impels the Soviet government to allocate funds—limited though they may be—from the state budget to the Northern Sea Route is the latter's strategic value. Since, however, the resources of the Soviet Union are limited and there are many other projects which are equally important in "assuring the independence of the U.S.S.R.," the severance of service areas from the Northern Sea Route must necessarily militate against its optimum development.

NOTES

[1] Imports from abroad could also have helped to meet these needs, but this was prohibited by the Soviet Government beginning with the Second Five-Year Plan.

[2] "Amuro-Yakutskaya Magistral' (AYaM)" [The Amur-Yakutsk Highway (AYaM)] *Bol'shaya Sovetskaya entsiklopediya* [Large Soviet Encyclopediya], 2d ed., Moscow, Vol. II, 1950, p. 308. The total length of the road is 1,177 kilometers (*ibid.*).

[3] *Kursy politupravleniya dlya komandnovo sostava Glavsevmorputi: ekonomgeografiya Krainevo Severa* [Courses in Political Administration for Executive Personnel of Glavsevmorput': Economic Geography of the Extreme North], Leningrad-Moscow, Glavsevmorput', 1940, p. 35.

[4] Margolin, A., "Puti zavoza gruzov na krainyi Sever" [Freight Routes to the Extreme North], *Sovetskaya Arktika* [Soviet Arctic], Moscow, No. 6, 1939, pp. 35-36. For other details on the theoretical advantages of the Route, see pp. 14-15.

[5] For example, the Taimyr and Evenki National Okrugs are in Krasnoyarsk Krai, the Chukotsk and Koryak National Okrugs are part of Khabarovsk Krai, and the Yamal-Nenets and Khanty-Mansi National Okrugs are part of Tyumen' Oblast.

[6] Molodykh's cost analyses are in the archives of Komseverput'. For a published study on these lines, see Molodykh, I. F., *Puti svyazi i snabzheniya Kolymsko-Indigirskovo kraya* [Communications and Supply Routes of the Kolyma-Indigirka Region], Irkutsk, 1931.

[7] In a conference in the Economics and Law Branch of the U.S.S.R. Academy of Sciences in October 1949, V. F. Vasyutin, a prominent economic geographer and Gosplan official, warned against "overevaluating the role of the geographical milieu in the development of the productive forces of society," and demanded instead that economic geographers take as a point of departure the "decisive role of the policy of the Party and government in matters of economic development." In the same report Vasyutin complained of the lack of studies on the place and role of individual regions in the national economy. "O koordinatsii nauchnoi raboty v oblasti ekonomiki" [On the Coordination of Research in the Field of Economics], *Voprosy ekonomiki* [Problems of Economics], Moscow, No. 1, 1950, p. 96. Vasyutin was not in a position to say that the need to discount facts and to conform to government policy was probably one of the major causes for the lack of studies of which he complained.

[8] Baranski, N. N., *Ekonomicheskaya geografiya SSSR* [Economic Geography of the U.S.S.R.], 14th ed., Moscow, Uchpedgiz, 1953, pp. 91-92; see also *ibid.*, 10th ed., 1949, p. 244.

[9] Balzak, S. S., *et al.*, eds., *Economic Geography of the U.S.S.R.*, trans. by Robert M. Hankin and Olga A. Titelbaum, New York, Macmillan, 1949, pp. 439, 488, 492-493. A feature article in the Soviet press in 1954 gave the credit to the Northern Sea Route for "supplying the northern fringes of Siberia and shipping out local production from these areas." Gordiyenko, P., "Pokoreniye vysokikh shirot" [The Conquest of the High Latitudes], *Krasnaya zvezda* [Red Star], Moscow, May 18, 1954.

[10] On the need for southern supply for Kolyma, see Margolin, A., "Puti zavoza gruzov na Krainyi Sever," *op. cit.*, p. 41. A photograph of trucks and trailers hauling freight on the Kolyma road can be found in the ninth edition of Baranski's text (Moscow, 1948, p. 264). This photograph was deleted in subsequent editions, as was the reference to gold mining in Kolyma on the preceding page.

[11] Data from the Planning Department of the Krasnoyarsk Krai Executive Committee.

[12] See p. 162.

[13] "Yeniseiskoye rechnoye parokhodstvo" [Yenisei River Shipping Administration], *Bol'shaya Sovetskaya entsiklopediya*, 2d ed., Vol. XV, 1952, p. 516. The timber shipments constitute 65-70 per cent of the cargo turnover; the remainder consists mostly of shipments of grain, coal, oil products and building materials; "Yenisei," *ibid.*, p. 514. Not all these shipments are made to or from the extreme North. The coal

movements, for example, refer to shipments from Minusinsk to Krasnoyarsk and Yeniseisk. From the first article cited in this note (p. 516) it is evident that perishable products for the North (such as meat and butter) come from the south.

[14] "Lenskoye rechnoye parokhodstvo" [Lena River Shipping Administration], *ibid.*, Vol. XXIV, 1953, p. 559.

[15] "Po Severnomu morskomu puti" [Along the Northern Sea Route], *Izvestiya*, September 1, 1954.

[16] "Lena," *Bol'shaya Sovetskaya entsiklopediya*, 2d ed., Vol. XXIV, 1953, p. 487. For press reports evidencing the movement of supplies from the south, see "Na rekakh Sibiri" [On the Rivers of Siberia], *Pravda*, May 21, 1950; "Navigatsiya na Yenisei" [Navigation on the Yenisei], *Izvestiya*, August 7, 1949; "Na rekakh Vostochnoi Sibiri" [On the Rivers of Eastern Siberia], *Izvestiya*, May 26, 1951; Vernikovski, N., "Neporyadki v Lenskom rechnom parokhodstve" [Disorders in the Lena River Shipping Administration], *Izvestiya*, September 13, 1952.

[17] ". . . The rich fur, taiga and tundra zones of the Olenyok and Yana owe their development to a considerable extent to the self-sacrificing work of the river workers of the Lena River Basin." Serzhantov, N., "Na rechnykh putyakh strany: Ot Yakutska do Ust'-Kuta" [On the River Routes of the Country: From Yakutsk to Ust'-Kut], *Izvestiya*, October 13, 1954.

[18] "Karskaya ekspeditsiya" [The Kara Run], *Sibirskaya Sovetskaya entsiklopediya* [Siberian Soviet Encyclopedia], Novosibirsk, Vol. II, 1931, pp. 548-49.

[19] A resolution of the Eighteenth Party Congress in March 1939 ordered that shipments of lumber from Siberia to the European U.S.S.R. were to be discontinued. *XVIII S"yezd Vsesoyuznoi Kommunisticheskoi Partii (b) 10-21 marta 1939 g.; stenograficheskii otchot* [Eighteenth Congress of the All-Union Communist Party (Bolsheviks), March 10-21, 1939: Stenographic Report], Moscow-Leningrad, OGIZ, 1939, p. 663. The resolution referred only to shipments from areas such as the southern part of the Ob' and Yenisei Basins, not to lumber shipments via the Northern Sea Route, which were not being sent to the European U.S.S.R. at that time. In the twenties intermittent shipments went from Igarka to the Murmansk area, merely as a stop-gap measure before the development of the lumber industry in Karelia, which has abundant timber resources. The Party resolution is of interest here in that it underscores the prewar policy of allocating Siberian lumber to Siberian needs.

[20] According to Glavsevmorput' data, Igarka lumber exports averaged 100,000 tons or slightly more per year in the late thirties.

[21] Calculated from the figures for lumber export through the Kara Sea given in "The Kara Sea Route," *The Polar Record*, Cambridge, Scott Polar Research Institute, Vol. VI, No. 46, July, 1953, pp. 826-29.

[22] *Ibid.*

[23] Evidently the usual level of Kara Sea lumber exports was main-

tained in 1940. Shipments leaving the Arctic in that year totaled 80,-600 tons, which is not far below the annual average (see Table II).

²⁴ Calculated from figures in "The Kara Sea Route," *op. cit.*

²⁵ See for example "K Sovetsko-Niderlandskim torgovym otnosheni-yam" [Soviet-Netherlands Trade Relations], *Pravda*, April 29, 1954; "K Sovetsko-Vengerskim torgovym otnosheniyam" [Soviet-Hungarian Trade Relations], *Izvestiya*, April 8, 1954; "K Sovetsko-Livanskim torgovym otnosheniyam" [Soviet-Lebanese Trade Relations], *Izvestiya*, May 1, 1954.

²⁶ Data from Glavsevmorput'.

²⁷ *Ibid*. See also *Kursy politupravleniya*, p. 22.

²⁸ Data from the Department of the North, R.S.F.S.R. Gosplan.

²⁹ Lutski, S. L., *Geograficheskiye ocherki russkoi taigi* [Geographic Sketches of the Russian Taiga], Moscow, Geografgiz, 1947, pp. 150-51.

³⁰ Lavrov, B. V., and P. Ye Shadrin, "Ekonomika gruzooborota Sever-novo morskovo puti" [The Economics of Cargo Turnover on the Northern Sea Route], *Sovetskaya Arktika*, No. 4, 1936, pp. 11-12.

³¹ *Byulleten' Arkticheskovo instituta* [Bulletin of the Arctic Institute], Leningrad, No. 9, 1935, p. 291.

³² *Ibid.*, No. 10, 1935, p. 341.

³³ *Ibid.*

³⁴ *Ibid.*, No. 9, 1935, p. 291.

³⁵ Orlov, V. I., *Severnyi morskoi put' (zapadnaya chast')* [The North-ern Sea Route (Western Sector)], Moscow, 1924 *(Materialy Gosplana* [Materials of Gosplan], Vol. VII).

³⁶ "O dal'neishem uvelichenii proizvodstva zerna v strane i ob osvo-yenii tselinnykh i zalezhnykh zemel': Postanovleniye Plenuma TsK KPSS, prinyatoye 2 marta 1954 g. po dokladu tov. N. S. Krushchova" [On the Further Increase of the Production of Grain and on the Development of Virgin and Idle Lands: Resolution of the Plenum of the Central Committee of the CPSU Adopted on March 2, 1954, on the Basis of the Report of N. S. Khrushchov], *Izvestiya*, March 6, 1954.

³⁷ "Vsesoyuznoye soveshchaniye aktiva rabotnikov morskovo i rech-novo flota" [All-Union Conference of the *Aktiv* of Personnel of the Maritime and River Fleet], *Izvestiya*, March 7, 1954.

³⁸ Data for Archangel from "Arkhangel'sk," *Bol'shaya Sovetskaya ent-siklopediya*, 2d ed., Vol. III, 1950, p. 151; data for Murmansk from *Kursy politupravleniya*, p. 42.

³⁹ The entire monograph was never published, but part of it appeared in the article by Lavrov and Shadrin entitled "Ekonomika gruzoobo-rota Severnovo morskovo puti" [The Economics of Cargo Turnover on the Northern Sea Route], *Sovetskaya Arktika*, No. 4, 1936, pp. 11-24.

⁴⁰ Lavrov, who was sincerely interested in the development of an economically sound Northern Sea Route (primarily on the basis of grain exports), was constantly criticized in Glavsevmorput' for the policies

he advocated toward this end. On May 28, 1937, as a last resort, he addressed a meeting in the Moscow House of Scientists in order to enlist the support of the academic world for his position. His argument was so persuasive that the audience did not subject it to any criticism. In an article which later appeared in *Sovetskaya Arktika,* criticizing the speaker for his speech and the audience for failing to rebut him, the author was himself unable to refute Lavrov's economic thesis. The main argument was that "Lavrov is indifferent to the economic, political and military significance of the Northern Sea Route for our country." Zhdanov, N. T., "Vrednaya vylazka B. V. Lavrova v Moskovskom dome uchonykh" [Harmful Sortie by B. V. Lavrov in the Moscow House of Scientists], *Sovetskaya Arktika,* No. 9, 1937, p. 9.

[41] Lavrov and Shadrin, "Ekonomika gruzooborota Severnovo morskovo puti," *op. cit.,* p. 16.

[42] Natsarenus, S. P., "Takova li ekonomika gruzooborota?" [Are Such the Economics of Cargo Turnover?], *Sovetskaya Arktika,* No. 10, 1936, pp. 25-28.

[43] "Postanovleniye Sovnarkoma SSSR ob uluchshenii raboty Glavnovo Upravleniya Severnovo morskovo puti ot 29 avgusta 1938 g." [Decree of August 29, 1938 of the Council of People's Commissars of the U.S.S.R. on Improving the Work of Glavsevmorput'], *Pravda,* August 30, 1938. See also Lyubarskaya, R., "Arkticheskomu khozyaistvu—strogii khozrashchot" [For the Arctic Economy—Strict Cost Accounting], *Sovetskaya Arktika,* No. 7, 1939, pp. 27-30.

[44] "Severnyi morskoi put'" [The Northern Sea Route] *Bol'shaya Sovetskaya entsiklopediya,* Vol. L, 1944, col. 590.

[45] From Table IA it is evident that the cargo turnover on the Route from 1920 to 1942 totaled a little over 2,590,800 tons (computing from data in Table IB the total is 2,597,700, a discrepancy of about 6,900 tons which does not significantly alter the picture); according to data from Glavsevmorput', cargo turnover from 1920 to 1940 totaled 2,145,700 tons (see Table II). If the plans for cargo turnover on the Route for 1941 (240,400 tons) were carried out by at least 65 per cent, the cargo turnover in 1942 would not have reached 300,000 tons. Although it has not been possible to provide precise and reliable data for each individual year between 1933-1938, the author can attest from his contacts with Glavsevmorput' that in no year during this period did the annual cargo turnover on the Route reach 300,000 tons. The method of deducing annual cargo turnover from scattered sources has been discarded not only because inaccuracies inevitably result therefrom but also because the reliable data already at hand are adequate for an interpretation of the economic value of the Northern Sea Route. For references to various other Soviet articles and statements on cargo turnover, see Armstrong, Terence, *The Northern Sea Route: Soviet Exploitation of the North East Passage,* Cambridge, Cambridge University Press, 1952, Appendixes I-IV (Scott Polar Research Institute, Special Publication No. 1).

[46] This figure is also supported by the statement that "cargo turnover on the Northern Sea Route in 1939 totaled 127,700 tons (excluding

the shipments of lumber from Igarka over the Kara Sea)." *Kursy pol. itupravleniya*, p. 35.

[47] *Gosudarstvennyi plan razvitiya narodnovo khozyaistva SSSR na 1941 god* [State Plan for the Development of the National Economy of the U.S.S.R. for 1941], Photo-Lithoprint by Universal Lithographers, Baltimore, Md., Supplement No. 116, p. 465 (American Council of Learned Societies Reprints: Russian Series No. 30). The 88,700 tons to be shipped to the Arctic in 1941 were assigned to the following organizations in the proportions indicated: Glavsevmorput', 31,500 tons; Dal'stroi (Far Eastern Development Project), 22,500 tons; Union of Yakut Cooperatives "Kholbos," 2,400 tons; Narkompishcheprom (People's Commissariat of the Food Industry), 5,500 tons; Glavnikeleolovo (Main Administration for the Nickel and Tin Industries), 10,000 tons; Narkomtorg RSFSR (People's Commissariat of Trade of the R.S.F.S.R.), 16,800 tons. *Ibid.*, Supplement No. 118, p. 467. The 10,000 tons to be shipped by Glavnikeleolovo probably were destined for a tin mining combine at Verkhoyansk, which was under construction in 1940. *Kursy politupravleniya*, p. 37.

[48] The shipping between ports (3,400 tons) probably refers to shipping between ports of different seas, and the local coastal shipping (71,000 tons) to coastal shipping within the confines of one sea.

[49] Data from Glavsevmorput'.

[50] This situation was expressed as follows in the Soviet literature: "A general defect in the work of river transportation in the extreme North is the inadequate amount of return cargo. Cargo goes mainly in one direction." *Kursy politupravleniya*, p. 37.

[51] The planned figures for river shipping are available in the 1941 plan, but they include a large volume of freight shipments originating and terminating in the southern areas, thus making it impossible to compare the role of the Yenisei and Ob' with that of the Northern Sea Route in supplying the northern regions of these river basins.

[52] Data from Glavsevmorput', 1939. Apart from the economic unsoundness of this practice, a "light" vessel has greater difficulty proceeding through Arctic waters. Since she rides too high, her propeller leaves the water. She loses speed and incurs the constant risk of damage from ice.

[53] Data from Glavsevmorput'. See also Molodetski, K. G., "Voprosy ekonomiki eksploatatsii Severnovo morskovo puti" [Problems of the Economics of the Exploitation of the Northern Sea Route], *Sovetskii Sever* [Soviet North], Leningrad, No. 3, 1939, pp. 3-17.

[54] Sibirtsev, N., and V. Itin, *Severnyi morskoi put' i Karskiye ekspeditsii* [The Northern Sea Route and the Kara Runs], Novosibirsk, Zapadno-Sibirskoye krayevoye izd-vo, 1936, p. 72.

[55] *Ibid.*, pp. 100-1.

[56] Data from Glavsevmorput'. Lavrov, in his 1937 speech in the House of Scientists, declared that the further enlargement of the icebreaker fleet was inexpedient; see Zhdanov, N. T., "Vrednaya vylazka B. V. Lavrova," *op. cit.* This statement was prompted by the unfavorable cargo turnover situation in relation to icebreaker costs. Symptomatic

of this difficulty were the suggestions by some Glavsevmorput' officials that all icebreaker and aviation expenditures be transferred to the state budget. Stepanov, N., "Tarify Severnovo morskovo puti" [Freight Charges on the Northern Sea Route], *Sovetskaya Arktika,* No. 10, 1939, p. 26.

⁵⁷ Papanin, V., "Vo l'dakh Arktiki" [On the Ice of the Arctic], *Pravda,* December 3, 1945.

⁵⁸ See "Na arkticheskikh liniyakh" [On the Arctic Lines], *Izvestiya,* August 24, 1947; "V portu Tiksi" [In the Port of Tiksi], *ibid.,* August 28, 1947; "Pervye parokhody v zapolyarnom portu" [The First Ships in a Polar Port], *Pravda,* July 3, 1953; "Poslednyi reis na Novuyu Zemlyu" [The Last Trip to Novaya Zemlya], *ibid.,* October 3, 1953. In 1954, however, the formula on the yearly increase in cargo turnover was reiterated. See Gordiyenko, *op. cit.*

⁵⁹ Pinkhenson, D. M., "Istoricheskiye etapy zavoyevaniya Severnovo morskovo puti" [Historical Stages in the Conquest of the Northern Sea Route], *Izvestiya Vsesoyuznovo geograficheskovo obshchestva* [News of the All-Union Geographical Society], Moscow-Leningrad, Vol. LXXXII, fasc. 4, July/August 1950, pp. 410-11.

⁶⁰ Papanin, V., "Vo l'dakh Arktiki," *op. cit.*

⁶¹ This computation is based on a cargo turnover of 197,600 tons for 1940.

⁶² Shashkov, Z., "Uluchshit' ispol'zovaniye morskovo i rechnovo flota" [Make Better Use of the Maritime and River Fleet], *Pravda,* June 22, 1954.

⁶³ In the 1941 Plan, shipping for the Route was set at 240,400 tons (see Table II) and in the Far Eastern Basin at 1,910,000 tons. *Gosudarstvennyi plan razvitiya narodnovo khozyaistva SSSR na 1941 god,* Supplement No. 113, p. 464.

⁶⁴ See Novikov, V. D., "K istorii osvoyeniya Severnovo morskovo puti v pervye gody sovetskoi vlasti" [On the History of the Conquest of the Northern Sea Route in the Early Years of the Soviet Power], *Letopis' Severa* [Chronicle of the North], Moscow-Leningrad, Glavsevmorput', No. 1, 1949, pp. 3-41.

⁶⁵ Archives of Komseverput'. *Obzor severnykh morskikh plavanii za 1917-27: Materialy k sostavleniyu pervovo pyatiletnevo plana* [Review of Northern Sea Navigation During 1917-27: Materials for the Drawing Up of the First Five-Year Plan], pp. 9-10.

⁶⁶ For details on the "Komet" and its voyage see Thorwald, Juergen, "Das Gespensterschiff im Pazifik," *Revue- die Weltillustrierte,* Munich, No. 33, August 19, 1950, p. 18.

⁶⁷ Webster, C. J., "The Economic Development of the Soviet Arctic and Sub-Arctic," *The Slavonic and Eastern European Review,* London, Vol. XXIX, No. 72, December 1950, p. 207.

⁶⁸ Former sailors of the northern fleet now in the West state that many of the vessels coming from the Kara Sea carried only coal as their cargo. They also testify that Noril'sk coal was much superior to the Pechora coal of that time.

⁶⁹ Zubov, N. N., *V tsentre Arktiki: Ocherki po istorii issledovaniya i*

Role of the Northern Sea Route

fizicheskoi geografi tsentral'noi Arktiki [In the Center of the Arctic: Notes on the History of Exploration and Physical Geography of the Central Arctic], Moscow-Leningrad, Glavsevmorput', 1948, p. 133.

[70] Armstrong, T., *op. cit.,* Appendix V.

[71] Zubov, *op. cit.,* p. 133.

[72] *XVIII S"yezd Vsesoyuznoi Kommunisticheskoi Partii (b) 10-21 marta 1939 g.: Stenograficheskii otchot* [Eighteenth Congress of the All-Union Communist Party (Bolsheviks), March 10-21, 1939: Stenographic Report], Moscow-Leningrad, OGIZ, 1939, p. 330.

[73] For further details on the canal, see *Malaya Sovetskaya entsiklopediya* [Small Soviet Encyclopedia], 2d ed., Moscow, Vol. I, 1933, col. 802.

[74] The fifteenth anniversary of the Polyarnoye base was celebrated in 1948. "Leningrad, 22 iyulya, 1948 g." [Leningrad, July 22, 1948], *Izvestiya,* July 23, 1948. The other naval bases are at Kronstadt, Sevastopol', and Vladivostok.

[75] "The Stalin White Sea—Baltic Canal," *Soviet Calendar: Thirty Years of the Soviet State,* Moscow, Foreign Languages Publishing House, 1947, Section "August 2."

[76] Author's evaluation of materials on file in the Karelian A.S.S.R. Planning Commission and the Leningrad Oblast Planning Commission in 1938. From a postwar report it is evident that the prerequisites for full commercial use of the canal have not been met: the necessary water approach routes to the canal have still not been adequately developed. Koldomasov, Yu., "Kompleksnoye razvitiye i ispol'zovaniye razlichnykh vidov transporta" [Balanced Development and Use of Various Types of Transport], *Planovoye khozyaistvo* [Planned Economy], Moscow, No. 4, 1954, p. 69.

[77] Voznesenski, N., *Voyennaya ekonomika SSSR v period otechestvennoi voiny* [The War Economy of the U.S.S.R. in the Period of the Patriotic War], Moscow, OGIZ, 1948, p. 52.

[78] *Zakon o pyatiletnem plane vosstanovleniya i razvitiya narodnovo khozyaistva SSSR na 1946-1950 g.g.* [Law on the Five-Year Plan for the Reconstruction and Development of the National Economy of the U.S.S.R. for 1946-1950], Moscow, OGIZ, 1946, p. 6.

[79] *Sovetskaya Arktika: Obzor nauchno-issledovatel'skoi raboty Vsesoyuznovo arkticheskovo instituta v Sovetskom sektore Arktiki* [The Soviet Arctic: A Survey of the Scientific Research of the All-Union Arctic Institute in the Soviet Sector of the Arctic], Leningrad, Vsesoyuznyi Arkticheskii Institut, 1934, p. 11.

[80] "Aviatsionnye recordy" [Aviation Records], *Bol'shaya Sovetskaya entsiklopediya,* 2d ed., Vol. I, 1949, p. 82.

[81] Akkuratov, V., *Pokoryonnaya Arktika* [The Conquered Arctic], Moscow, Molodaya Gvardiya, 1948, p. 7.

[82] "Arkticheski reis M. Kozlova" [The Arctic Flight of M. Kozlov], *Sovetskaya Sibir'* [Soviet Siberia], Novosibirsk, October 24, 1945.

[83] Akkuratov, *op. cit.,* p. 121.

[84] Obraztsov, V. N., and F. I. Shaul'ski, *Vodnyi, vozdushnyi, avtodo-*

The Northern Sea Route

rozhnyi gorodskoi i promyshlennyi transport [Municipal and Industrial Transport by Water, Air and Highway], Moscow, Transzheldorizdat, 1948, p. 18.

[85] Akkuratov, *op. cit.,* pp. 116-17.

[86] See for example Shcherbakov, D. I., "V serdtse Arktiki" [In the Heart of the Arctic], *Nauka i zhizn'* [Science and Life], Moscow, No. 9, September 1954, p. 30.

[87] Up to 1940 the Soviet efforts to transform the northern native population culturally and politically and to draw them into industrial work and kolkhozes brought only minor results. See Krypton, Constantine, "Soviet Policy in the Northern National Regions After World War II," *American Slavic and East European Review,* New York, Vol. XIII, No. 3, October 1954, pp. 343, 346.

[88] See Krylov, P., "Protiv burzhuaznoi metodologii v voprosakh ekonomiki transporta" [Against Bourgeois Methodology in the Economics of Transportation], *Planovoye khozyaistvo,* No. 4, July-August 1949, p. 87.

[89] *Ibid.,* pp. 85-91, *passim.* For an attempt, criticized by Krylov, to establish a quantitative rate of return for capital investments in railway transport, see Lur'ye, A., "Metody sopostavleniya eksploatatsionnykh raskhodov i kapitalovlozhenii pri ekonomicheskoi otsenke tekhnicheskikh meropriyatii" [Methods of Comparing Operating Expenditures and Capital Investments in the Economic Appraisal of Technical Measures], *Voprosy ekonomiki zheleznodorozhnovo transporta* [Problems of the Economics of Railroad Transportation], ed. by Ye. D. Khanukov and V. I. Chernyshev, Moscow, Transzheldorizdat, 1948. The result of the preponderance of non-economic criteria in making Soviet capital investments is that "an objective method of evaluating the effectiveness of capital investments has not been worked out to this day." Chilikin, M., "Ukreplat' yedinstvo uchebnoi i nauchnoi raboty v vysshei shkole" [Classroom Work and Research Must be More Closely Unified in the Higher School], *Pravda,* December 18, 1953.

BIBLIOGRAPHY

The bibliography contains works cited in the text. An extensive list of other books and articles on the Soviet Arctic may be found in the comprehensive *Arctic Bibliography: Prepared For and in Cooperation With the Department of Defense Under the Direction of the Arctic Institute of North America,* Washington, U.S. Government Printing Office, Vol. I-V, 1953-1955. Use has also been made of unpublished information obtained from the following organizations at various times between 1931 and 1941:

Komseverput';

Glavsevmorput' and its various subdivisions (Planning Department, Maritime Department, Arctic Institute, and Institute for the Economy of the North);

The Scientific Research Association of the Institute for the Peoples of the North in Leningrad;

Archives of the Committee of the North;

Department of the North, R.S.F.S.R. Gosplan;

Planning and Economic Department of Aeroflot in Moscow;

Igarka City Soviet;

Igarka Port Administration;

Planning Department, Krasnoyarsk Krai Executive Committee;

Taimyr Okrug Executive Committee;

Yenisei River Shipping Administration.

Abbreviations used in the bibliography are as follows:

BSE—Bol'shaya Sovetskaya entsiklopediya [Large Soviet Encyclopedia], Moscow.

BSE: SSSR—Bol'shaya Sovetskaya entsiklopediya: SSSR [Large Soviet Encyclopedia: The U.S.S.R.], Moscow, OGIZ [Associated State Publishing Houses], 1947.

MSE—Malaya Sovetskaya entsiklopediya [Small Soviet Encyclopedia], Moscow.

Ned. Ark.—Nedra Arktiki [Mineral Resources of the Arctic], Moscow-Leningrad.

Plan. khoz.—Planovoye khozyaistvo [Planned Economy], Moscow.

Prob. Ark.—Problemy Arktiki [Problems of the Arctic], Leningrad

Sib. SE—Sibirskaya Sovetskaya entsiklopediya [Siberian Soviet Encyclopedia], Novosibirsk.

BIBLIOGRAPHY

Sov. Ark.—Sovetskaya Arktika [Soviet Arctic], Moscow.
Sov. Sev.—Sovetskii Sever [Soviet North], Moscow.

"Agitsamolyoty v Zapolar'ye" [Propaganda Airplanes in the Polar Regions], *Izvestiya,* January 29, 1950.
Akkuratov, V., *Pokoryonnaya Arktika* [The Conquered Arctic], Moscow, Molodaya Gvardiya [Young Guard], 1948.
Aktivist O. A. Kh., "Imperializm na polyarnom Severe i interesy SSSR" [Imperialism in the Polar North and the Interests of the U.S.S.R.], *Sov. Sev.,* No. 1-2, 1932.
Aleksandrov, A., "Nasushchnye zadachi mestnoi promyshlennosti i promyslovoi kooperatsii" [Urgent Tasks of Local Industry and Producers' Cooperatives], *Pravda,* November 21, 1953.
"Alyaska v planakh amerikanskikh agressorov" [Alaska in the Plans of the American Aggressors], *Izvestiya,* September 8, 1950.
"Amderma," *BSE,* 2d ed., Vol. II, 1950.
Amerikanskii Sever [The American North], Moscow, Izdatel'stvo inostrannoi literatury [Publishing House of Foreign Literature], 1950.
"Amuro-Yakutskaya Magistral' (AYaM)" [The Amur-Yakutsk Highway (AYaM)], *BSE,* 2d ed., Vol. II, 1950.
"Anadyr'," *BSE,* 2d ed., Vol. II, 1950.
Anan'yev, P. M., "Nordvikskaya sol' real'na" [Nordvik Salt is Real], *Sov. Ark.,* No. 4, 1936.
Anikeyev, N. P., and A. I. Gusev, *Geologicheskii ocherk yugo-zapadnoi chasti Taimyrskovo poluostrova* [Geologic Outline of the Southwestern Part of the Taimyr Peninsula], 1939 (*Trudy ANII* [Works of the Arctic Scientific Research Institute], Vol. CXL).
Anikeyev, N. P., and G. G. Moor, "Sushchestvuyet li Taimyrskii shariazh?" [Is There a Taimyr Overthrust Sheet?], *Prob. Ark.,* No. 4, 1939.
Annin, N., and K. Yevtyukhov, "Vazhneisheye zveno v podgotovke k navigatsii 1940 goda: O sudoremonte" [The Most Important Part of the Preparations for the 1940 Navigation Season: Concerning Ship Repair], *Sov. Ark.,* No. 11, 1939.
Anvel't, Ya. Ya., *et al.,* eds., *Vozdushnye puti Severa* [Air Routes of the North], Moscow, Sovetskaya Aziya [Soviet Asia], 1933.
"Apel'siny zhitelyam zapolyar'ya" [Oranges for Polar Residents], *Pravda,* January 10, 1950.
Archives of Glavsevmorput'. "O moshchnom istochnike energii v Arktike" [On an Abundant Source of Power in the Arctic], 1936.
Archives of Komseverput'. *Obzor severnykh plavanii za 1917-27: Materialy k sostavleniyu pervovo pyatiletnevo plana* [Review of

BIBLIOGRAPHY

Northern Sea Navigation During 1917-27: Materials for the Drawing Up of the First Five-Year Plan].

———, *Plan Komseverputi na 1932 god* [Plan of Komseverput' for 1932].

———, *Spravka ob uzakoneniyakh i rasporyazheniyakh sovetskovo pravitel'stva po voprosu morskikh plavanii vdol' sibirskikh beregov 1917-1927* [Memoranda on Laws and Ordinances of the Soviet Government Concerning Navigation Along the Siberian Coasts, 1917-1927].

Archives of the Committee for Assistance to the Nationalities of the Northern Borderlands. *Klassovaya bor'ba na Chukotskom poluostrove* [The Class Struggle on the Chukotsk Peninsula], Official Memorandum, File for 1929.

———, *Snabzheniye severnovo promyslovovo naseleniya posle grazhdanskoi voiny* [Supplying the Northern Trading Population After the Civil War], Official Memorandum, File for 1927.

"Arkhangel'sk," *BSE,* 2d ed., Vol. III, 1950.

"Arkticheskii reis M. Kozlova" [The Arctic Flight of M. Kozlov], *Sovetskaya Sibir'* [Soviet Siberia], Novosibirsk, October 24, 1945.

"Arktika" [The Arctic], *BSE,* 2d ed., Vol. III, 1950.

———, *Kratkaya Sovetskaya entsiklopediya* [Short Soviet Encyclopedia], Moscow, OGIZ [Associated State Publishing Houses], 1943.

Armstrong, Terence, *The Northern Sea Route: Soviet Exploitation of the North East Passage,* Cambridge, Cambridge University Press, 1952 (Scott Polar Research Institute, Special Publication No. 1).

Assberg, F. F., and E. T. Krenkel', *Dirizhabl' v Arktike* [The Dirigible in the Arctic], Moscow-Leningrad, Gosmashmetizdat, 1933.

"Aviatsionnye rekordy" [Aviation Records], *BSE,* 2d ed., Vol. I, 1949.

"Aviatsiya" [Aviation], *BSE,* 2d ed., Vol. I, 1949.

"Aziya" [Asia], *BSE,* 2d ed., Vol. I, 1949.

Badigin, K. S., *Tri zimovki vo l'dakh Arktiki* [Three Winters in the Arctic Ice], Moscow, Molodaya Gvardiya [Young Guard], 1950.

Baidakov, B., "Novosibirsk," *Pravda,* December 13, 1954.

Balzak, S. S., *et al.,* eds., *Economic Geography of the U.S.S.R.,* trans. by Robert M. Hankin and Olga A. Titelbaum, New York, Macmillan, 1949.

Baranski, N. N., *Ekonomicheskaya geografiya SSSR* [Economic Geography of the U.S.S.R.], Moscow, Uchpedgiz [State Educational and Pedagogical Publishing House], 1936; 9th ed., Moscow, 1948; 12th ed., Moscow, 1951; 14th ed., Moscow, 1953.

———, "Ob izuchenii raionov Sibiri" [On the Study of the Districts of Siberia], *Geografiya v shkole* [Geography in School], Moscow, No. 5, 1952.

BIBLIOGRAPHY

——, and B. Kaminski, *Sotsialisticheskaya rekonstruktsiya oblastei, krayov i respublik SSSR v postanovleniyakh partiinykh i sovetskikh organov* [Socialist Reconstruction of Oblasts, Krais and Republics of the U.S.S.R. in Decrees of Party and Soviet Organs], Moscow, Sotsekgiz [State Publishing House of Social Sciences and Economics], 1932.

"Barentsburg," *BSE*, 2d ed., Vol. IV, 1950.

Baschin, O., "Die Arktiksfahrt des Luftschiffes 'Graf Zeppelin,'" *Naturwissenschaften*, Berlin, Vol. XX, No. 1, 1932.

"Beringovo more" [The Bering Sea], *BSE*, 2d ed., Vol. V, 1950.

Bernshtein-Kogan, S. V., *Ocherki geografii transporta* [Outlines of the Geography of Transport], Moscow-Leningrad, Gosizdat [State Publishing House], 1930.

Berzilov, N., "V storone ot nuzhd predpriyatii" [Apart from the Needs of Enterprises], *Pravda*, March 21, 1951.

Berzin, A. I., "Geologicheskoye issledovaniye neftenosnovo mestorozhdeniya Nordvik v 1934-35 godu" [Geologic Exploration of the Nordvik Oil Deposits During 1934-35], *Geologicheskiye issledovaniya Nordvik-Khatangskovo raiona i Taimyrskovo poluostrova* [Geologic Explorations in the Nordvik-Khatanga Area and the Taimyr Peninsula], 1939.

"Beseda tov. N. S. Khrushchova s angliiskim uchonym i obshchestvennym deyatelem Dzhonom Bernalom" [Conversation of N. S. Khrushchov with the English Scientist and Public Figure John Bernal], *Pravda*, December 24, 1954.

"Bol'shoi reserv morskovo transporta" [The Great Reserve of Sea Transport], *Izvestiya*, October 4, 1951.

Bruns, Walter, "Doklad o rezul'tatakh poyezdki na Kol'skii poluostrov v Murmansk" [Report on the Results of the Expedition to Murmansk on the Kola Peninsula], *Trudy vtoroi polyarnoi konferentsii 18-23 iyunya 1928 g.* [Transactions of the Second Polar Conference of June 18-23, 1928], Leningrad, Aeroarktik, 1930.

Bubleinikov, F., "Grafit v SSSR" [Graphite in the U.S.S.R.], *Gornyi zhurnal* [Mining Journal], Moscow, No. 1, 1926.

Buinitski, V. Kh., *812 dnei v dreifuyushchikh l'dakh* [812 Days on Drifting Ice], Moscow, Glavsevmorput', 1945.

Burkhanov, V., "Novye issledovaniya sovetskikh uchonykh v Arktike" [New Research of Soviet Scientists in the Arctic], *Pravda*, May 16, 1954.

Butuzov, S. M., "Krasnoyarskii krai," *BSE*, 2d ed., Vol. XXIII, 1953.

Buyalov, N. I., "Poiski nefti v Nordik-Khatangskom raione" [Prospecting for Oil in the Nordvik-Khatanga Area], *Razvedka Nedr* [Exploration for Mineral Resources], Moscow, No. 12, 1940.

186

BIBLIOGRAPHY

Bykhover, N., and M. Rozin, "Priroda: Mineral'nye resursy" [Nature: Mineral Resources], *BSE: SSSR.*

——, "Priroda: Toplivno-energeticheskiye resursy" [Nature: Fuel and Power Resources], *BSE: SSSR.*

Byulleten' Arkticheskovo instituta [Bulletin of the Arctic Institute], Leningrad, Nos. 9, 10, 1935. [On through freight shipments over the Northern Sea Route during the 1935 navigation season.]

Chaika, Ya., "Neispol'zovannye vozmozhnosti rybnoi promyshlennosti" [Unutilized Potentials of the Fishing Industry], *Pravda,* November 22, 1954.

Chapski, K. K., *Morskiye zveri sovetskoi Arktiki* [Sea Animals of the Soviet Arctic], Moscow-Leningrad, 1941.

Cherezov, I., "Polneye ispol'zovat' rybnye bogatstva Sibiri" [Make Fuller Use of the Fish Resources of Siberia], *Izvestiya,* November 23, 1954.

Chernov, A. A., *Mineral'no-syr'yevaya baza severo-vostoka yevropeiskoi chasti SSSR: Analiz i perspektivy* [The Mineral Raw Material Base of the Northeast Part of the European U.S.S.R.: Analysis and Prospects], Moscow-Leningrad, Akademiya Nauk SSSR [U.S.S.R. Academy of Sciences], 1948.

Chilikin, M., "Ukreplat' yedinstvo uchebnoi i nauchnoi raboty v vysshei shkole" [Classroom Work and Research Must Be More Closely Unified in the Higher School], *Pravda,* December 18, 1953.

Chirkin, G. F., *Transportno-promyshlenno-kolonizatsionnyi kombinat Murmanskoi zheleznoi dorogi* [The Transport-Industrial-Colonization Combine of the Murmansk Railroad], Moscow-Leningrad, NKPS, 1928 (*Trudy gosudarstvennovo nauchno-issledovatel'skovo instituta zemleustroistva i pereseleniya* [Works of the State Scientific Research Institute for Land Use and Resettlement], Vol. IX).

Chornykh, Ye., "O novom i otstalom na lesozagotovkakh Sibiri" [About the New and the Old in Siberian Lumbering], *Izvestiya,* November 16, 1949.

Dadykin, V. P., "Problema osevereniya zemledeliya" [The Problem of Adapting Agriculture to the North], *Priroda* [Nature], Leningrad, No. 4, October 1953.

"Direktivy XIX s"yezda partii po pyatomu pyatiletnemu planu razvitiya SSSR na 1951-1955 gody" [Directives of the Nineteenth Party Congress on the Fifth Five-Year Plan for the Development of the U.S.S.R. for 1951-1955], *Izvestiya,* August 20, 1952.

"Direktivy Gosplana RSFSR po sostavleniyu perspektivnovo pyatiletnovo plana po sotsialisticheskoi rekonstruktsii i razvitiyu narodnovo khozyaistva Krainevo Severa" [Directives of the R.S.F.S.R. Gosplan on the Drawing Up of a Prospective Five-Year Plan for the Socialist Reconstruction and Development of the National Economy of the Extreme North], *Sov. Sev.*, No. 1, 1930.

"Dreifuyushchiye nauchnye stantsii na l'dakh tsentral'noi Arktiki" [Drifting Research Stations on Central Arctic Ice], *Pravda*, July 17, 1954.

"Dudinka," *BSE*, 2d ed., Vol. XV, 1952.

Durdenevski, V. N., "Problemy pravovovo rezhima pripolyarnykh oblastei" [Problems of the Legal Status of the Arctic Regions], *Vestnik Moskovskovo universiteta* [The Moscow University Herald], Moscow, No. 7, 1950.

"Elektrifikatsiya Omskoi zheleznoi dorogi" [The Electrification of the Omsk Railroad], *Pravda*, July 16, 1948.

Ellsworth, L., and F. H. Smith, "Reports of the Preliminary Results of the Aeroarctic Expedition with the 'Graf Zeppelin,' " *Geographical Review*, New York, Vol. XXII, No. 1, 1932.

Fersman, A. Ye., "Apatit, yevo mestorozhdeniya, geokhimiya, zapasy i ekonomika" [Apatite, Its Occurrence, Geochemistry, Reserves and Economics], *Khibinskiye apatity* [Khibiny Apatites], Leningrad, Vol. III, 1931.

Frieden, K. K., "Sowjetische Hoheitsansprueche im noerdlichen Eismeer," *Svenska Dagbladt*, Stockholm, August 25, 1952, reprinted in *Ost-Probleme*, Bad Godesberg, No. 37, September 13, 1952.

Frolov, V., "Novye issledovaniya v Arktike" [New Studies in the Arctic], *Izvestiya*, June 25, 1954.

Gakkel', Ya. Ya., "Oshibki v arkticheskoi navigatsii 1937 g." [Mistakes of the 1937 Navigation Season], *Sov. Ark.*, No. 3, 1938.

Galitski, A., *Planirovaniye sotsialisticheskovo transporta* [The Planning of Socialist Transport], Moscow, Gosplanizdat [Publishing House of the State Planning Commission], 1950.

Garf, A. L., and V. V. Pokshishevski, *Sever* [The North], ed. by N. N. Mikhailov, Moscow, Molodaya Gvardiya [Young Guard], 1948.

Gedroits, N. A., "Perspektivi neftenosnosti severa Sibiri" [Prospects of Oil Deposits in the North of Siberia], *Ned. Ark.*, No. 1, 1946.

——, "Ust'-Yeniseiskii port i perspektivi yevo neftenosnosti" [The Ust'-Yeniseisk Port and Its Oil Bearing Prospects], *Prob. Ark.*, No. 13, 1940.

Geograficheskii atlas SSSR [Geographical Atlas of the U.S.S.R.], Moscow, Glavnoye Upravleniye Geodezii i Kartografii MVD SSSR [Main Administration of Geodesy and Cartography of the Ministry of Internal Affairs of the U.S.S.R.], 1954.

BIBLIOGRAPHY

"Geologo-s"yomochnye raboty v Olekminskom raione" [Geologic Survey Work in the Olekma District], *Otchot Neftyanovo Instituta za 1934 god* [Report of the Oil Institute for 1934], 1936.

Gerasimov, S. K., *Patrioty Dal'nevo Vostoka* [Patriots of the Far East], Moscow, Pishchepromizdat [State Food Industry Publishing House], 1946.

Golant, V., "Polyarnaya likhoradka v Amerike" [Polar Fever in America], *Zvezda* [The Star], Leningrad, No. 11, November 1947.

Gordiyenko, P., "Pokoreniye vysokikh shirot" [The Conquest of the High Latitudes], *Krasnaya zvezda* [Red Star], Moscow, May 18, 1954.

"Gorod v Zapolar'ye" [City Above the Arctic Circle], *Sovetskii Soyuz* [The Soviet Union], Moscow, No. 2, February 1951.

Gosudarstvennyi plan razvitiya narodnovo khozyaistva SSSR na 1941 god [State Plan for the Development of the National Economy of the U.S.S.R. for 1941], Photo-Lithoprint by Universal Lithographers, Baltimore, Md. (American Council of Learned Societies Reprints: Russian Series No. 30).

"Grafit," *MSE*, 2d ed., Vol. III, 1935.

Gurvich, I. Ya., "Poslevoyennye izmeneniya v geografii lesov" [Postwar Changes in the Geography of Forests], *Izvestiya Vsesoyuznovo Geograficheskovo obshchestva* [News of the All-Union Geographic Society], Leningrad, Vol. LXXXII, No. 4, July-August, 1950.

Gusev, A. I., "Bulunskii uglenosnyi raion" [The Bulun Coal District], *Tezisy dokladov sessii Uchonovo Soveta VAI* [Theses of Reports at the Session of the Learned Council of the All-Union Arctic Institute], Moscow-Leningrad, Glavsevmorput', 1935.

——, *Bulunskii uglenosnyi raion Yakutskoi ASSR* [The Bulun Coal District of the Yakut A.S.S.R.], Leningrad, Glavsevmorput', 1936, (*Trudy ANII* [Works of the Arctic Scientific Research Institute], Vol. LIX).

Harris, C. D., "Growing Food by Decree in Soviet Russia," *Foreign Affairs*, New York, Vol. XXXIII, No. 2, January 1955.

"Indigirka," *BSE*, 2d ed., Vol. XVIII, 1953.

Internationale Studiengesellschaft zur Erforschung der Arktis mit dem Luftschiff "Aeroarktik," *Verhandlung der 1. ordentlichen Versammlung in Berlin, 9-13. November, 1926,* Supplement to *Petermans Mitteilungen*, Gotha, 1927.

"Iz Tyumeni" [From Tyumen'], *Izvestiya*, October 22, 1949.

"K Sovetsko-Livanskim torgovym otnosheniyam" [Soviet-Lebanese Trade Relations], *Izvestiya*, May 1, 1954.

BIBLIOGRAPHY

"K Sovetsko-Niderlandskim torgovym otnosheniyam" [Soviet-Netherlands Trade Relations], *Pravda*, April 29, 1954.

"K Sovetsko-Vengerskim torgovym otnosheniyam" [Soviet-Hungarian Trade Relations], *Izvestiya*, April 8, 1954.

"K voprosu o rezhime Antarktiki" [On the Problem of the Status of the Antarctic], *Sovetskoye gosudarstvo i pravo* [Soviet State and Law], Moscow, No. 3, March 1951.

"Kamchatskaya oblast'," *MSE*, 2d ed., Vol. V, 1936.

"Kamvol'no-sukonnyi kombinat v Sibiri" [Worsteds Combine in Siberia], *Pravda*, August 7, 1954.

"The Kara Sea Route," *The Polar Record*, Cambridge, Scott Polar Research Institute, Vol. VI, No. 46, July 1953.

Karavayev, A., "Narodnoye khozyaistvo: Sel'skoye khozyaistvo" [The National Economy: Agriculture], *BSE: SSSR*.

Karelin, D. B., *Ledovaya aviatsionnaya razvedka* [Air Ice Reconnaissance], Moscow, Glavsevmorput', 1946.

Karmishin, A., "O vetrodvigatelyakh" [On Wind Generators], *Izvestiya*, October 19, 1951.

"Karskaya ekspeditsiya" [The Kara Run], *Sib. SE*, Vol. II, 1931.

Kazakov, George, *Soviet Peat Resources: A Descriptive Study*, New York, Research Program on the U.S.S.R., 1953.

Khrapal', A., "K navigatsii 1940 goda gotovitsya seichas" [Preparations for the 1940 Navigation Season Are Now Being Made], *Sov. Ark.*, No. 10, 1939.

——, "Vetroenergiya v predpriyatiyakh Glavsevmorputi" [Wind Power in the Enterprises of Glavsevmorput'], *Sov. Ark.*, No. 7, 1940.

Khrenov, N. I., and M. I. Vilenski, "Novostroiki khlopchatobumazhnoi promyshlennosti" [New Construction in the Cotton Industry], *Nauka i zhizn'* [Science and Life], Moscow, No. 4, 1954.

"Kirovsk," *MSE*, 2d ed., Vol. V, 1936.

"Kirovskaya zheleznaya doroga" [The Kirov Railroad], *BSE*, 2d ed., Vol. XXI, 1953.

Klimaticheskii ocherk Karskovo morya [Climatic Outline of the Kara Sea], ed. by Ye. I. Tikhomirov, Moscow, Glavsevmorput', 1946 (*Trudy Arkticheskovo Nauchno-Issledovatel'skovo Instituta Glavnovo upravleniya Severnovo morskovo puti pri Sovete Ministrov SSSR* [Works of the Arctic Scientific Research Institute of Glavsevmorput' of the U.S.S.R. Council of Ministers], Vol. 187).

Klyuchnikov, Yu. V., and A. V. Sabanin, eds., *Mezhdunarodnaya politika noveishevo vremeni v dogovorakh, notakh i deklaratsiyakh* [Recent International Politics in Agreements, Notes and Declarations], Moscow, Narkomindel [People's Commissariat of Foreign Affairs], 1928.

Kogan, A., "Narodnoye khozyaistvo: zhivotnovodstvo" [The National Economy: Animal Breeding], *BSE: SSSR.*

Koldomasov, Yu., "Kompleksnoye razvitiye i ispol'zovaniye razlichnykh vidov transporta" [Balanced Development and Use of Various Types of Transport], *Plan. khoz.,* No. 4, 1954.

"Kolyma," *BSE,* 2d ed., Vol. XXII, 1953.

"Komitet Severnovo morskovo puti" [Committee for the Northern Sea Route], *Sib. SE,* Vol. II, 1931.

"Komitet sodeistviya narodnostyam severnykh okrain" [Committee for Assistance to the Nationalities of the Northern Borderlands], *BSE,* Vol. XXXIII, 1938.

"Kommyunike o prebyvanii v Finlyandii zamestitelya Soveta Ministrov SSSR A. I. Mikoyan" [Communique on the Stay in Finland of the Vice-Chairman of the Council of Ministers of the U.S.S.R., A. I. Mikoyan], *Pravda,* December 2, 1954.

Kondakov, Zh., "O dobyche soli v raione bukhty Kozhevnikova" [On the Mining of Salt in the Kozhevnikovo Gulf Area], *Sov. Ark.,* No. 7, 1940.

Kornilyuk, Yu. I., T. P. Kochetkov and T. M. Yemel'yantsev, "Nordvik-Khatangskii neftenosnyi raion" [The Nordvik-Khatanga Oil Bearing Area], *Ned. Ark.,* No. 1, 1946.

Korovin, E., ed., *Mezhdunarodnoye pravo* [International Law], Moscow, Institut prava Akademii Nauk SSSR [Institute of Law of the U.S.S.R. Academy of Sciences], 1951.

Koshelev, I., "O rukovodstve raionami Krainevo Severa" [On the Management of Regions of the Extreme North], *Izvestiya,* January 17, 1948.

"Kotui," *BSE,* 2d ed., Vol. XXIII, 1953.

Kovalkin, I., "V raionakh Krainevo Severa" [In Areas of the Extreme North], *Pravda,* October 1, 1952.

——, "Za polyarnym krugom" [Above the Arctic Circle], *Izvestiya,* November 5, 1953.

"Krasnoyarsk," *BSE,* 2d ed., Vol. XXIII, 1953.

Krasovski, N. V., *Kak ispol'zovat' energiyu vetra* [How to Utilize the Power of the Wind], Moscow-Leningrad, 1936.

——, "Vetroenergeticheskiye resursy SSSR i perspektivi ikh ispol'-zovaniya" [Wind Power Resources of the U.S.S.R. and the Prospects for Their Utilization], *Atlas energeticheskikh resursov SSSR* [Atlas of the Power Resources of the U.S.S.R.], ed. by A. V. Vinter and G. M. Krzhizhanovski, Moscow-Leningrad, 1935, Vol. 1, Part 3.

Kruglov, A., "Severnoye zakonodatel'stvo" [Northern Legislation], *Sov. Sev.,* No. 1, 1931.

Krylov, P., "Protiv burzhuaznoi metodologii v voprosakh ekonomiki transporta" [Against Bourgeois Methodology in the Economics of

Transportation], *Plan. khoz.*, No. 4, July-August 1949.

Krypton, Constantine, *The Northern Sea Route: Its Place in Russian Economic History Before 1917*, New York, Research Program on the U.S.S.R., 1953.

——, "Soviet Policy in the Northern National Regions After World War II," *The American Slavic and East European Review*, New York, Vol. XIII, No. 3, October 1954.

Kurski, V. I., *Ryby v prirode i khozyaistve cheloveka* [Fish in Nature and in the Economy of Man], ed. by L. Averintsev, Moscow, Uchpedgiz [State Educational and Pedagogical Publishing House], 1949.

Kursy politupravleniya dlya komandnovo sostava Glavsevmorputi: Ekonomgeografiya Krainevo Severa [Courses in Political Administration for Executive Personnel of Glavsevmorput': Economic Geography of the Extreme North], Moscow-Leningrad, Glavsevmorput', 1940.

"Kuznetskii ugol'nyi bassein" [The Kuznetsk Coal Basin], *BSE*, 2d ed., Vol. XXIII, 1953.

Lakhtin, V. L., *Prava na severnye polyarnye prostranstva* [Rights to North Pole Areas], Moscow, Narkomindel [People's Commissariat of Foreign Affairs], 1928.

Lappo, S. D., *Spravochnaya knizhka polyarnika* [Manual for Polar Personnel], Moscow-Leningrad, Glavsevmorput', 1945.

Lappo, V. I., "Neftyanoye mestorozhdeniye Nordvik" [The Nordvik Oil Deposit], *Ned. Ark.*, No. 1, 1946.

Lavrov, B. V., and P. Ye. Shadrin, "Ekonomika gruzooborota Severnovo morskovo puti" [The Economics of Cargo Turnover on the Northern Sea Route], *Sov. Ark.*, No. 4, 1936.

"Lena," *BSE*, Vol. XXXVI, 1938.

"Lena," *BSE*, 2d ed., Vol. XXIV, 1953.

"Leningrad, 22 iyulya, 1948 g." [Leningrad, July 22, 1948], *Izvestiya*, July 23, 1948.

"Lenskoye rechnoye parokhodstvo" [The Lena River Shipping Administration], *BSE*, 2d ed., Vol. XXIV, 1953.

"Lesopil'naya promyshlennost'" [The Sawmill Industry], *BSE*, 2d ed., Vol. XXV, 1954.

Lur'ye, A., "Metody sopostavleniya eksploatatsionnykh raskhodov i kapitalovlozhenii pri ekonomicheskoi otsenke tekhnicheskikh meropriyatii" [Methods of Comparing Operating Expenditures and Capital Investments in the Economic Appraisal of Technical Measures], *Voprosy ekonomiki zheleznodorozhnovo transporta* [Problems of the Economics of Railroad Transportation], ed. by Ye. D. Khanukov and V. I. Chernyshev, Moscow, Transzheldorizdat, 1948.

Lutski, S. L., *Geograficheskiye ocherki russkoi taigi* [Geographic

BIBLIOGRAPHY

Sketches of the Russian Taiga], Moscow, Geografiz [State Publishing House of Geographical Literature], 1947.

———, *Kol'skii gornopromyshlennyi raion* [The Kola Mining District], Moscow, 1939 *(Uchonye zapiski Moskovskovo gosudarstvennovo universiteta* [Scientific Notes of the Moscow State University], No. 21).

———, *Ostrov Sakhalin* [Sakhalin Island], Moscow, Glavsevmorput', 1946.

Lyapin, N. [Minister of Food Supply of the Yakut A.S.S.R.], "Vopros zhdyot resheniya Ministerstva" [The Question Awaits Decision by the Ministry], *Izvestiya*, December 8, 1950.

Lyubarskaya, R., "Arkticheskomu khozyaistvu—strogii khozraschot" [For the Arctic Economy—Strict Cost Accounting], *Sov. Ark.*, No. 7, 1939.

Lyutkevich, Ye. M., "Yeniseisko-Pyasinskaya geologicheskaya ekspeditsiya" [The Yenisei-Pyasina Geologic Expedition], *Prob. Ark.*, No. 3, 1938.

Machikhin, V., "Razvitiye proizvodstva predmetov narodnovo potrebleniya po predpriyatiyam mestnoi promyshlennosti i promyslovoi kooperatsii" [The Development of the Production of Consumer Goods at Enterprises of Local Industry and Producers' Cooperatives], *Plan. khoz.*, No. 1, 1954.

Makhotkin, V., "Ob oshibkakh navigatsii 1938 g." [On the Mistakes of the 1938 Navigation Season], *Sov. Ark.*, No. 4, 1939.

Malov, F., "Gorod na Yeniseye" [City on the Yenisei], *Izvestiya*, April 8, 1953.

Margolin, A., "Goroda Zapolyar'ya" [Cities Above the Arctic Circle], *Sov. Ark.*, No. 7, 1937.

———, "Nuzhen li karbososplav po reke Lene?" [Are High-Walled Barges Needed on the Lena River?], *Sov. Ark.*, No. 10, 1940.

———, "Puti zavoza gruzov na krainyi Sever" [Freight Routes to the Extreme North], *Sov. Ark.*, No. 6, 1939.

Materialy k general'nomu planu razvitiya narodnovo khozyaistva Sibirskovo kraya [Materials for the General Plan for the Development of the National Economy of the Siberian Krai], Novosibirsk, Sibkraiizdat [The Siberian Krai State Publishing House], 1930.

Meshcherin, V., "Za chotkuyu organizovannuyu rabotu" [For the Efficient Organization of Work], *Sov. Ark.*, No. 5, 1939.

"Michurintsy Severa" [Michurinites of the North], *Pravda*, September 18, 1948.

Mikhailov, A. P., "Set' polyarnykh stantsii v tret'yei pyatiletke" [The Network of Polar Stations in the Third Five-Year Plan], *Sov. Ark.*, No. 10, 1937.

193

BIBLIOGRAPHY

Mikhailov, S., "Puti pod"yoma rybnoi promyshlennosti" [Paths to the Expansion of the Fishing Industry], *Plan. khoz.*, No. 4, 1953.

——, "Rybnyi promysel i yevo vozmozhnosti" [The Fishing Industry and Its Potentialities], *Izvestiya,* February 25, 1953.

Mikhailov, S. V., and S. P. Udovenko, "Kamchatskaya oblast'" [Kamchatka Oblast], *BSE,* 2d ed., Vol. XIX, 1953.

Mineyev, A. I., *Ostrov Vrangelya* [Wrangel Island], Moscow, Glavsevmorput', 1946.

Molodetski, K. G., "Kamennougol'nye bazy Severnovo morskovo puti" [Coal Bases of the Northern Sea Route], *Izvestiya Vsesoyuznovo geograficheskovo obshchestva* [News of the All-Union Geographic Society], Moscow, Vol. LXXIII, No. 1, 1941.

——, *Prava i interesy Sovetskovo Soyuza v polyarnykh prostranstvakh Severa* [Rights and Interests of the Soviet Union in the Polar Regions of the North], Leningrad, NIAI UKGVF [Air Research Institute of the Training Combine, Civil Air Fleet], 1931.

——, "Voprosy ekonomiki eksploatatsii Severnovo morskovo puti" [Problems of the Economics of the Exploitation of the Northern Sea Route], *Sovetskii Sever* [Soviet North], Leningrad, No. 3, 1939.

——, "Vozdushnye linii Kol'skovo poluostrova" [Air Routes of the Kola Peninsula], *Aerofikatsiya Leningradskoi oblasti vo vtoroi pyatiletke* [Development of Aviation in Leningrad Oblast in the Second Five-Year Plan], Leningrad, Lenosoaviakhim [The Leningrad Society for the Promotion of Defense and Aero-Chemical Development], 1934.

Molodykh, I. F., *Puti svyazi i snabzheniya Kolymsko-Indigirskovo kraya* [Communications and Supply Routes of the Kolyma-Indigirka Region], Irkutsk, 1931.

Monastyrski, A. S., "Ugol'nye resursy Yakutska" [Coal Resources of Yakutsk], *Sov. Ark.*, No. 7, 1937.

Morozov, S., "K poslednim parallelyam" [At the Last Parallels], *Ogonyok,* Moscow, Nos. 31-33, August, 1954.

"Murmanskaya oblast'" [Murmansk Oblast], *BSE,* 2d ed., Vol. XXVIII, 1954.

Mutafi, N. N., "Pyasinskoye mestorozhdeniye uglei v obshchem komplekse Yeniseiskovo uglenosnovo polya" [The Pyasina Coal Deposit in the General Complex of the Yenisei Coal Field], *Prob. Ark.*, No. 2, 1938.

"Na arkticheskikh liniyakh" [On the Arctic Lines], *Izvestiya,* August 24, 1947.

"Na Kamchatke" [On Kamchatka], *Izvestiya,* December 30, 1949.

"Na magistrali Taishet-Lena" [On the Taishet-Lena Main Line], *Izvestiya,* December 2, 1954.

194

BIBLIOGRAPHY

"Na rekakh Sibiri" [On the Rivers of Siberia], *Pravda,* May 21, 1950.
"Na rekakh Vostochnoi Sibiri" [On the Rivers of Eastern Siberia], *Izvestiya,* May 26, 1951.
"Na Severe otkrylas' navigatsiya" [Navigation Has Begun in the North], *Morskoi Flot* [Maritime Fleet], Moscow, May 1949.
"Na stupen' vyshe" [A Step Up], *Sov. Ark.,* No. 5, 1935.
"Na Taimyre" [On Taimyr], *Izvestiya,* July 19, 1951.
"Na vozdushnykh liniyakh" [On the Air Lines], *Izvestiya,* June 16, 1948.
"Na vozdushnykh magistralyakh" [On the Main Air Routes], *Izvestiya,* July 19, 1952.
"Na vozdushnykh magistralyakh strany" [On the Main Air Routes of the Country], *Pravda,* October 6, 1948.
"Na zapadnom poberezh'i Kamchatki" [On the Western Coast of Kamchatka], *Pravda,* August 20, 1949.
"Nakanune vesennei putiny" [On the Eve of the Spring Fishing Season], *Izvestiya,* March 4, 1954.
Natsarenus, S. P., "Takova li ekonomika gruzooborota?" [Are Such the Economics of Cargo Turnover?], *Sov. Ark.,* No. 10, 1936.
"Navigatsiya na Yenisei" [Navigation on the Yenisei], *Izvestiya,* August 7, 1949.
"Neotlozhnye zadachi mestnykh sovetov Urala, Sibiri i Dal'nevo Vostoka" [Urgent Tasks of Local Soviets in the Urals, Siberia and the Far East], *Izvestiya,* September 7, 1948.
"Neporyadki na morskom vokzale" [Disorder in the Maritime Station], *Morskoi Flot* [Maritime Fleet], Moscow, August 9, 1949.
Nesterov, V., "Narodnoye khozyaistvo: Lesnoye khozyaistvo" [The National Economy: The Timber Economy], *BSE: SSSR.*
New York Times, December 29, 1949; December 16, 17, 19, 1951; February 26, 1952. [On the return of U. S. Lend-Lease icebreakers by the U.S.S.R.].
Nikitin, M., "Reis vo l'dakh" [Voyage in the Ice], *Pravda,* March 2, 1955.
Nikitin, N. V., *Lesnaya promyshlennost' Arkhangel'skoi oblasti za 30 let i perspektivy yeyo dal'neishevo razvitiya* [Thirty Years of the Lumber Industry of Archangel Oblast and the Prospects for Its Further Development], Archangel, 1948.
Notkin, A. I., "Severnyi morskoi put' " [The Northern Sea Route], *Severnaya Aziya* [Northern Asia], Moscow, No. 1-2, 1925.
Novikov, V. D., "K istorii osvoyeniya Severnovo morskovo puti v pervye gody sovetskoi vlasti" [On the History of the Conquest of the Northern Sea Route in the Early Years of the Soviet Power], *Letopis' Severa* [Chronicle of the North], Moscow-Leningrad, Glavsevmorput', No. 1, 1949.

BIBLIOGRAPHY

"Novosibirskii port pered navigatsiyei" [The Novosibirsk Port Before the Navigation Season], *Pravda,* April 15, 1953.

"Novostroiki samovo molodovo goroda v Zapolar'ye" [New Construction in the Newest City Above the Arctic Circle], *Pravda,* November 22, 1953.

"Novye goroda Yakutii" [New Cities of Yakutiya], *Izvestiya,* October 7, 1948.

"O dal'neishem uvelichenii proizvodstva zerna v strane i ob osvoyenii tselinnykh i zalezhnykh zemel': Postanovleniye Plenuma TsK KPSS, prinyatoye 2 marta 1954 g. po dokladu tov. N. S. Khrushchova" [On the Further Increase of the Production of Grain and on the Development of Virgin and Idle Lands: Resolution of the Plenum of the Central Committee of the CPSU, Adopted on March 2, 1954, on the Basis of the Report of N. S. Khrushchov], *Izvestiya,* March 6, 1954.

"O koordinatsii nauchnoi raboty v oblasti ekonomiki" [On the Coordination of Research in the Field of Economics], *Voprosy ekonomiki* [Problems of Economics], Moscow, No. 1, 1950.

"O rabote Glavsevmorputi za 1937 god" [Concerning the Work of Glavsevmorput' in 1937], *Sov. Ark.,* No. 5, 1938.

"Ob itogakh vypolneniya gosudarstvennovo plana razvitiya narodnovo khozyaistva SSSR v 1954 godu: Soobshcheniye Tsentral'novo statisticheskovo upravleniya pri Sovete Ministrov SSSR" [On the Results of the Fulfillment of the State Plan for the Development of the National Economy of the U.S.S.R. in 1954: Statement of the Central Statistical Administration Under the Council of Ministers of the U.S.S.R.], *Pravda,* January 21, 1955.

"Ob uvelichenii proizvodstva produktov zhivotnovodstva: Doklad tovarishcha N. S. Khrushchova na Plenume Tsentral'novo Komiteta KPSS 25 yanvarya 1955 goda" [On Increasing the Output of Animal Husbandry Products: Report of N. S. Khrushchov at the Plenum of the Central Committee of the CPSU on January 25, 1955], *Izvestiya,* February 3, 1955.

Obraztsov, V. N., and F. I. Shaul'ski, *Vodnyi, vozdushnyi, avtodorozhnyi gorodskoi i promyshlennyi transport* [Municipal and Industrial Transport by Water, Air and Highway], Moscow, Transzheldorizdat, 1948.

Obruchev, S. B., "Problema Tunguskovo basseina" [The Problem of the Tunguska Basin], *Angaro-Yeniseiskaya problema* [The Angara-Yenisei Problem], Moscow, Gosplanizdat [Publishing House of the State Planning Commission], 1932 *(Trudy I konferentsii po razmeshcheniyu proizvoditel'nykh sil SSSR* [Transactions of the First

BIBLIOGRAPHY

Conference on the Geographic Distribution of Productive Forces of the U.S.S.R.], Vol. XVI).

"Ocherednye zadachi kul'turnovo stroitel'stva na Krainem Severe: Po dokladu T. Davydova na IX Plenume Komiteta Severa" [The Next Tasks of Cultural Construction in the Extreme North: From the Report of Comrade Davydov at the Ninth Plenum of the Committee of the North], *Sov. Sev.*, No. 4, 1932.

"Ogni na Yeniseye" [Lights on the Yenisei], *Izvestiya*, August 7, 1952.

Orlov, V. I., *Severnyi morskoi put' (zapadnaya chast')* [The Northern Sea Route (Western Sector)], Moscow, 1924 *(Materialy Gosplana* [Materials of Gosplan], Vol. VII).

Orlovski, P., "2-oi mezhdunarodnyi polyarnyi god" [The Second International Polar Year], *Sov. Sev.*, No. 1-2, 1932.

"Ostrov Vrangelya" [Wrangel Island], *Izvestiya*, November 4, 1924.

"Osvoyeniye malykh rek" [The Development of Small Rivers], *Izvestiya*, June 4, 1953.

Papanin, V., "Vo l'dakh Arktiki" [On the Ice of the Arctic], *Pravda*, December 3, 1945.

Perov, G., "Stalin i sotsialisticheskoye planirovaniye narodnovo khozyaistva" [Stalin and Socialist Planning of the National Economy], *Narodnoye khozyaistvo SSSR* [The National Economy of the U.S.S.R.], Sbornik [Symposium] No. 3, ed. by B. I. Eidel'man, Moscow, Gosplanizdat [Publishing House of the State Planning Commission], 1950.

"Pervye parokhody v zapolyarnom portu" [The First Ships in a Polar Port], *Pravda*, July 3, 1953.

"Pervye ploty v Arkhangel'ske" [The First Rafts in Archangel], *Izvestiya*, May 20, 1948.

Pinkhenson, D. M., "Istoricheskiye etapy zavoyevaniya Severnovo morskovo puti" [Historical Stages in the Conquest of the Northern Sea Route], *Izvestiya Vsesoyuznovo geograficheskovo obshchestva* [News of the All-Union Geographical Society], Moscow-Leningrad, Vol. LXXXII, fasc. 4, July/August, 1950.

"Plan osvoyeniya Arktiki" [Plan for the Conquest of the Arctic], *Izvestiya*, March 16, 1933.

"Plan raboty Komiteta Severa na 1935 g." [Work Plan of the Committee of the North for 1935], *Sov. Sev.*, Moscow, No. 1, 1935.

Pletnyov, V., "Medno-nikelevye mestorozhdeniya Norilya" [The Copper and Nickel Deposits of Noril'sk], *Sovetskaya Zoloto-promyshlennost'* [The Soviet Gold Industry], Irkutsk, No. 2-3, 1932.

"Plovuchii lektorii" [Floating Lecture Hall], *Izvestiya*, June 22, 1949.

197

BIBLIOGRAPHY

"Plovuchiye kul'tbazy" [Floating Culture Bases], *Izvestiya*, August 18, 1951.

"Po Severnomu morskomu puti" [Along the Northern Sea Route], *Izvestiya*, September 1, 1954.

"Political Rights in the Arctic," *Foreign Affairs*, New York, Vol. IV, No. 1, October 1925.

"Polneye ispol'zovat' lesnye bogatstva Dal'nevo Vostoka" [Make Fuller Use of the Lumber Resources of the Far East], *Izvestiya*, February 24, 1952.

Polovinkin, A. A., *Obshchaya fizicheskaya geografiya: Uchebnik dlya uchitel'skikh institutov* [General Physical Geography: A Textbook for Teachers' Institutes], Moscow, Gosuchebizdat RSFSR [The R.S.F.S.R. State Educational Publishing House], 1948.

Popov, V. S., "Tunguskii uglenosnyi bassein" [The Tunguska Coal Basin], *Poleznye iskopayemye Krasnoyarskovo kraya* [Useful Minerals of Krasnoyarsk Krai], Tomsk, 1938.

"Port na Lene" [A Port on the Lena], *Izvestiya*, July 13, 1954.

"Poslednyi reis na Novuyu Zemlyu" [The Last Trip to Novaya Zemlya], *Pravda*, October 3, 1953.

"Postanovleniya TsK partii i SNK v ikh primenenii k Severu" [Decrees of the Central Committee of the Party and of the Council of People's Commissars and Their Application to the North], *Sov. Sev.*, No. 3, 1932.

"Postanovleniye Sovnarkoma SSSR ob uluchshenii raboty Glavnovo upravleniya Severnovo morskovo puti ot 29 avgusta 1938 g." [Decree of August 29, 1938, of the Council of People's Commissars of the U.S.S.R. on Improving the Work of Glavsevmorput'], *Pravda*, August 30, 1938.

"Preobrazhonnaya Pechenga" [Transformed Pechenga], *Pravda*, December 21, 1949.

"Promysel sel'di na Severe" [The Herring Industry in the North], *Izvestiya*, August 9, 1951.

"Pyasina," *BSE*, Vol. XLVII, 1940.

"Raport nachal'nika Arkticheskoi Ekspeditsii, Pompolita i Nachal'nika morskoi provodki—Predsedatelyu Soveta Ministrov SSSR, I. V. Stalinu" [Report of the Head of the Arctic Expedition, the Assistant for Political Affairs, and the Head of the Sea Escort to the Chairman of the Council of Ministers of the U.S.S.R., J. V. Stalin], *Pravda*, September 9, 1949.

Raport nachal'nika Glavsevmorputi O. Yu. Shmidta I. V. Stalinu [Report of the Head of Glavsevmorput' O. Yu. Shmidt to J. V. Stalin], *Sov. Ark.*, No. 1, 1935 (Supplement).

"Razvedka Noril'skovo medno-nikelevovo mestorozhdeniya" [Explora-

BIBLIOGRAPHY

tion of the Noril'sk Copper and Nickel Deposits], *Izvestiya GK (1925)* [News of the Geological Committee (1925)], Leningrad, Vol. XLIV, No. 2, 1927.

"Rech' deputata S. A. Nemtseva ot Krasnoyarskovo Kraya" [Address by Deputy S. A. Nemtsev of Krasnoyarsk Krai], *Izvestiya*, May 31, 1949.

"Rechnaya flotiliya v vodakh Arktiki: Beseda s ministrom rechnovo flota SSSR tov. Z. A. Shashkovym" [The River Fleet in the Waters of the Arctic: An Interview with the Minister of the River Fleet of the U.S.S.R., Z. A. Shashkov], *Ogonyok*, Moscow, No. 38, September 1949.

"Rechnoi transport v 1949 godu" [River Transport in 1949], *Izvestiya*, February 8, 1949.

"Rechnoi vokzal na Yeniseye" [River Station on the Yenisei], *Izvestiya*, February 24, 1951.

Rezolyutsii XVIII s"yezda VKP(b) [Resolutions of the Eighteenth Congress of the All-Union Communist Party (Bolsheviks)], Moscow, Gosudarstvennoye izdatel'stvo politicheskoi literatury [State Publishing House of Political Literature], 1939.

Rozanov, M., "V kholodnykh prostorakh Sibiri" [In the Cold Expanses of Siberia], *Novoye russkoye slovo*, New York, February 26, 1949.

Ryabukhin, G. Ye., "Geologicheskoye stroyeniye i neftenostnost' raiona Ust'-Porta na reke Yeniseye" [Geologic Structure and Oil Resources of the Ust'-Port Area on the Yenisei River], *Prob. Ark.*, No. 3, 1939.

———, "Novye dannye po geologii nizhnevo techeniya R. Yeniseya" [New Data on the Geology of the Lower Reaches of the Yenisei], *Sovetskaya geologiya* [Soviet Geology], Leningrad, No. 11, 1940.

"Rybolovetskaya baza v Gizhiginskoi gube" [A Fishing Base in Gizhiga Bay], *Pravda*, August 8, 1948.

Ryumkin, Ya., and S. Morozov, "Na l'dakh tsentral'noi Arktiki" [On the Central Arctic Ice], *Ogonyok*, Moscow, No. 30, July 1954.

Saks, V. N., "Osnovnye etapy formirovaniya Taimyrskoi depressii" [Principal Stages in the Formation of the Taimyr Depression], *Prob. Ark.*, No. 10, 1940.

"Samolyoty dostavlyayut gruz kolkhozam" [Planes Deliver Freight to the Kolkhozes], *Izvestiya*, August 9, 1949.

Savin, V., "Protiv povtoreniya oshibok navigatsii 1938 g." [Against the Repetition of the Mistakes of the 1938 Navigation Season], *Sov. Ark.*, No. 2, 1939.

Sbornik po trudovomu zakonodatel'stvu dlya rabotnikov Severnovo morskovo puti [Collection of Labor Laws for Personnel of the

BIBLIOGRAPHY

Northern Sea Route], comp. by P. I. Nedzvedski, Moscow-Leningrad, Glavsevmorput', 1948.

"Sdelano na Kolyme" [Made in Kolyma], *Kamchatskaya pravda*, Petropavlovsk, December 7, 1945.

XVII konferentsiya Vsesoyuznoi kommunisticheskoi partii (b): stenograficheskii otchot [Seventeenth Conference of the All-Union Communist Party (Bolsheviks): Stenographic Report], Moscow, Partizdat, [Party Publishing House], 1932.

Senyukov, V. M., "Novaya neftenosnaya oblast' kembriiskikh otlozhenii severnovo sklona Aldanskovo massiva" [The New Oil-Bearing Region of the Cambrian Deposits of the Northern Slope of the Aldan Massif], *Neftyanoi Institut* [The Oil Institute], No. 7, 1937.

——, "Problema neftenosnosti Kembriiskikh otlozhenii Sibiri v basseine r.r. Lena-Aldan" [The Problem of Oil Resources of the Cambrian Deposits of Siberia in the Lena and Aldan River Basin], *Neftyanoye khozyaistvo* [Oil Economy], Moscow, Vol. XXVII, No. 2, 1935.

——, "Reka Tolba i neftenosnost' severnovo sklona Aldanskovo massiva" [The Tolba (Tuolba) River and the Oil Deposits of the Northern Slope of the Aldan Massif], *Trudy neftyanovo Geologorazvedochnovo instituta* [Works of the Oil Geologic Exploration Institute], Leningrad, Series A, No. 107, 1938.

Serzhantov, N., "Na rechnykh putyakh strany: Ot Yakutska do Ust'-Kuta [On the River Routes of the Country: From Yakutsk to Ust'-Kut], *Izvestiya*, October 13, 1954.

"Severnyi morskoi put' " [The Northern Sea Route], *BSE*, Vol. L, 1944.

Shabad, Theodore, "Secret Siberian City Linked to Uranium," *New York Times*, January 16, 1955.

Shapiro, I. O., "O tekhnicheskoi i ekonomicheskoi vozmozhnosti promyshlennovo ispol'zovaniya kureiskovo mestorozhdeniya grafita" [Concerning the Technical and Economic Possibilities for the Industrial Utilization of the Kureika Graphite Deposits], *Gornyi zhurnal* [Mining Journal], Moscow, No. 6, 1926.

Shashkov, Z., "Uluchshit' ispol'zovaniye morskovo i rechnovo flota" [Make Better Use of the Maritime and River Fleet], *Pravda*, June 22, 1954.

——, "Vazhneishiye zadachi rechnikov" [Most Important Tasks of River Workers], *Pravda*, September 10, 1949.

Shatski, N. S., "Neft' Yakutskoi ASSR" [Oil of the Yakut A.S.S.R.], *Atlas energeticheskikh resursov SSSR: Dal'nevostochnyi krai, Yakutskaya ASSR* [Atlas of the Power Resources of the U.S.S.R.: The

BIBLIOGRAPHY

Far Eastern Krai, the Yakut A.S.S.R.], Moscow-Leningrad, Vol. II, No. 14, 1934.

Shcherbakov, D. I., "V serdtse Arktiki" [In the Heart of the Arctic], *Nauka i zhizn'* [Science and Life], Moscow, No. 9, September 1954.

Shekhovtsov, N., "Ob ispol'zovanii energii vetra na Krainem Severe" [On the Utilization of Wind Power in the Extreme North], *Sov. Ark.*, No. 10, 1939.

Shevno, Ye., "Uvelichit' proizvodstvo vetrodvigatelei" [Increase the Production of Wind Generators], *Izvestiya*, May 16, 1953.

Shmidt, O. Yu., "Nashi zadachi v 1936 godu" [Our Tasks in 1936], *Sov. Ark.*, No. 3, 1936.

Shorokhov, L., "Tunguskii uglenosnyi bassein" [The Tunguska Coal Basin], *Atlas energeticheskikh resursov SSSR: Vostochno-Sibirskii krai* [Atlas of the Power Resources of the U.S.S.R.: The Eastern Siberian Region], Moscow-Leningrad, Vol. II, No. 13, 1934.

"Sibirskiye bakenshchiki" [The Siberian Buoy Attendants], *Izvestiya*, May 28, 1953.

"Sibirskiye sudostroiteli" [Siberian Shipbuilders], *Izvestiya*, August 5, 1949.

Sibirtsev, N., and V. Itin, *Severnyi morskoi put' i Karskiye ekspeditsii* [The Northern Sea Route and the Kara Runs], Novosibirsk, Zapadno-Sibirskoye krayevoye izd-vo [Western Siberian Krai Publishing House], 1936.

Skachko, A., *Narody Krainevo Severa i rekonstruktsiya severnovo khozyaistva* [The Peoples of the Extreme North and the Reconstruction of the Northern Economy], Leningrad, Institut narodov Severa [Institute of the Peoples of the North], 1934.

Sobraniye zakonov i rasporyazhenii pravitel'stva SSSR [Collection of Laws and Ordinances of the Government of the U.S.S.R.], Moscow, 1932-1936.

"Sodoklad predsedatelya Byudzhetnoi Komissii Soveta Soyuza, deputata P. L. Korniyetsa" [Co-Report of the Chairman of the Budget Commission of the Soviet of the Union, Deputy P. L. Korniyets], *Izvestiya*, March 12, 1949.

Sokolov, A. A., "Belogorskii lesokombinat" [The Belogor'ye Lumber Combine], *Sov. Ark.*, No. 9, 1936.

Solomin, V., "Ratsionalizatsiya perevozok—krupnyi reserv transporta" [The Rationalization of Shipping—an Important Transport Reserve], *Izvestiya*, April 19, 1953.

Soobshcheniye gosudarstvennovo planovovo komiteta SSSR i Tsentral'novo Statisticheskovo Upravleniya SSSR: Ob itogakh vypolneniya chetvyortovo (pervovo poslevoyennovo) pyatiletnevo plana SSSR na 1946-1950 g.g. [Statement of the State Planning Committee of the

BIBLIOGRAPHY

U.S.S.R. and the Central Statistical Administration of the U.S.S.R.: On the Results of the Fulfillment of the Fourth (First Postwar) Five-Year Plan of the U.S.S.R. for 1946-1950], Moscow, Gospolitizdat [State Publishing House of Political Literature], 1951.

"Soobshcheniye iz Yakutska" [Report from Yakutsk], *Izvestiya,* August 11, 1948.

"Soobshcheniye Tsentral'novo Komiteta KPSS i Soveta Ministrov SSSR o vypolnenii gosudarstvennovo plana khlebozagotovok kolkhozami i sovkhozami Sovetskovo Soyuza iz urozhaya 1954 goda" [Statement of the Central Committee of the CPSU and the Council of Ministers of the U.S.S.R. on the Fulfillment of the State Plan for Grain Procurements by the Kolkhozes and Sovkhozes of the Soviet Union from the 1954 Harvest], *Pravda,* November 8, 1954.

Sovetskaya Arktika: Obzor nauchno-issledovatel'skoi raboty Vsesoyuznovo arkticheskovo instituta v Sovetskom sektore Arktiki [The Soviet Arctic: A Survey of the Scientific Research of the All-Union Arctic Institute in the Soviet Sector of the Arctic], Leningrad, Vsesoyuznyi Arkticheskii Institut [All-Union Arctic Institute], 1934.

Spirin, I., *Pokoreniye Severnovo polyusa* [The Conquest of the North Pole], Moscow, Gosudarstvennoye izdatel'stvo geograficheskoi literatury [State Publishing House of Geographical Literature], 1950.

Stalin, I. V., *Marksizm i natsional'no-kolonial'nyi vopros* [Marxism and the National and Colonial Question], Moscow, Partizdat [Party Publishing House], 1937.

"The Stalin White Sea—Baltic Canal," *Soviet Calendar: Thirty Years of the Soviet State,* Moscow, Foreign Languages Publishing House, 1947, Section "August 2."

Stefansson, Vilhjalmur, *The Adventure of Wrangel Island,* New York, Macmillan, 1925.

Stepanov, N., "Tarify Severnovo morskovo puti" [Freight Charges on the Northern Sea Route], *Sov. Ark.,* No. 10, 1939.

Stsepuro, N. V., "Lesnaya promyshlennost' v tret'yem pyatiletii na Krainem Severe" [The Lumber Industry in the Third Five-Year Plan in the Extreme North], *Sov. Ark.,* No. 2, 1937.

Sudnitsyn, I., "Mekhanizatsiya lesnoi promyshlennosti" [Mechanization of the Lumber Industry], *Plan. khoz.,* No. 3, 1949.

Suslov, S. P., *Fizicheskaya geografiya SSSR: Zapadnaya Sibir', Vostochnaya Sibir', Dal'nii Vostok, Srednyaya Aziya* [Physical Geography of the U.S.S.R.: Western Siberia, Eastern Siberia, the Far East, Central Asia], Moscow-Leningrad, Uchpedgiz [State Educational and Pedagogical Publishing House], 1947.

Sverdrup, Kh. [Sverdrup, von, H.], *Vo l'dy na podvodnoi lodke* [In the Ice with a Submarine], Leningrad, Vsesoyuznyi Arkticheskii Institut [All-Union Arctic Institut], 1932.

BIBLIOGRAPHY

Sverdrup, von, H., and K. Wagener, *Polarbuch: Neue Forschungsfahrten in Arktis und Antarktis mit Luftschiff, U-Boot, Schlitten und Forschungsschiff*, Berlin, 1933.

Taracouzio, T. A., *Soviets in the Arctic: An Historical, Economic and Political Study of the Soviet Advance into the Arctic*, New York, Macmillan, 1938.

"Taz," *BSE*, Vol. LIII, 1946.

Thorwald, Juergen, "Das Gespensterschiff im Pazifik," *Revue-die Weltillustrierte*, Munich, No. 33, August 19, 1950.

Tikhomirov, B., "Sibirskii les—na sluzhbu narodnomu khozyaistvu strany" [Siberian Lumber—In the Service of the National Economy of the Country], *Izvestiya*, April 16, 1953.

"Tiksi," *BSE*, Vol. LIV, 1946.

Titunov, P. S. and F. A. Terent'yev, eds., *Severnoye olenevodstvo* [Northern Reindeer Farming], Moscow, Sel'khozgiz, [State Publishing House of Sovkhoz and Kolkhoz Literature], 1948.

Treshnikov, A., "Sevodnya na dreifuyushchikh nauchnykh stantsiyakh" [Today at the Drifting Research Stations], *Pravda*, July 19, 1954.

Trudy dreifuyushchei stantsii "Severnyi Polyus": Nauchnye otchoty i rezul'taty nablyudenii dreifuyushchei ekspeditsii Glavsevmorputi 1937-1938 g.g. [Works of the Drifting Station "North Pole": Scientific Reports and Results of Observations of the Drifting Expedition of Glavsevmorput' in 1937-1938], Leningrad-Moscow, Glavsevmorput', 2 vols., 1940-1945.

"Tseremoniya spuska na vodu ledokola, stroyashchevosya v Finlyandii dlya Sovetskovo Soyuza" [Launching Ceremony for the Icebreaker Built in Finland for the Soviet Union], *Pravda*, December 16, 1953.

Tuayev, N. P., "Ocherk geologii i neftenosnosti Zapadno-Sibirskoi nizmennosti" [Outline of the Geology and Oil Resources of the West Siberian Lowland], *Trudy neftyanovo Geologorazvedochnovo instituta* [Works of the Oil Geologic Exploration Institute], Moscow-Leningrad, New Series, No. 4, 1941.

"Tunguskii uglenosnyi bassein" [The Tunguska Coal Basin], *BSE*, Vol. LV, 1947.

"Tunguskii uglenosnyi bassein" [The Tunguska Coal Basin], *Za industrializatsiyu Sovetskovo Vostoka* [For the Industrialization of the Soviet East], Moscow, No. 2, 1932.

"Turkestano-Sibirskaya zheleznaya doroga" [The Turkestan-Siberian Railroad], *BSE*, Vol. LV, 1947.

"Tyulenskiye rybaki" [Seal Fishermen], *Izvestiya*, February 3, 1953.

"U rybakov Zapolyar'ya" [With the Fishermen Above the Arctic Circle], *Izvestiya*, March 10, 1949.

BIBLIOGRAPHY

"U yeniseiskikh bakenshchikov" [With the Yenisei Buoy Attendants], *Izvestiya*, July 12, 1949.

Urinson, M., "Soveshchaniye predsedatelei planovykh komissii oblastei, krayov i avtonomnykh respublik v Gosplane RSFSR" [Conference of Chairmen of Planning Commissions of Oblasts, Krais, and Autonomous Republics in the R.S.F.S.R. Gosplan], *Plan. khoz.*, No. 5, 1950.

Urvantsev, N. N., "Gde iskat' neft' v Sovetskoi Arktike?" [Where to Prospect for Oil in the Soviet Arctic?], *Problemy Sovetskoi geologii* [Problems of Soviet Geology], Leningrad, No. 3, 1933.

——, "Geofizika na sluzhbe osvoyeniya nedr Arktiki" [Geophysics in the Service of the Development of the Mineral Resources of the Arctic], *Byulleten' ANII* [Bulletin of the Arctic Scientific Research Institute], Leningrad, No. 12, 1935.

——, "Geologiya i poleznye iskopayemye Khatangskovo raiona" [The Geology and Useful Minerals of the Khatanga Area], *Prob. Ark.*, No. 2, 1937.

——, "Geologiya i poleznye iskopayemye Taimyrsko-Vilyuiskoi depressii" [The Geology and Useful Minerals of the Taimyr-Vilyui Depression], *Tezisy dokladov sessii Uchonovo Soveta VAI* [Theses of Reports at the Session of the Learned Council of the All-Union Arctic Institute], Moscow-Leningrad, Glavsevmorput', 1935.

——, "K probleme promyshlennovo osvoyeniya soli v vostochnom sektore polyarnoi zony SSSR" [On the Problem of Industrial Utilization of Salt in the Eastern Sector of the Polar Zone in the U.S.S.R.], *Arktika* [The Arctic], Leningrad, No. 3, 1935.

——, "Khatanga—novyi gornopromyshlennyi raion" [Khatanga—A New Mining District], *Sov. Ark.*, No. 1, 1935.

——, *Klimat i usloviya rabot v raione Noril'skovo kamennougol'novo i polimetallicheskovo mestorozhdeniya* [Climate and Working Conditions in the Area of the Noril'sk Coal and Polymetallic Deposits], Leningrad, 1934 (*Trudy Polyarnoi Komissii AN SSSR* [Works of the Polar Commission of the Academy of Sciences of the U.S.S.R.], Vol. XIV).

——, Raboty po khozyaistvennomu osvoyeniyu Leno-Taimyrskovo raiona v 1933 godu" [Work During 1933 on the Economic Exploitation of the Lena-Taimyr Area], *Byulleten' ANII* [Bulletin of the Arctic Scientific Research Institute], Leningrad, No. 5, 1933.

Ushakov, A., "Ostrov Vrangelya" [Wrangel Island], *Sov. Ark.*, No. 8, 1936.

"Uspekhi okhotnikov Zapolyar'ya" [Successes of the Polar Hunters], *Pravda*, April 16, 1953.

Ustyugov, P., "Samokritika na suglanakh" [Self-Criticism at *Suglany* (Meetings)], *Sov. Sev.*, No. 7-8, 1930.

BIBLIOGRAPHY

"V molodom raione Kamchatki" [In a New Raion of Kamchatka], *Pravda*, June 14, 1950.

"V nevedomuyu gornuyu stranu" [Into Unknown Mountain Country], *Izvestiya*, July 9, August 13, 20 and 27, 1947.

"V portu Tiksi" [Into the Port of Tiksi], *Izvestiya*, August 28, 1947.

"V Prezidiume Akademii Nauk SSSR" [In the Presidium of the Academy of Sciences of the U.S.S.R.], *Izvestiya*, April 29, 1954.

"V Prezidiume Verkhovnovo Soveta SSSR" [In the Presidium of the Supreme Soviet of the U.S.S.R.], *Pravda*, August 29, 1954.

"V severnykh lesakh" [In the Northern Forests], *Izvestiya*, December 19, 1952.

"V Sovete Ministrov SSSR i Tsentral'nom Komitete KPSS: O rasshirenii proizvodstva promyshlennykh tovarov shirokovo potrebleniya i uluchshenii ikh kachestva" [In the Council of Ministers of the U.S.S.R. and the Central Committee of the CPSU: On the Expansion of the Production of Industrial Consumer Goods and the Improvement of Their Quality], *Pravda*, October 28, 1953.

"V Sovete Narodnykh Komissarov Soyuza SSR: O Rabote Glavsevmorputi za 1937 g." [In the Council of People's Commissars of the U.S.S.R.: On the Work of Glavsevmorput' for 1937], *Izvestiya*, March 29, 1938.

"V Sovetskoi Arktike" [In the Soviet Arctic], *Novoye Russkoye Slovo*, New York, December 24, 1953.

"V Sovetskoi Yakutii" [In Soviet Yakutiya], *Ogonyok*, Moscow, No. 13, March 1951.

"V Tsentral'nom Komitete Kommunisticheskoi partii Sovetskovo Soyuza i Sovete Ministrov Soyuza SSR: O dal'neishem osvoyenii tselinnykh i zalezhnykh zemel' dlya uvelicheniya proizvodstva zerna" [In the Central Committee of the CPSU and the Council of Ministers of the U.S.S.R.: On the Further Development of Virgin and Idle Lands for Increased Grain Production], *Izvestiya*, August 17, 1954.

"V tsentral'nuyu Arktiku" [To the Central Arctic], *Pravda*, April 4, 1955.

Vasil'yev, P., "Vetrosilovye ustanovki v Arktike" [Wind Power Installations in the Arctic], *Sov. Ark.*, No. 6, 1940.

"Vdvoye bol'she konservov chem do voiny" [Twice as Much Canned Food as Before the War], *Pravda*, November 18, 1949.

Velichko, V., *Siyaniye Severa* [Northern Lights], Moscow, Izdatel'stvo "Pravda" [Pravda Publishing House], 1946.

Vernikovski, N., "Neporyadki v lenskom rechnom parokhodstve" [Disorders in the Lena River Shipping Administration], *Izvestiya*, September 13, 1952.

BIBLIOGRAPHY

Vinogradov, M. P., *Morskiye mlekopitayushchiye Arktiki* [Sea Mammals of the Arctic], Moscow-Leningrad, 1949.

Vinter, A. V., "Ispol'zovaniye energii vetra" [Utilization of Wind Power], *Priroda* [Nature], Leningrad, No. 2, February 1953.

Vittenburg, P. V., ed., *Trudy vtoroi polyarnoi konferentsii 18-23 iyunya 1928 g.* [Transactions of the Second Polar Conference of June 18-23, 1928], Leningrad, Aeroarktik, 1930.

Vize, V. Yu., *Morya Sovetskoi Arktiki* [Seas of the Soviet Arctic], Moscow-Leningrad, Glavsevmorput', 1948.

———, *Na "Sibiryakove" i "Litke" cherez Ledovitye morya* [Through Arctic Seas in the "Sibiryakov" and "Litke"], Moscow-Leningrad, Glavsevmorput', 1946.

Volkov, N., "Port v Osetrove" [A Port in Osetrovo], *Pravda,* March 4, 1954.

Vologdin, A. G., "K poiskam nefti v Turukhanskom raione" [Explorations for Oil in the Turkhansk Area], *Vestnik Zapadno-Sibirskovo geologicheskovo upravleniya* [Courier of the West Siberian Geologic Administration], Novosibirsk, No. 2, 1940.

———, "Novyi Turukhanskii neftenosnyi raion" [The New Turukhansk Oil Bearing Area], *Sovetskaya geologiya* [Soviet Geology], Leningrad, No. 12, 1938.

———, "Problema nefti v Krasnoyarskom kraye" [The Problem of Oil in Krasnoyarsk Krai], *Poleznye iskopayemye Krasnoyarskovo kraya* [Useful Minerals of Krasnoyarsk Krai], Tomsk, 1938.

"Vorkuta," *BSE,* 2d ed., Vol. IX, 1951.

XVIII S"yezd Vsesoyuznoi Kommunisticheskoi partii (b) 10-21 marta 1939 g.: Stenograficheskii otchot [Eighteenth Congress of the All-Union Communist Party (Bolsheviks), March 10-21, 1939: Stenographic Report], Moscow, Leningrad, OGIZ [Associated State Publishing Houses], 1939.

Voznesenski, N., *Voyennaya ekonomika SSSR v period otechestvennoi voiny* [The War Economy of the U.S.S.R. in the Period of the Patriotic War], Moscow, OGIZ [Associated State Publishing House], 1948.

"Vsesoyuznoye soveshchaniye aktiva rabotnikov morskovo i rechnovo flota" [All-Union Conference of the *Aktiv* of Personnel of the Maritime and River Fleet], *Izvestiya,* March 7, 1954.

"Vydayushchiisya uspekh sovetskikh rechnikov" [An Outstanding Success of Soviet River Workers], *Izvestiya,* September 28, 1952.

"Vydayushchiyesya nauchnye trudy" [Outstanding Scientific Studies], *Pravda,* May 16, 1953.

Vyshepol'ski, S. A., "K probleme pravovovo rezhima arkticheskoi oblasti" [On the Problem of the Legal Status of the Arctic Region],

BIBLIOGRAPHY

Sovetskoye gosudarstvo i pravo [Soviet State and Law], Moscow, No. 7, July 1952.

Vysotski, N. K., "O korennykh mestorozhdeniyakh platiny na Urale i v Sibiri" [Basic Deposits of Platinum in the Urals and Siberia], *Izvestiya GK* [News of the Geological Committee], Vol. XLII, No. 1, 1923, pp. 15-21.

Waultrin, René, "Le problème de la souveraineté des pôles," *Revue générale de droit international public*, Paris, Vol. XVI, 1909.

——, "La question de la souveraineté des terres arctiques," *Revue générale de droit international public*, Paris, Vol. XV, 1908.

Webster, C. J., "The Economic Development of the Soviet Arctic and Sub-Arctic," *The Slavonic and East European Review*, London, Vol. XXIX, No. 72, December 1950.

"Yakutsk," *Pravda*, June 5, 1953.

"Yakutskaya ekspeditsiya" [The Yakutsk Expedition], *Razvedka nedr* [Exploration for Mineral Resources], Moscow, No. 6, 1938.

Yankin, V., "Ob otgruzke tovarov raionam Krainevo Severa" [On Freight Shipments to the Extreme North], *Izvestiya*, June 29, 1948.

Yemel'yantsev, T. M., "Geologicheskiye issledovaniya v raione Nordvika i ostrova Begicheva v 1933 godu" [Geologic Exploration in the Area of Nordvik and Begichev Island in 1933], *Geologicheskiye issledovaniya Nordvik-Khatangskovo raiona i Taimyrskovo poluostrova* [Geologic Explorations in the Nordvik-Khatanga Area and the Taimyr Peninsula], 1939.

——, "Geologicheskiye issledovaniya v raione rek Khety, Khatangi, Taimyrskovo poluostrova v 1935-36 godakh" [Geologic Explorations in the Areas of the Kheta and Khatanga Rivers and the Taimyr Peninsula During 1935-36], *Geologicheskiye issledovaniya Nordvik-Khatangskovo raiona i Taimyrskovo poluostrova* [Geologic Explorations in the Nordvik-Khatanga Area and the Taimyr Peninsula], 1939.

"Yenisei," *BSE*, 2d ed., Vol. XV, 1952.

"Yeniseiskoye rechnoye parokhodstvo" [Yenisei River Shipping Administration], *BSE*, 2d ed., Vol. XV, 1952.

Yermashov, I. I., *Polyarnaya strategiya i polyarnaya ekspansiya* [Polar Strategy and Polar Expansion], Moscow, Izdatel'stvo "Pravda" [Pravda Publishing House], 1947.

"Za polyarnym krugom" [Above the Arctic Circle], *Pravda*, March 13, 1950.

Zakharov, F. A., *Grazhdanskaya aviatsiya na sluzhbe narodnomu khozyaistvu SSSR* [Civil Aviation in the Service of the National Economy of the U.S.S.R.], Moscow, 1948.

BIBLIOGRAPHY

"Zakon o preobrazovanii ministerstv SSSR" [Law on the Reorganization of the Ministries of the U.S.S.R.], *Vedomosti Verkhovnovo Soveta SSSR* [News of the Supreme Soviet of the U.S.S.R.], March 20, 1953.

Zakon o pyatiletnem plane vosstanovleniya i razvitiya narodnovo khozyaistva SSSR na 1946-1950 g.g. [Law on the Five-Year Plan for the Reconstruction and Development of the National Economy of the U.S.S.R. for 1946-1950], Moscow, OGIZ [Associated State Publishing Houses], 1946.

"Zamechatel'naya pobeda krasnoyarskikh kolkhoznikov" [A Remarkable Victory of Krasnoyarsk Kolkhoz Members], *Pravda,* October 2, 1948.

"Zamechatel'nyi uspekh sovetskikh rechnikov" [The Remarkable Success of Soviet River Workers], *Pravda,* September 10, 1949.

Zarzar, V. A., "Noveisheye v sovremennom aeronautizme" [The Latest in Contemporary Aeronautism], *Voprosy vozdushnovo prava* [Problems of Air Rights], Moscow-Leningrad, No. 2, 1930.

Zarzar, V. A., and V. L. Lakhtin, *Bor'ba za vozdukh* [Struggle for the Air], Moscow, Osoaviakhim [Society for the Promotion of Defense and Aero-Chemical Development], 1927.

"Zasedaniya Verkhovnovo Soveta RSFSR: Rech' deputata F. P. Shchurova" [Sessions of the Supreme Soviet of the R.S.F.S.R.: Speech of Deputy F. P. Shchurov], *Izvestiya,* May 31, 1949.

"Zasedaniya Verkhovnovo Soveta RSFSR: Rech' ministra lesnoi promyshlennosti RSFSR" [Sessions of the Supreme Soviet of the R.S.F.S.R.: Address of the Minister of the Lumber Industry of the R.S.F.S.R.], *Izvestiya,* March 29, 1952.

"Zasedaniya Verkhovnovo Soveta RSFSR: Rech' nachal'nika upravleniya promkooperatsii pri Sovete ministrov RSFSR P. F. Kravchuka" [Sessions of the Supreme Soviet of the R.S.F.S.R.: Address by P. F. Kravchuk, Head of the Administration for Producers' Cooperatives Under the Council of Ministers of the R.S.F.S.R.], *Izvestiya,* June 1, 1949.

Zasedaniya Verkhovnovo Soveta RSFSR 20-25 iyunya 1946 g. (sed'maya sessiya): Stenograficheskii otchot [Sessions of the Supreme Soviet of the R.S.F.S.R. of 20-25 June 1946 (Seventh Session): Stenographic Report], Moscow, Izdaniye Verkhovnovo Soveta RSFSR [Publication of the Supreme Soviet of the R.S.F.S.R.], 1946.

"Zasedaniya Verkhovnovo Soveta SSSR: Rech' deputata A. P. Yefimova" [Sessions of the Supreme Soviet of the U.S.S.R.: Address by Deputy A. P. Yefimov], *Pravda,* June 18, 1950.

"Zasedaniya Verkhovnovo Soveta SSSR: Rech' deputata L. M. Kaganovicha" [Sessions of the Supreme Soviet of the U.S.S.R.: Speech of Deputy L. M. Kaganovich], *Izvestiya,* April 27, 1954.

BIBLIOGRAPHY

"Zasedaniya Verkhovnovo Soveta SSSR: Rech' deputata R. G. Vasil'-yeva" [Sessions of the Supreme Soviet of the U.S.S.R.: Address of Deputy R. G. Vasil'yev], *Izvestiya*, April 25, 1954.

"Zasedaniye Verkhovnovo Soveta SSSR: V Sovete natsional'nostei: Rech' deputata Komi ASSR V. K. Shishonkov" [Session of the Supreme Soviet of the U.S.S.R.: In the Soviet of Nationalities: Speech of the Deputy of the Komi A.S.S.R. V. K. Shishonkov], *Pravda*, July 19, 1950.

"Zasedaniye Verkhovnovo Soveta SSSR: V Sovete natsional'nostei: Rech' ministra rechnovo flota SSSR Z. A. Shashkova" [Session of the Supreme Soviet of the U.S.S.R.: In the Soviet of Nationalities: Address of the Minister of the River Fleet Z. A. Shashkov], *Pravda*, March 12, 1951.

Zhdanova, N. T., "Vrednaya vylazka B. V. Lavrova v Moskovskom dome uchonykh" [Harmful Sortie by B. V. Lavrov in the Moscow House of Scientists], *Sov. Ark.*, No. 9, 1937.

"Zheleznaya doroga Taishet—Ust'-Kut" [The Taishet—Ust'-Kut Railroad], *Pravda*, November 4, 1954.

"Zheleznodorozhnaya magistral' v polyarnoi tundre" [The Railroad Trunk Line in the Polar Tundra], *Byulleten' Arkticheskovo Instituta* [Bulletin of the Arctic Institute], Leningrad, No. 6-7, 1933.

"Znatnye lyudi Arktiki" [Eminent Men of the Arctic], *Izvestiya*, November 23, 1950.

Zubov, N. N., *V tsentre Arktiki: Ocherki po istorii issledovaniya i fizicheskoi geografii tsentral'noi Arktiki* [In the Center of the Arctic: Notes on the History of Exploration and Physical Geography of the Central Arctic], Moscow-Leningrad, Glavsevmorput', 1948.

Zubrikov, A. F., "Uspekhi Polyarnoi MRS" [Success of the Polar Motor-Fishing Stations], *Rybnoye khozyaistvo* [Fishing Economy], Moscow, No. 8, August 1952.

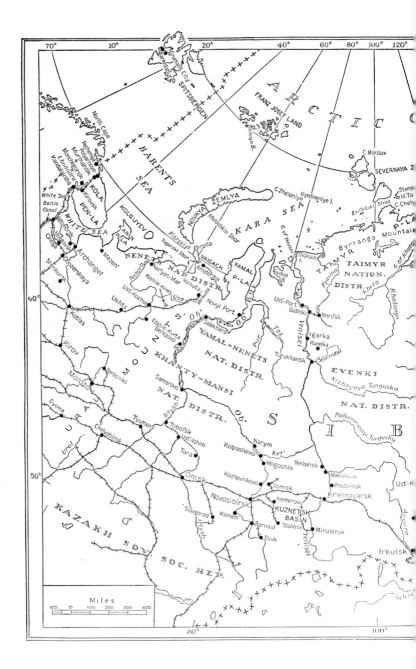

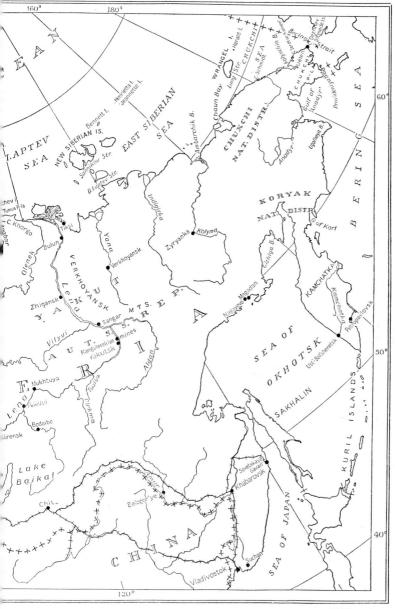

N. Krijanovsky.

INDEX

Index

Central Asia, 31-32, 88
Central Executive Committee, see All-Union Central Executive Committee
Chaidak Dome, 53
Chaun Bay, 120
Chelyabinsk, 31, 32, 87
Chelyabinsk-Chkalov Railway Line, 31
"Chelyushkin" (vessel), 25
Chelyuskin, Cape, 110, 113, 118, 123-24
Chernogorsk, 49
Chinese People's Republic, 158
Chita Oblast, 87
"Chita" (vessel), 118
Chkalov, 31
Chkalov, Valeri, 170
Chukotsk Fish Trust, 68, 77
Chukotsk National Okrug, 63, 66, 175 n. 5
Chukotsk Peninsula, 3, 23, 46, 48, 55, 66-67, 150, 153, 159, 170, 172
Chukotsk Sea, 10, 22, 61-62, 110
Claude, Prof. Georges, 81
Commission for the Northern Sea Route, 167
Committee for Assistance to the Nationalities of the Northern Borderlands Attached to the All-Union Central Executive Committee, 2-3, 36
Committee of the North, see Committee for Assistance to the Nationalities of the Northern Borderlands
Council of People's Commissars, 15 n. 1, 33-35, 160
Crawford, Allan Rudyard, 5
Dal'stroi (Far Eastern Development Project), 46, 107 n. 244, 179 n. 47

Department of the North, R.S.F.S.R. Gosplan, 104 n. 207, 132
Department of Wind Power Installation of the Ministry of Agriculture, 83
"Desna" (vessel), 118
Dezhnov, Cape, 167
Dickson, 22, 43, 49-51, 82, 119
Dickson Island, 48, 109, 112-14, 120, 123, 153
Dmitri Laptev Strait, 22, 114
Dnepr River, 37 n. 7

Donbass, see Donets Basin
Donets Basin, 41, 48-49, 86, 89 n. 4
Dudinka, 43, 59, 78, 105 n. 218, 125, 130, 149
Dvina River, 37 n. 7
Dyoma, 32

East Siberian Sea, 10, 22, 61-62, 109-110
European U.S.S.R., 14, 25, 32, 41-43, 49, 58-59, 68-69, 74, 86, 137, 147-149, 155-56, 158-59, 169, 173, 176 n. 19
Evenki National Okrug, 175 n. 5
Extreme North, 16 n. 2, 17 n. 7-8, 33-36, 40, 52, 56, 58, 61, 68-69, 70-73, 74-75, 77-81, 83, 125, 127, 130, 132, 135, 137, 148, 154, 162, 173, 175 n. 13, 179 n. 50

Far East (Soviet), 33, 46-47, 55-56, 58-59, 63-64, 67, 75, 84, 86-89, 153, 159, 170, 173
Far Eastern Basin 36 n. 1, 165-66
Finland, 20 n. 45, 115, 154
Fleet of the Arctic Expedition, 133
"Fram" (vessel), 138 n. 13
Franz Josef Land, 6, 171
Frolov, V., 112

General Vil'kitski Island, 18 n. 15
Germany, 20, n. 45, 58, 116, 155, 167
Glavnikeleolovo, see Main Administration for the Nickel and Tin Industries
Glavsevmorput' (*Glavnoye upravleniye severnovo morskovo puti* [Main Administration for the Northern Sea Route]), 7, 33-36, 40-43, 44-46, 49, 51, 53-54, 61-63, 70, 76-78, 81, 110, 112-14, 116-20, 122-24, 127, 131-32, 134, 148-49, 155-57, 160-62, 164-65, 179 n. 47; Administration of Polar Stations, 82, 112; Agricultural Administration, 82; Arctic Institute, 3, 7, 12, 51, 53-54, 111-12, 120, 170; Department of Mining and Geology, 51; Department of Polar Aviation,

The Northern Sea Route

127, 172; Hydrographic Institute, 111; Institute of Economics, 160; Krasnoyarsk Territorial Administration, 134; Maritime Department, 114; Omsk Territorial Administration, 77, 134; Planning Department, 160
Golant, V., 14
Gromiv, M. M., 170
Grumant, 48
Gyda Bay, 61-62

Hamburg, 25, 27
Hansen, F., 11
Henrietta Island, 18 n. 15
Herald Island, 18 n. 15

Igarka, 22, 30-31, 35, 43, 49, 51, 58, 69-70, 77, 82, 105 n. 218, 116-18, 120, 125-26, 129-30, 149, 154-55, 157
Igarka-Dudinka Air Line, 125
Imandra, Lake, 51
Indiga, 61
Indigirka River, 121, 136-37, 153, 168
Inskaya, 32
Institute for the Peoples of the North (Leningrad), 57, 104 n. 207
Institute of Frost Study of the U.S.S.R. Academy of Sciences, 74; see also Scientific Frost Research Station
"Iosif Stalin" (vessel), 144 n. 98
Irkutsk, 15, 56, 126, 128
Irkutsk Oblast, 87
"Irtysh" (vessel), 137
Irtysh River, 27, 69, 130-31, 133, 143 n. 90
"Iskra" (vessel), 157
Izhma River, 57

Japan, 20 n. 45, 144 n. 97, 165
Jeannette Island, 18 n. 15

Kachuga, 128, 131, 152
"Kaganovich" (icebreaker), 115
Kaganovich, L. M., 38 n. 24
Kamchatka Peninsula, 46-47, 63-65, 79, 99 n. 152
Kamen', 27
Kamenev, S. S., 124
Kandalaksha, 16 n. 2, 93 n. 58

Kangalasskiye Kopi, 44-45
Kansk, 86
"Kapitan Belousov" (icebreaker), 115
"Kapitan Belousov" (new icebreaker), 115-16
"Kapitan Melekhov" (icebreaker), 115
"Kapitan Voronin" (icebreaker), 115
Kara Sea, 3-4, 10, 22-31, 33, 61-62, 69, 92 n. 51, 100 n. 162, 109, 114, 116, 122, 154-56, 158-59, 162-63, 167-68, 180 n. 68
Kara Strait, 10
Karaganda, 89 n. 4
Karelia, 9, 176 n. 19
Karskiye Vorota, 22
Kazakh S.S.R. (Kazakhstan), 27, 32, 85-86, 88, 105 n. 229
Kemerovo Oblast, 105 n. 229, 146 n. 125
Khabarovsk, 87
Khabarovsk Krai, 72, 78, 175 n. 5
Khanty-Mansi National Okrug, 103 n. 194, 175 n. 5
Khatanga River, 53-54, 121, 126, 136, 153, 168
Kheta River, 53, 145 n. 116
Khibiny Experimental Agricultural Station, 74
Khibiny Mountains, 51
Khorgo, Cape, 121
Khruschov, N. S., 106 n. 230-31, 107 n. 251
Kikhchikhsk Combine, 64
Kirov Combine, 64
Kirov Railroad, 1, 52, 167; see also Murmansk Railroad
Kirov-Kotlas Rail Line, 159
Kirovsk, 51, 158
Klyuchevski Lumber Combine, 64
Kola, 74
Kola Peninsula, 11, 41, 51-52, 69, 74, 167-69
Kolpashevo, 154
Kolyma River, 23, 46, 49-51, 55, 70, 79, 107 n. 244, 120-21, 136-37, 148, 150-51, 157
Kolyuchin Bay, 110
"Komet" (German auxiliary cruiser), 26, 138 n. 5, 167

214

Index

Index

217

Index